FOR REFERENCE

VIOLENT RELATIONSHIPS

BATTERING AND ABUSE AMONG ADULTS

ISSN 1534-1615

VIOLENT RELATIONSHIPS
BATTERING AND ABUSE AMONG ADULTS

Melissa J. Doak

INFORMATION PLUS® REFERENCE SERIES
Formerly published by Information Plus, Wylie, Texas

THOMSON
GALE

Detroit • New York • San Francisco • San Diego • New Haven, Conn. • Waterville, Maine • London • Munich

THOMSON
★
GALE™

Violent Relationships: Battering and Abuse among Adults
Melissa J. Doak
Paula Kepos, Series Editor

Project Editor
John McCoy

Permissions
Margaret Abendroth, Edna Hedblad, Emma Hull

Composition and Electronic Prepress
Evi Seoud

Manufacturing
Drew Kalasky

LIBRARY OF CONGRESS CATALOGING-IN-PUBLICATION DATA

ISBN 0-7876-5103-6 (set)
ISBN 0-7876-9083-X
ISSN 1534-1615

Printed in the United States of America
10 9 8 7 6 5 4 3 2 1

TABLE OF CONTENTS

PREFACE

Violent Relationships: Battering and Abuse among Adults is part of the *Information Plus Reference Series*. The purpose of each volume of the series is to present the latest facts on a topic of pressing concern in modern American life. These topics include today's most controversial and most studied social issues: abortion, capital punishment, care for the elderly, crime, the environment, health care, immigration, minorities, national security, social welfare, women, youth, and many more. Although written especially for the high school and undergraduate student, this series is an excellent resource for anyone in need of factual information on current affairs.

By presenting the facts, it is Thomson Gale's intention to provide its readers with everything they need to reach an informed opinion on current issues. To that end, there is a particular emphasis in this series on the presentation of scientific studies, surveys, and statistics. These data are generally presented in the form of tables, charts, and other graphics placed within the text of each book. Every graphic is directly referred to and carefully explained in the text. The source of each graphic is presented within the graphic itself. The data used in these graphics are drawn from the most reputable and reliable sources, in particular from the various branches of the U.S. government and from major independent polling organizations. Every effort has been made to secure the most recent information available. The reader should bear in mind that many major studies take years to conduct, and that additional years often pass before the data from these studies are made available to the public. Therefore, in many cases the most recent information available in 2005 dated from 2002 or 2003. Older statistics are sometimes presented as well, if they are of particular interest and no more-recent information exists.

Although statistics are a major focus of the *Information Plus Reference Series*, they are by no means its only content. Each book also presents the widely held positions and important ideas that shape how the book's subject is discussed in the United States. These positions are explained in detail and, where possible, in the words of their proponents. Some of the other material to be found in these books includes: historical background; descriptions of major events related to the subject; relevant laws and court cases; and examples of how these issues play out in American life. Some books also feature primary documents, or have pro and con debate sections giving the words and opinions of prominent Americans on both sides of a controversial topic. All material is presented in an even-handed and unbiased manner; the reader will never be encouraged to accept one view of an issue over another.

HOW TO USE THIS BOOK

People have suffered abuse at the hands of family members and caretakers throughout human history. Women have suffered a great deal of this abuse as in most cultures they were, and in many places still are, considered little more than the property of their husbands or fathers, who could do whatever they pleased to them. While this idea gradually fell out of favor in the United States during the 19th century, many American women continued to suffer, for the most part silently. Only in the 1960s did Americans begin to recognize that the abuse of women by intimate partners was a major social problem and to take steps to reduce its prevalence. Since then, scientists have researched many troubling questions that this abuse raises, such as: Why do men abuse women that they are close to? Why do women stay with men who abuse them? What are the physical and mental effects of abuse? At the same time, activists have established shelters to help abuse victims, and politicians have enacted laws to protect them. This book examines the many controversies that surround these efforts. In addition, as society became more aware of the abuse of women by their partners, it became more sensitive to the possibility of other forms of abuse, most notably the abuse of men by their female partners, the abuse of people by their same-sex partners, and the abuse of the elderly and the infirm by their caretakers. These issues are also discussed in this volume.

Violent Relationships: Battering and Abuse among Adults consists of ten chapters and three appendices. Each of the chapters is devoted to a particular aspect of violent relationships in the United States. For a summary of the information covered in each chapter, please see the synopses provided in the Table of Contents at the front of the book. Chapters generally begin with an overview of the basic facts and background information on the chapter's topic, then proceed to examine sub-topics of particular interest. For example, Chapter 3: The Causes of Wife Abuse begins with a description of the typical characteristics of abuse victims and perpetrators in the United States. It then moves on to examine research into the causes of abuse. Thus there is a section on the struggle for power within relationships and importance of traditional gender roles, followed by sections on psychological and sociological explanations for violent relationships. The latest scientific studies—both pro and con—on various sociological theories are incorporated. Other major sub-topics in this chapter include: substance abuse as it relates to domestic violence; abuse of pregnant women; abusive behavior by adults who were abused in childhood; stress as a factor in spouse abuse; the inverse relationship between partner abuse and increasing age; and personality characteristics that may predict future violence. Readers can find their way through a chapter by looking for the section and sub-section headings, which are clearly set off from the text. Or, they can refer to the book's extensive index, if they already know what they are looking for.

Statistical Information

The tables and figures featured throughout *Violent Relationships: Battering and Abuse among Adults* will be of particular use to the reader in learning about this topic. These tables and figures represent an extensive collection of the most recent and important statistics on abusive relationships, as well as related issues—for example, graphics in the book cover the percentage of all violent crime victims whose assailant was an intimate partner; the differences between what sorts of behaviors men and women consider to be sexual harassment; why some stalking victims do not report the stalking to the police; and the estimated percentage of all abuse that goes unreported. Thomson Gale believes that making this information available to the reader is the most important way in which we fulfill the goal of this book: to help readers understand the issues and controversies surrounding violent relationships in the United States and reach their own conclusions.

Each table or figure has a unique identifier appearing above it, for ease of identification and reference. Titles for the tables and figures explain their purpose. At the end of each table or figure, the original source of the data is provided.

In order to help readers understand these often complicated statistics, all tables and figures are explained in the text. References in the text direct the reader to the relevant statistics. Furthermore, the contents of all tables and figures are fully indexed. Please see the opening section of the index at the back of this volume for a description of how to find tables and figures within it.

Appendices

In addition to the main body text and images, *Violent Relationships: Battering and Abuse among Adults* has three appendices. The first is the Important Names and Addresses directory. Here the reader will find contact information for a number of government and private organizations that can provide further information on aspects of violent relationships. The second appendix is the Resources section, which can also assist the reader in conducting his or her own research. In this section, the author and editors of *Violent Relationships: Battering and Abuse among Adults* describe some of the sources that were most useful during the compilation of this book. The final appendix is the index.

ADVISORY BOARD CONTRIBUTIONS

The staff of Information Plus would like to extend their heartfelt appreciation to the Information Plus Advisory Board. This dedicated group of media professionals provides feedback on the series on an ongoing basis. Their comments allow the editorial staff who work on the project to continually make the series better and more user-friendly. Our top priorities are to produce the highest-quality and most useful books possible, and the Advisory Board's contributions to this process are invaluable.

The members of the Information Plus Advisory Board are:

- Kathleen R. Bonn, Librarian, Newbury Park High School, Newbury Park, California
- Madelyn Garner, Librarian, San Jacinto College—North Campus, Houston, Texas
- Anne Oxenrider, Media Specialist, Dundee High School, Dundee, Michigan
- Charles R. Rodgers, Director of Libraries, Pasco-Hernando Community College, Dade City, Florida
- James N. Zitzelsberger, Library Media Department Chairman, Oshkosh West High School, Oshkosh, Wisconsin

COMMENTS AND SUGGESTIONS

The editors of the *Information Plus Reference Series* welcome your feedback on *Violent Relationships: Batter-*

ing and Abuse among Adults. Please direct all correspon-
dence to:

Editors
Information Plus Reference Series
27500 Drake Rd.
Farmington Hills, MI 48331-3535

CHAPTER 1

THE ABUSE OF WOMEN—A WORLDWIDE ISSUE

"Violence against women" means any act of gender-based violence that results in, or is likely to result in, physical, sexual or psychological harm or suffering to women, including threats of such acts, coercion or arbitrary deprivation of liberty, whether occurring in public or private life.

—United Nations Declaration on the Elimination of Violence against Women, 1993

Domestic violence has existed in almost all societies throughout history. Its origin can be traced back centuries to the development of patriarchal and hierarchical systems of authority in which males controlled all property. In such systems, women and children were often considered to be the property of men. The growth of male-oriented societies promoted the widely accepted belief in male superiority that in turn formed the basis for women's subordination (Vivian C. Fox, "Historical Perspectives on Violence against Women," *Journal of International Women's Studies,* vol. 4, November 2002). This belief in men's domination over women, which was often supported by economic, social, cultural, and religious institutions, made it acceptable for men to use violence as a way to control women. As the United Nations Declaration on the Elimination of Violence against Women stated,

> Violence against women is a manifestation of historically unequal power relations between men and women, which have led to domination over and discrimination against women by men and to the prevention of the full advancement of women. . . . [V]iolence against women is one of the crucial social mechanisms by which women are forced into a subordinate position compared with men.

In fact, until the end of the nineteenth century, the law supported a man's right to control his wife by force, and it was not until the advent of the women's liberation movement during the late 1960s and 1970s that domestic violence gained recognition as a social issue. Today, there are social service and justice system resources, including shel-

ters and counseling, available to victims of abuse. In the United States, victims also have legal options. Yet despite this relatively recent progress in the United States, the use of violence in family and intimate partner relationships is still regarded as a man's right in many parts of the world.

An international examination of male violence against women reveals that it is a universal constant—it appears in practically every culture throughout the world and is tolerated by many governments. Many groups, including the United Nations (UN), believe that collaborative international efforts are needed to address this far-reaching health and social problem.

EUROPEAN TRADITIONS

The subservient role of women was well established by the Middle Ages. During the fourteenth century in France, a man could legally beat his wife for failing to obey his orders as long as he did not kill or permanently maim her. The 1371 tale of Geoffrey de la Tour de Landry reflected the contemporary attitude toward "the wickedness of a nagging wife" and the proper punishment for her behavior:

> Here is an example to every good woman that she suffer and endure patiently, nor strive with her husband, nor answer him before strangers, as did once a woman who did answer her husband before strangers with short words: and he smote her with his fist down to earth; and then with his foot he struck her in her visage and broke her nose, and all her life after she had her nose crooked, which so shent [spoiled] and disfigured her visage after, that she might not for shame show her face, it was so foul blemished. And this she had for her language that she was wont to say to her husband, and therefore the wife ought to suffer, and let the husband have the words, and to be her master, for that is her duty.

There were some, however, who cautioned men to treat women with some restraint. Bernard of Siena, Italy, advised the husband in 1427 to treat his wife as well as he did his fowl and livestock. It is doubtful whether his advice was heeded, though, since Siena was also home to the Rules on Marriage, which declared:

> When you see your wife commit an offense, don't rush at her with insults and violent blows, rather, first correct the wrong lovingly. [If this doesn't work] scold her sharply, bully and terrify her. And if this still doesn't work . . . take up a stick and beat her soundly. It is better to punish the body and correct the soul than to damage the soul and spare the body. You should beat [your wife] only when she commits a serious wrong. Then readily beat her, not in rage but out of charity and concern for her soul.

Social and religious values were designed to teach women that it was their duty to yield to their husbands' desires. If they resisted, however, those values also taught that it was in a woman's best interest to have the badness beaten out of her. Violence was justified if an appeal to reason or faith was unsuccessful. Wife beating was rarely viewed as the first recourse.

AMERICAN TRADITIONS

Early Laws Allow "Chastisement"

In colonial America, English common law allowed physical "chastisement," as long as the husband did not inflict permanent damage on his wife. The early Puritans, however, forbade wife beating. According to a Massachusetts Bay Colony edict, "No man shall strike his wife nor any woman her husband on penalty of such fine not exceeding ten pounds for one offense, or such corporal punishment as the County shall determine."

Calvin Bradley v. The State (of Mississippi) resulted in the first American legal ruling on the subject of "reasonable chastisement." In that 1824 case, the court found that Bradley, convicted by a lower court of assault and battery against his wife, had gone too far in chastising his wife. "If the defendant now before us could shew from the record, in this case he confined himself within reasonable bounds, when he thought proper to chastise his wife, we would deliberate long before an affirmance of the judgment," the court noted. While criticizing Bradley for bringing shame to his family, the court ruled:

> Family broils and dissensions cannot be investigated before the tribunals of the country, without casting a shade over the character of those who are unfortunately engaged in the controversy. To screen from public reproach those who may be thus unhappily situated, let the husband be permitted to exercise the right of moderate chastisement in cases of great emergency and use salutary restrains in every case of misbehavior, without being subjected to vexatious prosecutions, resulting in mutual discredit and shame of all parties concerned.

Early Feminists Fail to Improve Wives' Legal Status

The first women's rights movement, inaugurated in 1848 at the Seneca Falls Woman's Rights Convention, was the first movement to analyze the husband's right to chastise his wife as a symbol of the political system of male dominance over females. In the *Declaration of Sentiments* (1848), the women objected to the status of married women: "In the covenant of marriage, she is compelled to promise obedience to her husband, he becoming, to all intents and purposes, her master — the law giving him power to deprive her of her liberty, and to administer chastisement."

A North Carolina High Court's ruling in *State v. Jesse Black* in 1864 illustrated the assertion of the Seneca Falls women, that upon marriage, husbands became the rulers of their wives. The case involved a man who abused his wife after she called him names. In its ruling the court said:

> A husband is responsible for the acts of his wife and he is required to govern his household, and for that purpose the law permits him to use towards his wife such a degree of force as is necessary to control an unruly temper and make her behave herself; and unless some permanent injury be inflicted, or there be an excess of violence, or such a degree of cruelty as shows that it is inflicted to gratify his own bad passions, the law will not invade the domestic forum, or go behind the curtain.

In 1874, just ten years later, the North Carolina court again expressed concern about excessive abuse but advised against public scrutiny of, or interference in, domestic and marital relationships. In *State v. Richard Oliver,* the court found:

> From motives of public policy and in order to preserve the sanctity of the domestic circle, the Courts will not listen to trivial complaints. . . . If no permanent injury has been inflicted, nor malice, cruelty, nor dangerous violence shown by the husband, it is better to draw the curtain, shut out the public gaze, and leave the parties to forget and forgive.

A Change in Direction

In a landmark Alabama case in 1871, a court found that a husband did not have the right to physically abuse his wife, even "moderately" or with "restraint." In *Fulgham v. State,* the court ruled that a married woman deserved protection under the law. The ruling stated:

> A rod which may be drawn through the wedding ring is not now deemed necessary to teach the wife her duty and subjection to the husband. The husband is therefore not justified or allowed by law to use such a weapon, or any other, for her moderate correction. The wife is not to be considered as the husband's slave. And the privilege, ancient though it be, to beat her with a stick, to pull her hair, choke her, spit in her face or kick her about the floor, or to inflict upon her like indignities, is not now acknowledged by our law.

In the same year (1871), the Massachusetts Supreme Court rejected a husband's manslaughter defense that he had a right to chastise his wife for drunkenness. He had hit his inebriated wife several times on the cheek and temple; she had fallen as a result, hit her head, and died. In *Commonwealth v. McAfee,* the Massachusetts Supreme Court announced that "beating or striking a wife violently with the open hand is not one of the rights conferred on a husband by the marriage, even if the wife be drunk or insolent."

Although the Alabama and Massachusetts cases declared husbands did not have the right to physically chastise their wives, no criminal penalties were yet attached to physical abuse. In fact, in a case three years earlier, *State v. Rhodes,* the North Carolina Supreme Court declared that although a husband's whipping of his wife "would without question have constituted a battery if the subject of it had not been the defendant's wife," they refused to convict him of assault and battery, ruling that if domestic assaults were prosecuted, "the evil of publicity would be greater than the evil involved in the trifles complained of."

Although Maryland enacted a law in 1882 that punished wife beaters with forty lashes with a whip or a year in jail, even in the early twentieth century courts still refused to convict wife batterers. In 1910 the U.S. Supreme Court ruled in *Thompson v. Thompson* that a wife had no cause for action on an assault and battery charge against her husband because it "would open the doors of the courts to accusations of all sorts of one spouse against the other and bring into public notice complaints for assaults, slander and libel."

Despite Laws, Little Recourse for Battered Wives

Thus, although court decisions affirmed that a husband could no longer legally beat his wife, in almost all cases a battered wife in the early twentieth century still had no legal recourse against her husband. Any criminal proceedings against a wife batterer had to be initiated by the state; women could not sue their husbands. Instead, the criminal justice system set up a separate court system—the family court—to deal with domestic complaints. According to author Reva B. Siegel, this act decriminalized physical abuse of women ("'The Rule of Love': Wife Beating as Prerogative and Privacy," *Yale Law Journal,* vol. 106, June 1996). Rather than punishing wife beaters, judges and social workers urged couples to reconcile, providing counseling designed to prevent divorce. Assault in this context was viewed as an inappropriate expression of emotions; wives and husbands needed to learn how to rechannel those emotions.

The ruling of a 1962 landmark case changed the legal consequences of physical abuse of a spouse. In *Self v. Self,* the Supreme Court of California agreed with earlier rulings, stating that a spouse's right to sue would "destroy the peace and harmony of the house." Despite that find-

ing, the court observed that this outdated assumption was based "on the bald theory that after a husband has beaten his wife there is a state of peace and harmony left to be disturbed." Therefore, "one spouse may maintain an action against the other" for physical abuse.

Despite the ruling enabling victims to seek legal recourse, by 1965 there had been little change. Jurisdictions throughout the United States ignored the complaints of battered women. For example, in Washington, D.C., 7,400 women filed official complaints and just two hundred arrest warrants were issued.

Social and Legal Recognition of Domestic Violence

In 1973 the first battered women's shelter in the United States opened in St. Paul, Minnesota. By 1976 there were four hundred programs for battered women operating in the United States. EMERGE, the first treatment program for male offenders, opened in Boston, Massachusetts, in 1977, and the following year many states enacted laws to protect victims of domestic violence. A decade later, in 1988, the U.S. surgeon general declared domestic abuse the leading health hazard to women in the United States. By the 1990s, there were well over a thousand battered women's programs in the United States.

In 1994 the Violence against Women Act granted female victims of violence, including battered women, federal civil rights protection. The civil rights section of the Violence against Women Act was tested in the U.S. Supreme Court in 1999, when Christy Brzonkala filed a civil suit after being raped by two football players from Virginia Polytechnic Institute. In a five-to-four decision in *U.S. v. Morrison,* the Supreme Court ruled that Congress could not enact a federal civil remedy "for victims of gender-motivated violence." Individuals who committed crimes motivated by a gender bias, the Court ruled, could not be held accountable at the federal level.

The U.S. Congress passed a revised act in October 2000, Victims of Trafficking and Violence Protection Act of 2000, which included sections on Strengthening Law Enforcement to Reduce Violence against Women, Strengthening Services to Victims of Violence, Limiting the Effects of Violence on Children, Strengthening Education and Training to Combat Violence against Women. The new legislation made no mention of women's civil rights. And although spouse abuse is illegal in the United States and women may now sue their abusers for damages at the state level, battering continues. Many women still feel helpless and trapped in abusive relationships, unable to tell others about their problems and unsure of where to seek and obtain help.

ABUSE IN OTHER CULTURES

Abuse threatens women's health and human rights throughout the world. Global estimates suggest as many as 30% of the world's women are at risk for violence (beatings, coerced sexual activity, or other physical abuse) at least once in their lives. It may occur in the home, the workplace, or the community and it may take different forms throughout the stages of a woman's life. (See Table 1.1.) Women of all races, ethnic backgrounds, and ages are subjected to forced abortion, rape, genital mutilation, and other acts of violence, often at the hands of their partners or persons known to them.

Data about violence against women are scarce. Most researchers agree that even when the data are available, rates of sexual abuse and domestic violence are significantly underestimated because many incidents are unreported. The official statistics that are collected by organizations such as the Statistical Commission and Economic Commission for Europe and the UN Interregional Crime and Justice Research Institute (UNICRI), are believed to be underreported—but still paint frightening pictures of the magnitude of the problem. For example, in industrialized countries, less than 1% of women were sexually assaulted in the past five years, and 1.3% of women had been victims of other offensive sexual behavior, according to J. N. van Kesteren, P. Mayhew, and P. Nieuwbeerta in *Criminal Victimisation in Seventeen Industrialised Countries: Key Findings from the 2000 International Crime Victims Survey* (The Hague: UN Interregional Crime and Justice Research Institute, 2000). The U.S. Department of State, in its 2003 *Country Reports on Human Rights Practices,* reported that between 10% and 15% of Ukrainian women had been raped. The report found that in Bosnia and Herzegovina as well as China, 30% of women were thought to have been victims of domestic violence; in Egypt, 67% of urban women and 30% of rural women had been victims of domestic violence. Another survey finds that reported instances of domestic abuse in the Ukraine rose by 16% in the five years ending January 1, 2000.

This section describes selected examples of violence against women practiced in various cultures. Although these practices are among the most extreme and dramatic instances of abuse, the fact that they have persisted into the twenty-first century is a shocking acknowledgment of a social problem of global proportions.

Bride Burning

In India, Pakistan, and Bangladesh, disputes over a bride's dowry—the money, property, or belongings given to the husband by the bride's family after marriage—has created a serious domestic violence crisis. The inability or unwillingness of a bride's family to meet dowry demands often results in brutality and sometimes death. The National Crime Bureau of the Government of India in 2002 estimated that each year about six thousand women are killed over dowry disputes (although they acknowl-

TABLE 1.1

Gender violence throughout the life cycle

Phase	Type of violence present
Prebirth	Sex-selective abortion (China, India, Republic of Korea); battering during pregnancy (emotional and physical effects on the woman; effects on birth outcome); coerced pregnancy (for example, mass rape in war)
Infancy	Female infanticide; emotional and physical abuse; differential access to food and medical care for girl infants
Girlhood	Child marriage; genital mutilation; sexual abuse by family members and strangers; differential access to food and medical care; child prostitution
Adolescence	Dating and courtship violence (for example, acid throwing in Bangladesh, date rape in the United States); economically coerced sex (African secondary school girls having to take up with "sugar daddies" to afford school fees); sexual abuse in the workplace; rape; sexual harassment; forced prostitution; trafficking in women
Reproductive age	Abuse of women by intimate male partners; marital rape; dowry abuse and murders; partner homicide; psychological abuse; sexual abuse in the workplace; sexual harassment; rape; abuse of women with disabilities
Elderly	Abuse of widows; elder abuse. (In the United States, the only country where data are now available, elder abuse affects mostly women)

SOURCE: Lori L. Heise, et al, "Gender Violence throughout the Life Cycle," in *Violence against Women: The Hidden Health Burden,* The International Bank for Reconstruction and Development, The World Bank, 1994

edge that the recorded number is a gross underestimate of actual murders of young women). Such women's groups as the International Society against Dowry and Bride Burning in India put the number closer to twenty-five thousand annually in India alone, according to Himendra Thakur in "Are Our Sisters and Daughters for Sale?" (http://www.indiatogether.org/wehost/nodowri/stats.htm [accessed November 16, 2004]). Many are victims of bride burning, a preplanned homicide committed by the groom and his family, in which women are doused with kerosene in the kitchen and set on fire; their deaths are later blamed on kitchen accidents. The risks for women are exacerbated by the unwillingness of many parents to shelter daughters in danger.

The phenomenon of burning brides who are unable to meet exorbitant dowry demands is alarming. Ahmed-Ghosh reported in "Chattels of Society: Domestic Violence in India" that in India a young bride is being beaten, burnt to death, or pushed to commit suicide every six hours (*Violence against Women,* vol. 10, January 2004). In the urban centers of Maharashtra state and greater Bombay, about one in five deaths of women aged fifteen to forty-four are due to "accidental burns"; the rate for younger women aged fifteen to twenty-four is one in four.

Although India has had an anti-dowry law since 1961, and Dowry Prohibition acts were passed in 1984 and 1986, the prohibition is not enforced. Dowry is still exchanged between the parents of newlyweds. Men usually only need to claim that their wives died as a result of a house fire or cooking accident or committed suicide to be freed from blame or suspicion. When cases are brought to court, it takes years for them to be heard. When they are heard, there is a high rate of acquittals. An Indian special public prosecutor quoted in "'Dowry Deaths' in Bangalore" said that in the first six months of 1999, out of 381 dowry death cases pending, fifty-one defendants had been acquitted and only eight convicted (*Frontline,* vol. 16, no. 17, August 14–27, 1999).

The lack of Indian society's recognition of domestic violence as a serious issue was graphically illustrated when the Indian Parliament unveiled the Protection from Domestic Violence Act of 2002. The act protected the right of husbands to beat their wives occasionally.

Wife Beating Still an Accepted Form of Discipline

In Iran and much of the Middle East, wife beating is an accepted form of discipline. The Koran, the basis of Islamic law, states:

> The men are placed in charge of the women, since God has endowed them with the necessary qualities and made them breadwinners. The righteous women will accept this arrangement obediently, and will honor their husbands in their absence, in accordance with God's commands. As for the women who show rebellion, you shall first enlighten them, then desert them in bed, and you may beat them as a last resort. Once they obey you, you have no excuse to transgress against them. God is high and most powerful.

Some interpret this passage of the Koran as allowing a Muslim husband to physically punish his wife whenever he determines she has misbehaved. For example, in his book, *The Woman in Islam,* Egyptian-born Sheikh Muhammad Kamal Mustafa states that wife beating can be used as a last resort, using "a rod that must not be stiff, but slim and lightweight so that no wounds, scars, or bruises are caused." The author was sentenced in January 2004 in a Barcelona court for publishing the book. The court found that the book contained incitement to violence against women and violated women's constitutional rights. The book was removed from bookstores in Spain.

The practice of wife beating is so culturally accepted that many women endorse the violence. In a 1996 study by Egypt's National Population Council, 86% of the 14,779 married women who responded said they believed a man is justified in beating his wife for refusing sex, talking back, talking to other men, neglecting his children, wasting money, or burning food. Agreement with a man's right to beat his wife varied according to the respondents' age, education, employment, and place of residence. The study also found that one out of every three married women had been beaten at least once by her spouse. Among pregnant women, 32% received a beating from their husbands; 44% of those women said they were beaten as often or more often during pregnancy than they had been before becoming pregnant.

Because premarital virginity and postmarital sexual fidelity are required of Islamic women, it is traditionally the role of male relatives to enforce chaste sexual conduct. In extreme cases, they do it through murder, known as "honor killing." In Islamic countries, men who kill a female relative because they perceive she is no longer chaste are generally given a lighter sentence than men convicted of other types of murders. Under a 1990 law, any Iraqi man who killed his own mother, sister, daughter, aunt, niece, or female cousin for adultery could receive immunity from prosecution.

The Hudood ordinances enacted in Pakistan in 1979 provided harsh punishments for violators of Islamic law; the ordinances replaced a system that included many more protections for women, according to Asma Jahangir in "Pakistan: The Women's Commission and the Hudood Ordinances," (http://www.ahrchk.net/hrsolid/mainfile.php/2003 vol13no04-05/2292/ [accessed September 18, 2004]). Under the Hudood ordinances, a female or non-Muslim witness is not allowed to testify in certain trials. Consequently, if a man rapes a woman in the presence of several females, he cannot be convicted by their testimony. In addition, rape of wives was made legal under the code, and women were liable for prosecution for adultery, or *zina.* In many cases, women alleging rape have been arrested and charged with *zina.* Punishment under the Hudood ordinances include death by stoning for unlawful sexual relations.

Increased conservatism in the Islamic world has forced more and more women to wear head scarves, undergo female circumcision, and avoid men in school and the workplace. The fundamentalist Taliban regime governing Afghanistan until 2002 banned women from any work outside the home, kept them from seeking and receiving needed medical care, and prevented girls from attending school. Women and girls could not appear outside the home unless they were accompanied by a male family member and wore a "burqa," a garment that covers the wearer from head to toe.

During 2002 Afghan women and girls took their first steps toward a new life by returning to school and work. Still, many women and girls remain trapped by poverty and rules imposed by strict husbands. In October 2002, CNN chief international correspondent Christiane Amanpour traveled to Afghanistan and broadcast a report on the CBS newsmagazine *Sixty Minutes* depicting impoverished families who sold their young daughters, as well as others who persisted in the belief that girls should not be educated.

Rape

In many parts of the world, women who are raped have nowhere to turn for help. In Colombia, for example, fewer than 0.5% of investigated rape cases in 1995 went to trial. Most cases—95%, according to Colombia's Institute for Legal Medicine—are never reported because the women know no action will be taken against their rapists.

RAPE IN WAR. The use of rape as a weapon of war occurs in many parts of the world. The high rates of rape in war are attributed to the idea that women are viewed as property, and men gain ownership of women by taking sexual liberties with them. Rape in the context of war is also provoked by the tendency to demonize and dehumanize the enemy, and by the climate of anger, hate, and immediate fear of death.

In Darfur, Sudan, rape has been used as a weapon of war by government-sponsored militia known as Janjawid since 2003 ("Darfur: Rape as a Weapon of War: Sexual Violence and Its Consequences," Amnesty International, July 19, 2004, http://web.amnesty.org/library/Index/ENGA FR540762004?open&of=ENG-373). The Janjawid, supported by the government army, attacks villages in Darfur, kills men, and rapes civilian women. The attacks are in response to the insurgency of two armed political groups and have led to the displacement of at least 1.2 million persons, according to Amnesty International. Women and girls are also targeted for abductions and sexual slavery.

During the Bosnian civil war it was estimated that Serbs, aware of how important chastity is to Muslims, raped more than twenty thousand Muslim women, forcing many women to bear Serbian children. Serbian "Rape Camps" existed across Bosnia, where Muslim women were held and routinely raped, according to Roy Gutman in "Rape Camps: Evidence Serb Leaders in Bosnia Oked Attacks" (*Newsday,* April 19, 1993). In Rwanda, as many as three hundred thousand ethnic Tutsi women were raped by the majority Hutu military during a bloody civil war in the 1990s, as reported by Llezlie L. Green in "Propaganda and Sexual Violence in the Rwandan Genocide: An Argument for Intersectionality in International Law" (*Columbia Human Rights Law Review,* Summer 2002, pp. 733-76). Many women became pregnant as a result of the rapes. Because abortion is illegal in Rwanda, women were forced to seek illegal abortions. Others abandoned their babies or committed infanticide. For those women who kept their children, survival has been precarious. Most of these women watched as their husbands and families were murdered at the same time they were raped. Now, their Tutsi neighbors shun their offspring and blame the mothers for their existence, according to Binaifer Nowrojee in *Shattered Lives: Sexual Violence during the Rwandan Genocide and its Aftermath* (Human Rights Watch, http://hrw.org/reports/1996/Rwanda.htm, September 1996).

The UN established war crimes tribunals for Rwanda and the former Yugoslavia, although neither has had much success. In 1997 the Rwanda Tribunal filed its first indict-ment for rape and sexual abuse. The international community has recently established a permanent International Criminal Court (ICC) to prosecute persons accused of crimes against humanity, including sexual violence, who are not brought to justice in their own countries. The ICC was to be formally established when sixty countries had ratified the Rome Statute of the International Criminal Court. On April 11, 2002, ten nations simultaneously ratified the statute, bringing the total to sixty-six and triggering its adoption. The Rome Statute entered into force on July 1, 2002. The first eighteen judges were sworn in on March 11, 2003. As of September, 2004, the ICC had been ratified by ninety-four nations.

The United States entered the ICC under the administration of President Bill Clinton. However, on May 6, 2002, the United States formally renounced its signature on the statute. President George W. Bush's administration cited serious reservations about the ICC and its functions, including concerns that it would have unchecked prosecutorial power and might undermine the UN Security Council's efforts to preserve international peace. Despite the U.S. decision to withdraw, there is widespread optimism about the establishment of the ICC and its potential global contribution to an effective justice system free of political influence. Some international affairs experts and historians mark the Rome Statute adoption as a historic achievement and the ICC as the most significant advance in international law since the founding of the UN.

CONSEQUENCES OF RAPE. The consequences of rape include immediate emotional symptoms, such as shock, anger, shame, fear, and helplessness. Rape also can trigger lasting psychological problems, such as confusion, disturbing or recurring memories, and self-blame. Physical injuries, sexually transmitted diseases, fatigue, and changes in appetite and sleep patterns may also occur in response to the trauma. Long-term consequences can be serious and debilitating. Rape victims may suffer from anger, distrust, and psychiatric disorders including:

- Post–traumatic stress disorder—Recurring memories and dreams, memory impairment, anxiety, sleep disorders, and social and emotional withdrawal

- Depression—Feelings of hopelessness, helplessness, loss of focus and purpose in life, fatigue, despair, and thoughts of suicide

- Alcohol and drug abuse—Substance abuse may occur as the victim attempts to self-medicate to relieve physical pain and dull the effects of bad memories and feelings or other emotional distress

Female Genital Mutilation

Female genital mutilation is practiced in twenty-eight African countries, in some parts of Asia and the Middle East, and among immigrant communities in Europe, Australia, Canada, and the United States. The World Health Organization estimates that between one hundred million and 140 million women and girls worldwide have undergone genital mutilation, and that each year another 2 million girls are at risk of undergoing genital mutilation of some type. Surveys of five African nations find that 93% of women in Mali and 89% of Sudanese women have been genitally mutilated. Slightly less than half the women of the Central African Republic and the Ivory Coast and 12% of Togo's women have also been "circumcised."

Different societies practice different rituals of so-called female circumcision, and young girls are subjected to a variety of procedures. Some procedures remove the foreskin of the clitoris; others involve "infibulation," in which the clitoris and labia minora are surgically removed and the two sides of the vulva are abraded and sewn together, usually with catgut. These procedures are performed without an anesthetic and often with primitive, unsterilized tools. Immediate health risks include hemorrhage, tetanus, blood poisoning, shock, and death. Women and girls who survive are left with terrible scarring, and their future sexual relationships are usually joyless and very painful. The inadequate openings the surgery leaves for the flow of urine and menstrual blood can cause vaginal and urinary tract infections and sometimes sterility, the ultimate disaster for women whose value is based on their fertility (ability to reproduce).

Infibulated women who do give birth must be surgically reopened, only to be resewn again after childbirth. In Somalia, a study of thirty-three infibulated women found that their final stage of labor was five times longer than normal, five of the babies died, and twenty-one babies suffered oxygen deprivation from the prolonged, obstructed labor. The information was reported by Lori L. Heise et al. in *Violence against Women: The Hidden Health Burden* (Washington, DC: The World Bank, 1994).

Some Muslims believe the Koran demands female genital mutilation (although, as the World Health Organization points out, the practice predates Islam); others see women's genitalia as unclean and believe infibulation is a ritual purification. Men in such cultures will not marry unmutilated women, believing them to be unclean, promiscuous, and sexually untrustworthy. Many women do not object to the procedure since they view it as a tradition and a natural part of their role in life. Some women, however, are trying to increase awareness about the procedure. They insist that female genital mutilation is not an important African tradition that must be maintained in the face of Western influence. Rather, they see it as violence directed against women. Many people believe that female genital mutilation stems from men's desire to control women's sexuality.

In June 1996 efforts to educate the public about this practice paid off when the U.S. Immigration and Naturalization Service (INS) recognized for the first time that the fear of genital mutilation was legitimate grounds for asylum. Fauziya Kasinga, a 19-year-old Tobago woman who feared she would be circumcised if she returned home, was detained in prison for one year while the INS made its decision. The ruling quoted an INS report that said that "women have little legal recourse and may face threats to their freedom, threats or acts of physical violence or social ostracism for refusing to undergo this harmful traditional practice or attempting to protect their female children."

The U.S. Congress outlawed infibulation in the United States under the Federal Prohibition of Female Genital Mutilation Act of 1996. Anyone found guilty of performing this surgery faces up to five years in jail. In addition, U.S. representatives to the World Bank and other international financial institutions are required to oppose loans to the twenty-eight African countries where the practice exists if those countries fail to conduct educational programs to prevent it.

In Egypt a 1995 government-supported study indicated that more than 97% of the 14,770 never-married women participants had undergone circumcision. Two years later, an Egyptian court overturned Egypt's ban on female genital mutilation. The ban was later restored through a decision from the Egyptian Supreme Court. Although it remains in effect, women's rights groups continue to work to change the Muslim tradition in villages where midwives and barbers still perform mutilations.

The Missing Women

In China, South Korea, India, Nepal, and other Asian countries, sons are favored over daughters for their economic value and their ability to carry on the family name. Some prospective parents believe that a female child is more likely to present a financial burden to her family, while a male child is a potential breadwinner who will not require such expenditures as a dowry. Preference for boys where resources are scarce can mean that daughters receive less food, education, and medical care than their brothers. The poor health care and nutrition daughters receive results in a higher child mortality rate among girls than boys.

In China, the problem is particularly acute. The U.S. Department of State, in its 2003 publication *Country Reports on Human Rights Practices,* stated: "Female infanticide, sex-selective abortions, and the abandonment and neglect of baby girls remained problems due to the traditional preference for sons and the birth limitation policy." This so-called "one child policy," established in 1979, imposed a variety of penalties on most couples who chose to have more than one child. The policy was instituted as law, with minor changes, in 2002. According to the Department of State report, the male-to-female birth ratio in China is about 116.9 to one hundred, as compared with a statistical norm of 106 to one hundred. For second births, which require parents to pay a social compensation fee of one-half to eight times the average worker's annual disposable income, the ratio was even higher, at 151.9 to one hundred.

In India, the male-to-female ratio has increased to one hundred males to every 92.7 females, a large demographic difference. Based on comparisons of male-to-female sex ratios, Princeton University demographer Ansley Coale estimated that at least sixty million women are missing, mainly from Asia and North Africa. These are females who have been aborted, given inferior care in childhood, underfed, and subjected to various forms of gender violence resulting in death.

CHAPTER 2
SPOUSE AND PARTNER ABUSE—WHO, WHAT, AND WHEN?

Although domestic violence has occurred for centuries, women have generally felt isolated, unsupported, and ashamed because of their victimization and frustrated in their attempts to deal with or escape the violence. The consciousness-raising groups that emerged during the rise of the second wave of U.S. feminism in the 1960s and 1970s provided small groups of women a place to discuss their problems as women. Their analysis of personal problems—including domestic violence—allowed them to understand women's collective oppression. This became the basis for feminist collective action.

Efforts to aid battered women arose out of this feminist consciousness. The first battered women's shelter was founded in 1971 by Erin Pizzey in London. Pizzey, the recognized founder of the modern women's shelter movement, published the first book on domestic violence, *Scream Quietly, or the Neighbors Will Hear,* in 1974. Authors in the United States followed suit. In 1975 Susan Brownmiller's *Against Our Will,* a book about the politics and sociology of rape, was published, and in 1976, Del Martin's book *Battered Wives* appeared, focusing specifically on violence within marriage functioning as part of male dominance of women.

In the late twentieth century, domestic violence was the subject of countless books, films, and stage plays. Of these, one of the most memorable was *The Burning Bed,* based on the true story of Francine Hughes, an East Lansing, Michigan, woman. After having suffered seventeen years of abuse, she burned her abusive husband to death in 1977 as he slept. Hughes was acquitted of murder based on a defense of temporary insanity caused by years of physical and psychological abuse. Her case gave rise to the "battered woman's defense," which subsequently was widely used to defend abused women who killed their partners. A made-for-television movie based on Hughes's case aired in 1984 to an audience of seventy-five million, giving momentum to the battered women's movement and significantly influencing legislative reform.

In 1978, the U.S. Commission on Civil Rights held a forum titled "Consultation on Battered Women" in Washington, D.C., considering violence against women as a civil rights issue. The testimony from that forum was published as *Battered Women—Issues of Public Policy.* The following year, the first Congressional hearings were held on the issue of domestic violence.

The subject dominated the media in 1995 with the highly publicized murder trial of O.J. Simpson, who was accused of the brutal slaying of his ex-wife, Nicole Brown, and her friend, Ronald Goldman. Simpson, a former football star and popular sports commentator, was acquitted of murder, but not until millions of Americans had heard a recording of Brown begging police for help and had seen a photo of her face, bruised and bloody from a beating, which was among the evidence presented at Simpson's trial.

Celebrities like O.J. Simpson from the sports and entertainment industries who have been convicted of domestic violence attract the media spotlight. According to the Family Violence Prevention Fund, a national nonprofit organization, when society continues to celebrate and reward actors and athletes who are violent to their partners, it not only condones their bad behavior, but also suggests that their abusive behavior is glamorous and desirable. The organization regularly updates a celebrity "Hall of Shame" on its Web site. As of September 2004, the Family Violence Prevention Fund's Hall of Shame listed almost one hundred celebrities, including:

- James Brown. In February 2004, this singer was arrested for assaulting his wife. His lifetime achievement award from the John F. Kennedy Center for the Performing Arts had been protested in November 2003 by advocates for victims of domestic violence. They protested because Brown had been charged with assaulting his previous wife in 1988, and had settled several sexual harassment lawsuits against him since then.

- Dwayne Carswell. In July 2003, the Denver Broncos football player was arrested for assaulting his girlfriend by picking her up by the neck and biting her. He had two previous arrests for assaulting other women.

- Dale Ellis. In February 2002 the former SuperSonics basketball player pleaded guilty to domestic violence charges. He had been convicted 13 years earlier of assaulting his wife and resisting arrest.

- Joe Frazier. The former heavyweight boxing champion was arrested in February 2004 for assaulting his girlfriend in front of their twelve-year-old son in their home.

- Michael Peterson. In October 2003, the novelist was found guilty of murdering his wife, whom he claimed had fallen down a flight of stairs.

- Charlie Sheen. In June 1997, the actor was given a one-year suspended sentence, a two-year probation, and ordered to perform three hundred hours of community service for physically abusing a former girlfriend.

In the summer of 2002, the wives of four soldiers based at Fort Bragg, North Carolina, were murdered over the course of six weeks. In all four cases, their husbands were alleged to have committed the murder; in two cases the soldiers apparently committed suicide after killing their wives. This rash of murders once again focused public and media attention on the issue of spousal violence. Three of the four husbands were special operations soldiers who had been deployed to Afghanistan, and some news media reports speculated that the murders may have been caused by stress. In September 2002 the U.S. Army and Congress launched an investigation of the crimes to determine their causes and prevent similar tragedies. In September 2004, no report had thus far been made public.

DEFINITIONS OF ABUSE

Early definitions of domestic abuse focused exclusively on physical assault and bodily injury. For example, the Colorado Committee of the Advisory Committee to the U.S. Commission on Civil Rights offered this definition of a battered wife in *The Silent Victims: Denver's Battered Women* (Washington, DC: U.S. Commission on Civil Rights, 1977): "a woman who has received deliberate, severe and repeated physical injury from her husband, the minimal injury being severe bruising." This definition excluded acts like pushing, slapping, pinching, or other violent acts perpetrated by husbands on their wives that produced no or minimal bruising, as well as threats of violence.

In their groundbreaking work based on the 1975 and 1985 National Family Violence Surveys (NFVS), Murray Straus and Richard Gelles defined "spousal violence" in specific actions, known as the Conflict Tactics Scale. That scale is now the measure most widely used to estimate the extent of spousal abuse. According to the scale, a spouse can be considered abusive if he or she:

- Throws something at a partner
- Pushes, grabs, or shoves
- Slaps
- Kicks, bites, or hits the partner with a fist
- Hits or tries to hit the partner with an object
- Beats up the partner
- Threatens the partner with a knife or a gun
- Uses a knife or fires a gun at the partner

Today, a broader interpretation is accepted and abuse is understood to include sexual and psychological actions and harm, such as marital rape and forced isolation. Feminist scholars and advocates have expanded the definition to encompass issues of intent, control, and power, conceptualizing the problem of violence against women as "coercive control" (Richard J. Gelles, "Estimating the Incidence and Prevalence of Violence against Women," *Violence against Women*, vol. 6, July 2000). The National Coalition against Domestic Violence defines battering as a pattern of behavior through which a person establishes power and control over another person by means of fear and intimidation. The incorrect belief that abusers are entitled to control their partners is a primary cause of aggression and abuse, according to the coalition.

The National Coalition against Domestic Violence also describes battering as emotional, economic, and sexual abuse, as well as using children, threats, male privilege, intimidation, isolation, and various other strategies to maintain power through fear and intimidation. The organization argues it is important to view all these behaviors as battering in order to understand how verbal threats, a single slap, or an insult can escalate to a life-threatening situation.

An international examination of violence by Lori Heise et al. in *Violence against Women: The Hidden Health Burden* (Washington, DC: World Bank, 1994) also defined abuse in terms broad enough to include the wide variety of abuses that occur throughout the world. Heise and colleagues observed that violence against women is tolerated partly because the victims are female. They distinguished between cultural customs and abuse intended to harm. Genital mutilation, for instance, is a ritual or tradition intended by its practitioners to guarantee marriage for the female victim, rather than abuse that is intended to harm. Still, whether it is considered custom or ritualized abuse, this practice can cause long-term physical and psychological harm, suffering, and even death. Table 2.1 shows definitions of violence against women developed by different organizations around the world.

Heise and colleagues cautioned against using the overly broad definitions of abuse proposed by some orga-

TABLE 2.1

Definitions of violence against women from around the world

Behavior by the man, adopted to control his victim, which results in physical, sexual and/or psychological damage, forced isolation, or economic deprivation or behavior which leaves a woman living in fear. (Australia, 1991)

Any act involving use of force or coercion with an intent of perpetuating/promoting hierarchical gender relations. (Asia Pacific Forum on Women, Law and Development, 1990)

Any act of gender-based violence that results in, or is likely to result in, physical, sexual or psychological harm or suffering to women, including threats of such acts, coercion or arbitrary deprivations of liberty, whether occurring in public or private life. Violence against women shall be understood to encompass but not be limited to:

Physical, sexual and psychological violence occurring in the family and in the community, including battering, sexual abuse of female children, dowry-related violence, marital rape, female genital mutilation and other traditional practices harmful to women, non-spousal violence, violence related to exploitation, sexual harassment and intimidation at work, in educational institutions and elsewhere, trafficking in women, forced prostitution, and violence perpetrated or condoned by the State. (UN Declaration against Violence against Women)

Any act, omission or conduct by means of which physical, sexual or mental suffering is inflicted, directly or indirectly, through deceit, seduction, threat, coercion or any other means, on any woman with the purpose or effect of intimidating, punishing or humiliating her or of maintaining her in sex-stereotyped roles or of denying her human dignity, sexual self-determination, physical, mental and moral integrity or of undermining the security of her person, her self-respect or her personality, or of diminishing her physical or mental capacities. (Draft Pan American Treaty against Violence against Women)

Any act or omission which prejudices the life, the physical or psychological integrity or the liberty of a person or which seriously harms the development of his or her personality. (Council of Europe, 1986)

SOURCE: Lori L. Heise, et al, "Appendix Box B. 1. Definitions of Violence against Women," in *Violence against Women: The Hidden Health Burden,* The International Bank for Reconstruction and Development, The World Bank, 1994

nizations, which encompass gender inequalities such as unequal pay or lack of access to contraception or other health care services. They termed such inequalities "discrimination," rather than "abuse." Abuse against women, according to their study, is verbal or physical force, coercion, or deprivation directed against a woman or girl that causes physical or psychological harm, humiliation, loss of liberty, or other female subordination.

HOW MUCH ABUSE OCCURS?

Because domestic violence is often unreported, it is impossible to be certain exactly how many domestic assaults occur each year. Variations in definitions of violence and abuse, the types of questions posed by researchers, and the context in which they are asked compound the difficulty. For example, when victims are questioned in the presence of their abusers, or even other family members, they are often more reluctant to report instances of violence. Studies on the subject are sometimes contradictory, but most show that domestic violence remains a growing concern. Many researchers fear that available data represent only the tip of the iceberg of a problem of glacial proportions.

To understand why there are so many varying estimates of domestic violence, it is necessary to consider the surveys, studies, and reports themselves. The source and purpose of the research, the definition of abuse used, the population surveyed, and the survey setting, as well as the political agendas of the surveyors and researchers, may elicit different data and varying interpretations of these data (Richard J. Gelles, "Estimating the Incidence and Prevalence of Violence against Women," *Violence against Women*, vol. 6, July 2000).

According to the World Health Organization, in countries where large-scale studies are conducted, between 10% and 50% of women report they have suffered physical abuse at the hands of an intimate partner (intimates include spouses, former spouses, boyfriends, and girlfriends). Population-based estimates suggest that from 12% to 25% of women experience attempted or completed forced sex with an intimate partner or former partner during their lives. The World Health Organization also observed that prostitution and trafficking for sex, activities strongly linked to violence against women and girls, appeared to be on the rise during the late 1990s and early twenty-first century.

The National Family Violence Surveys are among the most analyzed and cited data in the literature about intimate partner violence. The strength of these surveys lies in their ability to measure violent behavior that respondents might not classify as criminal. Using data from the 1975 and 1985 NFVS, Straus and Gelles estimated that about 1.6 million women were severely beaten by their partners in 1985, down from 2.1 million in 1975 ("Societal Change and Change in Family Violence from 1975 to 1985 As Revealed by Two National Surveys," *Journal of Marriage and the Family*, vol. 48, August 1986).

Other national data are derived from national sample surveys, such as the National Crime Victimization Surveys (NCVS), which measure violent assaults by intimate partners, including rape and sexual assault, and the Uniform Crime Reports, which supplement NCVS data with information about homicides. One advantage of these surveys is that they enable researchers to observe trends in interpersonal violence. For example, NCVS data reveal a decline in intimate partner violent victimizations during the 1990s (except for a slight increase from 1997 to 1998).

A joint effort of the U.S. Departments of Justice and Health and Human Services and the Centers for Disease Control and Prevention, the National Violence against Women Survey (NVAWS) collected data about intimate and non-intimate partner violence during the 1990s. The NVAWS and NCVS are considered the most reliable sources of data about intimate partner violence even though their differing approaches make data comparisons difficult. For example, the NCVS is a survey about crime, and since some victims do not consider instances of intimate partner violence crimes, they may be less likely to disclose them in the NCVS.

TABLE 2.2

Persons victimized by an intimate partner in lifetime and in previous 12 months, by type of victimization and gender, 1996

	In lifetime			
	Percent		Number[a]	
Type of victimization	Women (n = 8,000)	Men (n = 8,000)	Women (100,697,000)	Men (92,748,000)
Rape[b]***	7.7	0.3	7,753,669	278,244
Physical assault[b]***	22.1	7.4	22,254,037	6,863,352
Rape and/or physical assault[b]***	24.8	7.6	24,972,856	7,048,848
Stalking[b]***	4.8	0.6	4,833,456	556,488
Total victimized[b]***	25.5	7.9	25,677,735	7,327,092

	In previous 12 months			
	Percent		Number[a]	
Type of violence	Women (n = 8,000)	Men (n = 8,000)	Women (100,697,000)	Men (92,748,000)
Rape	0.2	—[c]	201,394	—[c]
Physical assault[b]*	1.3	0.9	1,309,061	834,732
Rape and/or physical assault[b]*	1.5	0.9[d]	1,510,455	834,732
Stalking[b]**	0.5	0.2	503,485	185,496
Total victimized[b]***	1.8	1.1	1,812,546	1,020,228

[a]Based on estimates of women and men 18 years of age and older: Wetrogen, S.I., *Projections of the Population of States by Age, Sex, and Race: 1988 to 2010*, Current Population Reports, Washington, D.C.: U.S. Bureau of the Census, 1988: 25–1017.
[b]Differences between women and men are statistically significant: χ^2, *$p \le .05$, **$p \le .01$, ***$p \le .001$.
[c]Estimates not calculated on fewer than five victims.
[d]Because only three men reported being raped by an intimate partner in the previous 12 months, the percentage of men physically assaulted and physically assaulted and/or raped is the same.

SOURCE: Patricia Tjaden and Nancy Thoennes, "Exhibit 1. Persons Victimized by an Intimate Partner in Lifetime and in Previous 12 Months, by Type of Victimization and Gender", in *Extent, Nature, and Consequences of Intimate Partner Violence: Findings from the National Violence against Women Survey*, National Institute of Justice and Centers for Disease Control and Prevention, July 2000, http://www.ncjrs.org/pdffiles1/nij/181867.pdf (accessed September 10, 2004)

The Bureau of Justice Statistics published results from the NCVS in *Intimate Partner Violence, 1993–2001* (Washington, DC: Bureau of Justice Statistics, February 2003). Researchers found that although the number of intimate violence victims decreased between 1993 and 2001, women still experienced about 588,490 nonfatal violent incidents at the hands of intimates in 2001, down from 1.1 million in 1993. More than 1,200 women were killed by an intimate partner in 2000.

The National Violence against Women Survey

The National Violence against Women Survey (NVAWS) collected information from interviews with eight thousand men and eight thousand women to assess their experiences as victims of various types of violence, including domestic violence. The NVAWS asked survey respondents about physical assaults and rape, but excluded other sexual assaults, murders, and robberies.

In *Extent, Nature and Consequences of Intimate Violence: Findings from the National Violence against Women Survey* (Washington, DC: National Institute of Justice and Centers for Disease Control and Prevention, July 2000), researchers Patricia Tjaden and Nancy Thoennes found that intimate violence is pervasive in American society, with women suffering about three times as much of this violence as men. They estimated that 22.1% of women (twenty-two million) are physically assaulted by a loved one during the course of their lifetimes, while about 7.4% of men (seven million) were physically assaulted by intimates over their lifetimes (See Table 2.2.) Women were also more likely to become victims of rape, stalking, and physical assault by intimates than their male counterparts at some time during their lifetimes. Furthermore, women physically assaulted by their partners averaged nearly seven assaults by the same person, as opposed to men, who averaged 4.4 assaults.

During the twelve months that preceded the interview, women also reported higher rates of rape, stalking, and physical assault than did men. Tjaden and Thoennes estimated based on NVAWS data that about 1.5% of the surveyed women (more than 1.5 million) and 0.9% of the men (834,732) reported they had been raped and/or physically assaulted by a partner in the twelve months preceding the survey. In other words, approximately 4.8 million women and 2.9 million men are assaulted every year.

The rates of violence between intimate partners varied by race. Asian/Pacific Islanders reported lower rates of violence than men and women from other minority groups, and African-American and American Indian/Alaska Natives reported higher rates. (See Table 2.3.)

Tjaden and Thoennes concluded that the majority of partner abuse and violence is not reported to the police.

TABLE 2.3

Persons victimized by an intimate partner in lifetime, by victim gender, type of victimization, and victim race, 1996

Victim gender/ Type of victimization	Persons victimized in lifetime (%)				
	White	African-American	Asian Pacific Islander	American Indian/ Alaska Native	Mixed Race
Women	(n = 6,452)	(n = 780)	(n = 133)	(n = 88)	(n = 397)
Rape[1]	7.7	7.4	3.8[2]	15.9	8.1
Physical assault[3,4]	21.3	26.3	12.8	30.7	27.0
Stalking	4.7	4.2	—[5]	10.2[2]	6.3
Total victimized[3]	24.8	29.1	15.0	37.5	30.2
Men	(n = 6,424)	(n = 659)	(n = 165)	(n = 105)	(n = 406)
Rape	0.2	0.9[2]	—[5]	—[5]	—[5]
Physical assault	7.2	10.8	—[5]	11.4	8.6
Stalking	0.6	1.1[2]	—[5]	—[5]	1.2[2]
Total victimized	7.5	12.0	3.0[2]	12.4	9.1

[1]Estimates for American Indian/Alaska Native women are significantly higher than those for white and African-American women: Tukey's B, $p \le .05$.
[2]Relative standard error exceeds 30 percent; estimates not included in statistical testing.
[3]Estimates for Asian/Pacific Islander women are significantly lower than those for African-American, American Indian/Alaska Native, and mixed-race women: Tukey's B, $p \le .05$.
[4]Estimates for African-American women are significantly higher than those for white women: Tukey's B, $p \le .05$.
[5]Estimates not calculated on fewer than five victims.

SOURCE: Patricia Tjaden and Nancy Thoennes, "Exhibit 6. Persons Victimized by an Intimate Partner in Lifetime, by Victim Gender, Type of Victimization, and Victim Race," in *Extent, Nature, and Consequences of Intimate Partner Violence: Findings from the National Violence against Women Survey*, National Institute of Justice and Centers for Disease Control and Prevention, July 2000, http://www.ncjrs.org/pdffiles1/nij/181867.pdf (accessed September 10, 2004)

Women reported about one-fifth of rapes, one-quarter of physical assaults, and one-half of stalking incidents to police, while men who had been victimized reported abuse to police even less frequently. Table 2.4 shows the reasons victims did not report their abuse to the police. Many victims said they felt the police would not or could not do anything on their behalf. These expressions of helplessness and hopelessness—feeling that others in a position to assist would be unwilling or unable to do so—is a common characteristic shared by many victims of intimate partner violence.

STATISTICS FOR VIOLENCE IN SAME-SEX COUPLES ARE PROBLEMATIC. The NVAWS also found that same-sex couples who lived together reported experiencing far more intimate violence in their lifetimes than heterosexual cohabitants. Among women, 39.2% of the same-sex cohabitants and 21.7% of the opposite-sex cohabitants reported being raped, physically assaulted, or stalked by a partner during their lifetimes. Among men, the comparative figures were 23.1% and 7.4%, respectively.

Although survey findings indicated that members of same-sex couples experience more intimate partner violence than do heterosexual couples, the reported violence does not necessarily occur within the same-sex relationship. When comparing intimate partner victimization rates among same-sex and opposite-sex cohabitants by the gender of the perpetrator, Tjaden and Thoennes found that 30.4% of the same-sex women cohabitants reported being victimized by a male partner sometime in their lifetimes, whereas 11.4% reported being victimized by a female partner. The researchers concluded that same-sex cohabit-ing women were three times more likely to report being victimized by a male partner than by a female partner. In comparison, women who lived with men were nearly twice as likely to report being victimized by a male than same-sex cohabiting women were to report being victimized by a female partner. (See Figure 2.1.)

Male same-sex partners reported more partner violence than men who lived with women. About 23% of men who lived with men said they had been raped, sexually assaulted, or stalked by a male cohabitant, as opposed to just 7.4% of men who reported comparable experiences with female cohabitants. This finding confirms the widely held observation that violence and abuse in intimate partner relationships is primarily inflicted by men, whether a partner is male or female.

In comparison with the research on intimate partner violence between men and women, the literature about same-sex violence is very sparse, in part because many respondents may consider disclosing same-sex relationships risky and revealing partner violence even more sensitive. Furthermore, not all persons who engage in same-sex relationships identify themselves as homosexual, leading to more questions about the quality of data gathered. The research that examines same-sex partner violence reveals that it is quite similar to heterosexual partner violence—abuse arises in the attempts of one partner to exert control over the other and it escalates throughout the course of the relationship.

The National Crime Victimization Surveys

The NCVS are ongoing federal surveys that interview eighty thousand persons from a representative sample of

TABLE 2.4

Distribution of rape, physical assault, and stalking victims who did not report their victimization to the police, by reasons for not reporting and gender, 1996

Reason for not reporting[2]	Rape victims (%)	Physical assault victims (%)		Stalking victims (%)	
	Women (n = 311)	Women (n = 2,062)	Men (n = 468)	Women (n = 165)	Men (n = 30)
Police couldn't do anything	13.2	99.7	100.0	100.0	100.0
Police wouldn't believe me	7.1	61.3[3]***	45.1	98.2	93.3
Fear of perpetrator	21.2	11.7[3]	1.9[4]	38.2[3]**	16.7[4]
Minor, one-time incident	20.3	37.9[3]***	58.5	33.9	36.7[4]
Ashamed, wanted to keep incident private	16.1	10.4[3]**	7.1	61.8	76.7
Wanted to handle it myself	7.7	7.3	5.8	7.9	—[5]
Victim or attacker moved away	—[5]	2.4	—[5]	12.1	—[5]
Attacker was a police officer	—[5]	4.7	3.8	7.9	—[5]
Too young, a child	3.5	2.2	1.5[4]	—[5]	—[5]
Reported to the military or someone else	—[5]	0.8[4]	—[5]	—[5]	—[5]
Didn't want police, court involvement	5.8	32.0[3]**	24.6	35.2	40.0
Wanted to protect attacker, relationship, or children	8.7	34.8[3]**	29.5	45.5	43.3

[1]Estimates are based on the most recent intimate partner victimization since age 18. Estimates not calculated for male rape victims because there were fewer than five victims when stratified by variables.
[2]Estimates exceed 100 percent because some victims gave multiple responses.
[3]Differences between women and men are statistically significant: χ^2, ***$p \le .001$, **$p \le .05$.
[4]Relative standard error exceeds 30 percent; statistical tests not performed.
[5]Estimates not calculated for fewer than five victims.

SOURCE: Patricia Tjaden and Nancy Thoennes, "Exhibit 17. Distribution of Rape, Physical Assault, and Stalking Victims Who Did Not Report Their Victimization to the Police, by Reasons for Not Reporting and Gender," in *Extent, Nature, and Consequences of Intimate Partner Violence: Findings from the National Violence against Women Survey*, National Institute of Justice and Centers for Disease Control and Prevention, July 2000, http://www.ncjrs.org/pdffiles1/nij/181867.pdf (accessed September 10, 2004)

households biannually to estimate the amount of crime committed against persons over age twelve in the United States. While the surveys cover all types of crime, they were extensively redesigned in 1992 to produce more accurate reports of rape, sexual assault, and other violent crimes committed by intimates or family members.

The 2003 report of NCVS trends found that the rate of violent crime fell by 54.7% from 1993 to 2003, although crime rates seem to have stabilized since 2001. Although the 2003 NCVS's criminal victimization estimates are among the lowest since the NCVS began in 1973, the numbers are still staggering: 5.4 million violent crimes were committed in 2003 (rape, sexual assault, robbery, aggravated assault, and simple assault). (See Figure 2.2.)

More than one in ten people (10.6%) who were victims of violent crimes in 2000 were victimized by intimate partners. Women were victimized by intimate partners at a greater rate than were men—19.9% of female victims named an intimate partner as the offender, compared with fewer than 2.5% of men. In sexual assault cases, 10.1% of women reported that the rapist was an intimate partner, 1.8% of female rape victims reported another relative was the perpetrator, and 57.3% reported a friend or acquaintance was the perpetrator. Among men, 52.2% of sexual assault/rape victims had been assaulted by a friend or acquaintance; no men reported having been assaulted or raped by an intimate or other family member. (See Table 2.5.)

In 2003, women continued to identify offenders as an intimate, friend, other relative, or acquaintance in about two-thirds of violent crimes (67%), while more than half of male victims identified the offender as a stranger (54%). This difference is largely accounted for by the fact that only 3% of male victims of violent crime identified their offender as an intimate, compared with 19% of female victims. Women were also considerably more likely to report that their offender was another relative (10%) than men were (5%). (See Table 2.6.)

Although men continued to experience higher rates of violent victimizations than women, the rates for both genders declined from 1993 to 2003. (See Figure 2.3.) Rates among persons from most racial, ethnic, and socioeconomic groups also declined from 1993 to 2001. The most significant annual declines in violent crime rates were observed among males and African-Americans. (See Table 2.7.)

According to the NCVS, almost half of all violent victimizations were reported to the police in 2003 (47.5%)—38.5% of rape and sexual assaults, 59.4% of aggravated assaults, and 42.1% of simple assaults. Women reported violent offenses more often than men did (49.4% and 45.7%, respectively).

The 1985 National Family Violence Survey

The National Family Violence Survey, considered by many to be the source of the most important research on

FIGURE 2.1

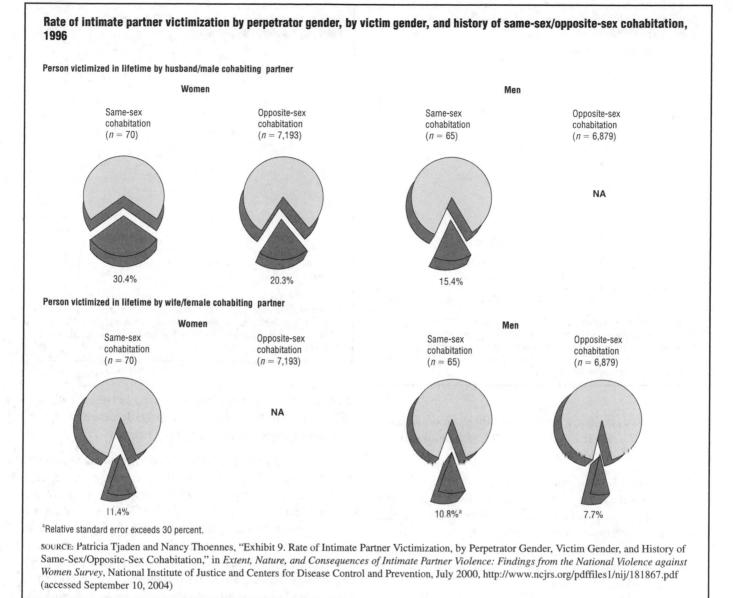

Rate of intimate partner victimization by perpetrator gender, by victim gender, and history of same-sex/opposite-sex cohabitation, 1996

Person victimized in lifetime by husband/male cohabiting partner

Women

Same-sex cohabitation (*n* = 70)

Opposite-sex cohabitation (*n* = 7,193)

30.4% 20.3%

Men

Same-sex cohabitation (*n* = 65)

Opposite-sex cohabitation (*n* = 6,879)

15.4% NA

Person victimized in lifetime by wife/female cohabiting partner

Women

Same-sex cohabitation (*n* = 70)

Opposite-sex cohabitation (*n* = 7,193)

11.4% NA

Men

Same-sex cohabitation (*n* = 65)

Opposite-sex cohabitation (*n* = 6,879)

10.8%[a] 7.7%

[a]Relative standard error exceeds 30 percent.

SOURCE: Patricia Tjaden and Nancy Thoennes, "Exhibit 9. Rate of Intimate Partner Victimization, by Perpetrator Gender, Victim Gender, and History of Same-Sex/Opposite-Sex Cohabitation," in *Extent, Nature, and Consequences of Intimate Partner Violence: Findings from the National Violence against Women Survey*, National Institute of Justice and Centers for Disease Control and Prevention, July 2000, http://www.ncjrs.org/pdffiles1/nij/181867.pdf (accessed September 10, 2004)

family violence, was originally conducted in 1975 for the Family Research Laboratory at the University of New Hampshire, Durham. Ten years later, in a follow-up to the landmark study, Straus and Gelles found that the rate of assaults by husbands on wives had dropped slightly during the decade, from 121 instances per one thousand couples in 1975 to 113 instances per one thousand couples in 1985. The rate of severe violence, such as hitting, kicking, or using a weapon, however, had declined sharply, from thirty-eight to thirty per one thousand couples—a 21% drop.

The study's most controversial finding indicated that women were initiating domestic violence at a rate equal to men. The 1985 study reported that in half of the cases, the abuse was mutual. After reassessing their data in 1990 and again in 1993, Straus and Gelles concluded that although there were similar levels of abuse between men and women, men were six times more likely to inflict serious injury.

In a paper presented in 1994 to the World Congress of Sociology titled *Changes in Spouse Assault Rates from 1975 to 1992: A Comparison of Three National Surveys in the United States*, Murray Straus and Glenda Kaufman Kantor compared the rates of abuse from the 1975 and 1985 NFVS and a 1992 survey conducted by Kantor. When the researchers reclassified "minor assault" to include pushing, grabbing, shoving, and slapping, and "severe assault" to include behavior likely to cause serious injury, such as kicking, punching, beating, and threatening with a weapon, they found some startling results.

The rates of reclassified minor assaults, which were considered less likely to cause injuries requiring medical treatment, decreased for husbands between the 1975 and 1985 surveys, yet remained constant for wives. The researchers found the same trend held true for severe assaults by husbands versus those by wives. While the

FIGURE 2.2

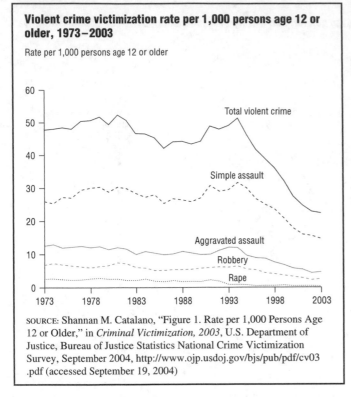

Violent crime victimization rate per 1,000 persons age 12 or older, 1973–2003

Rate per 1,000 persons age 12 or older

SOURCE: Shannan M. Catalano, "Figure 1. Rate per 1,000 Persons Age 12 or Older," in *Criminal Victimization, 2003*, U.S. Department of Justice, Bureau of Justice Statistics National Crime Victimization Survey, September 2004, http://www.ojp.usdoj.gov/bjs/pub/pdf/cv03 .pdf (accessed September 19, 2004)

FIGURE 2.3

Rate of violent victimization per 1,000 persons age 12 or older, by gender, 1993–2003

SOURCE: Shannan M. Catalano, "Figure 3. Violent Crime and Gender," in *Criminal Victimization, 2003*, U.S. Department of Justice, Bureau of Justice Statistics National Crime Victimization Survey, September 2004, http://www.ojp.usdoj.gov/bjs/pub/pdf/cv03.pdf (accessed September 19, 2004)

rate of severe assaults by men against their wives declined 50% in the 17 years from 1975 to 1992, severe assaults by women remained fairly steady.

Straus and Kantor concluded that the reason for the decline in severe assaults by husbands was that over time men became increasingly aware that battering was a crime and grew reluctant to admit the abuse. At the same time, women had been encouraged not to tolerate abuse and to report it, accounting for an increase in the reporting of even minor instances of abuse.

When abuse was measured based on separate reports by men and women, Straus and Kantor found that minor assaults by husbands decreased from 1975 to 1985. Based on the husbands' reports, these rates continued to decline from 1985 to 1992, but wives reported an increase over the same period. Men also reported a decrease in the rate of severe abuse between 1975 and 1985, while women reported no change. In contrast, between 1985 and 1992 men reported a slight increase in the rate of severe abuse while women reported a sharp drop of 43%. These findings appeared to contradict Straus and Kantor's hypothesis that the rate change was a result of men's reluctance to report abuse and women's greater freedom to report it.

According to women, minor abuse perpetrated by wives against their husbands declined from 1975 to 1985, but increased substantially from 1985 to 1992. Men, however, said the rate of minor abuse by their wives increased over both periods. Women also reported that the rate of severe assaults against their husbands remained steady

during the first decade but increased between 1985 and 1992. Husbands reported a steady decrease in severe assaults by their wives during both periods.

DRAWING CONCLUSIONS FROM THE DATA. Straus and Kantor observed that the large decrease in severe assaults by husbands was supported by Federal Bureau of Investigation (FBI) statistics showing an 18% drop in the number of women killed by their husbands during that period. Straus and Kantor speculated that strides made over several years, such as justice system interventions to punish abusive husbands, along with the greater availability of shelters and restraining orders, played a role in the decline of severe abuse. The lack of change in minor assaults by husbands may reflect the emphasis that has been placed on severe assaults, which could allow men to mistakenly assume that an occasional slap or shove did not constitute abusive behavior.

To explain the increase in minor assaults by women, Straus and Kantor suggested that there had been no effort to condemn assaults by wives, and with increasing gender equality, women might feel entitled to hit as often as their male partners. The decrease in severe abuse by wives as reported by their husbands, which is inconsistent with the wives' responses, might have reflected men's reluctance to admit they have been victims of abuse.

WHO STRIKES THE FIRST BLOW?

The NFVS data on violence by women triggered a firestorm of protest from feminist academicians, scholars, and activists, who claimed the analysis of survey data not

TABLE 2.5

Percent distribution of victimizations, by characteristics of victims, type of crime, and victim/offender relationship, 2000

Characteristic	Total victimizations	Percent of all victimizations					Don't know relationship
		Nonstrangers				Stranger	
		Total	Intimate	Other relative	Friend or acquaintance		
Both genders							
Crimes of violence	100%	54.0%	10.6%	5.0%	38.3%	44.4%	1.7%
Rape/sexual assault[2]	100	67.1	8.8[1]	1.6[1]	56.7	30.7	2.2[1]
Robbery	100	35.0	9.3	4.0[1]	21.7	62.5	2.5[1]
Assault	100	55.4	10.9	5.3	39.2	43.1	1.5
Aggravated	100	46.7	9.0	5.9	31.9	50.6	2.7[1]
Simple	100	57.8	11.4	5.2	41.2	41.0	1.2
Male							
Crimes of violence	100	42.6	2.5	3.5	36.6	56.1	1.3
Rape/sexual assault[2]	100	52.2[1]	0.0[1]	0.0[1]	52.2[1]	47.8[1]	0.0[1]
Robbery	100	23.5	3.6[1]	0.0[1]	19.9	74.0	2.5[1]
Assault	100	44.9	2.4	3.9	38.5	53.9	1.2[1]
Aggravated	100	38.9	2.3[1]	4.5[1]	32.1	59.9	1.2[1]
Simple	100	46.8	2.5	3.8	40.5	52.0	1.2[1]
Female							
Crimes of violence	100	67.1	19.9	6.9	40.3	30.9	2.0
Rape/sexual assault[2]	100	69.2	10.1[1]	1.8[1]	57.3	28.2	2.5[1]
Robbery	100	54.8	19.1	11.0[1]	24.7	42.8	2.4[1]
Assault	100	68.0	21.0	7.0	40.0	30.1	1.9
Aggravated	100	58.2	18.7	8.0	31.5	36.8	5.0[1]
Simple	100	70.3	21.5	6.8	42.0	28.5	1.2[1]
All races							
Crimes of violence	100	54.0	10.6	5.0	38.3	44.4	1.7
Rape/sexual assault[2]	100	67.1	8.8[1]	1.6[1]	56.7	30.7	2.2[1]
Robbery	100	35.0	9.3	4.0[1]	21.7	62.5	2.5[1]
Assault	100	55.4	10.9	5.3	39.2	43.1	1.5
Aggravated	100	46.7	9.0	5.9	31.9	50.6	2.7[1]
Simple	100	57.8	11.4	5.2	41.2	41.0	1.2
White							
Crimes of violence	100	53.7	10.5	4.9	38.3	44.9	1.4
Rape/sexual assault[2]	100	62.8	9.4[1]	2.4[1]	51.1	35.0	1.3[1]
Robbery	100	35.9	8.0[1]	5.6[1]	22.0	62.9	1.2[1]
Assault	100	55.0	10.8	5.0	39.3	43.5	1.4
Aggravated	100	47.5	9.2	5.8	32.5	49.9	2.6[1]
Simple	100	57.0	11.2	4.8	41.0	41.9	1.1
Black							
Crimes of violence	100	56.3	10.1	5.8	40.3	40.5	3.2[1]
Rape/sexual assault[2]	100	78.8	0.0[1]	0.0[1]	78.8	16.6[1]	4.6[1]
Robbery	100	32.5	11.9[1]	0.0[1]	20.6[1]	60.6	6.9[1]
Assault	100	58.2	11.0	7.6	39.6	39.4	2.4[1]
Aggravated	100	42.4	8.5[1]	6.7[1]	27.2	54.4	3.2[1]
Simple	100	65.4	12.1	8.1	45.2	32.6	2.0[1]
Other							
Crimes of violence	100	49.2	17.7[1]	4.3[1]	27.2	50.8	0.0[1]
Rape/sexual assault[2]	100[1]	54.9[1]	54.9	0.0[1]	0.0[1]	45.1[1]	0.0[1]
Robbery	100[1]	34.9[1]	16.8[1]	0.0[1]	18.0[1]	65.1[1]	0.0[1]
Assault	100	51.8	13.8[1]	5.7[1]	32.3	48.2	0.0[1]
Aggravated	100[1]	75.4[1]	0.1[1]	0.0[1]	75.4[1]	24.6[1]	0.0[1]
Simple	100	49.6	15.1[1]	6.2[1]	28.3[1]	50.4	0.0[1]
Ethnicity							
Crimes of violence	100	54.0	10.6	5.0	38.3	44.4	1.7
Rape/sexual assault[2]	100	67.1	8.8[1]	1.6[1]	56.7	30.7	2.2[1]
Robbery	100	35.0	9.3	4.0[1]	21.7	62.5	2.5[1]
Assault	100	55.4	10.9	5.3	39.2	43.1	1.5
Aggravated	100	46.7	9.0	5.9	31.9	50.6	2.7[1]
Simple	100	57.8	11.4	5.2	41.2	41.0	1.2
Hispanic							
Crimes of violence	100	50.2	7.2	7.0	35.9	49.4	0.4[1]
Rape/sexual assault[2]	100[1]	30.7[1]	0.0[1]	0.0[1]	30.7[1]	69.3[1]	0.0[1]
Robbery	100	31.0[1]	6.0[1]	0.0[1]	24.9[1]	69.0	0.0[1]
Assault	100	54.0	7.6	8.4	37.9	45.6	0.5[1]
Aggravated	100	49.6	2.2[1]	9.2[1]	38.3	48.8	1.6[1]
Simple	100	55.9	10.1	8.1[1]	37.7	44.1	0.0[1]

only ignored the context in which the violence occurred, but also failed to consider the fact that women often must resort to violence in self-defense. Other scholars supported the argument that domestic violence was usually mutual.

In his book *Abused Men: The Hidden Side of Domestic Violence* (Westport, CT: Greenwood, 1997), Philip W. Cook supported the mutual abuse argument. Using data from the 1985 NFVS and Murray Straus's 1993 work

TABLE 2.5

Percent distribution of victimizations, by characteristics of victims, type of crime, and victim/offender relationship, 2000 [CONTINUED]

		Percent of all victimizations					
		Nonstrangers					
Characteristic	Total victimizations	Total	Intimate	Other relative	Friend or acquaintance	Stranger	Don't know relationship
Non-Hispanic							
Crimes of violence	100	54.4	11.0	4.8	38.6	43.8	1.8
Rape/sexual assault[2]	100	70.2	9.6[1]	1.7[1]	58.9	27.4	2.4[1]
Robbery	100	36.0	10.0	4.9[1]	21.2	61.0	3.0[1]
Assault	100	55.4	11.2	5.0	39.3	42.9	1.7
Aggravated	100	46.2	10.3	5.3	30.6	50.9	2.9[1]
Simple	100	57.8	11.4	4.9	41.6	40.8	1.4

Note: Detail may not add to total shown because of rounding.
[1]Estimate is based on about 10 or fewer sample cases.
[2]Includes verbal threats of rape and threats of sexual assault.

SOURCE: "Table 43a. Personal Crimes of Violence, 2002: Percent Distribution of Victimizations, by Characteristics of Victims, Type of Crime, and Victim/Offender Relationship," in *Criminal Victimization in the United States, 2002 Statistical Tables, National Crime Victimization Survey,* U.S. Department of Justice, Bureau of Justice Statistics, December 2003, http://www.ojp.usdoj.gov/bjs/pub/pdf/cvus02.pdf (accessed September 21, 2004)

TABLE 2.6

Victim and offender relationship, 2003

	Violent crime		Rape/sexual assault		Robbery		Aggravated assault		Simple assault	
Relationship with victim	Number	Percent	Number	Percent	Number	Percent	Number	Percent	Number	Percent
Male victims										
Total	3,056,160	100%	19,670	100%	365,590	100%	688,420	100%	1,982,480	100%
Nonstranger	1,287,960	42%	14,500	74%*	118,300	32%	266,770	39%	888,400	45%
Intimate	83,750	3	5,940	30*	6,130	2*	21,910	3*	49,780	3
Other relative	138,310	5	0	0*	17,250	5*	12,490	2*	108,570	6
Friend/acquaintance	1,065,900	35	8,560	44*	94,910	26	232,370	34	730,050	37
Stranger	1,658,160	54%	5,170	26%*	226,110	62%	399,240	58%	1,027,630	52%
Relationship unknown	110,050	4%	0	0%*	21,180	6%*	22,420	3%*	66,450	3%
Female victims										
Total	2,345,550	100%	179,170	100%	230,540	100%	412,690	100%	1,523,150	100%
Nonstranger	1,562,010	67%	125,370	70%	110,670	48%	274,430	67%	1,051,540	69%
Intimate	437,990	19	21,440	12*	30,990	13*	101,400	25	284,170	19
Other relative	230,850	10	13,930	8*	17,430	8*	40,320	10	159,180	11
Friend/acquaintance	893,170	38	90,000	50	62,260	27	132,720	32	608,190	40
Stranger	745,930	32%	53,800	30%	103,630	45%	131,850	32%	456,640	30%
Relationship unknown	37,610	2%	0	0%*	16,240	7%*	6,400	2%*	14,970	1%*

Note: Percentages may not total to 100% because of rounding.
*Based on 10 or fewer sample cases.

SOURCE: Shannan M. Catalano, "Table 9. Victim and Offender Relationship, 2003," in *Criminal Victimization, 2003,* U.S. Department of Justice, Bureau of Justice Statistics National Crime Victimization Survey, September 2004, http://www.ojp.usdoj.gov/bjs/pub/pdf/cv03.pdf (accessed September 19, 2004)

"Physical Assault by Wives: A Major Social Problem" (*Current Controversies on Family Violence* [Newbury Park, CA: Sage, 1993]), Cook concluded that, in most cases, men and women shared equally when engaging in domestic abuse. Cook also found that women are 11% more likely to hit first during an argument.

Straus arrived at a similar conclusion in "Physical Assault by Wives." He observed that the number of women who hit first was about the same as the number of men, regardless of how dangerous the assault was. Straus concluded that self-defense did not account for all the attacks by women, and that 25% to 30% of violence is attributable to physical aggression by the wife.

Abuse by Women

Demie Kurz and Kersti Yllöo presented a feminist perspective in *Physical Assaults by Husbands: A Major Social Problem* (1987). Kurz and Yllöo observed that gender strongly influences how society functions, and they were critical of research that categorized "spouse abuse" as just one of several types of abuse that include elder and child abuse. They contended that this categorization reduced women to simply one victimized group among many. Instead, feminists believe, wife abuse should be grouped with other criminal acts of male dominance, such as marital and other types of rape, sexual harassment, and incest.

TABLE 2.7

Violent victimization rates of selected demographic categories, 1993–2003

Demographic category of victim	Number of violent crimes per 1,000 persons age 12 or older											Percent change, 1993–2003
	1993	1994	1995	1996	1997	1998	1999	2000	2001	2002	2003	
Gender												
Male	59.8	61.1	55.7	49.9	45.8	43.1	37.0	32.9	27.3	25.5	26.3	−56.0%
Female	40.7	43.0	38.1	34.6	33.0	30.4	28.8	23.2	23.0	20.8	19.0	−53.3
Race												
White	47.9	50.5	44.7	40.9	38.3	36.3	31.9	27.1	24.5	22.8	21.5	−55.1%
Black	67.4	61.3	61.1	52.3	49.0	41.7	41.6	35.3	31.2	27.9	29.1	−56.8
Other race	39.8	49.9	41.9	33.2	28.0	27.6	24.5	20.7	18.2	14.7	16.0	−59.8
Two or more races	—	—	—	—	—	—	—	—	—	—	67.7	—
Hispanic origin												
Hispanic	55.2	61.6	57.3	44.0	43.1	32.8	33.8	28.4	29.5	23.6	24.2	−56.2%
Non-Hispanic	49.5	50.7	45.2	41.6	38.3	36.8	32.4	27.7	24.5	23.0	22.3	−54.9
Annual household income												
Less than $7,500	84.7	86.0	77.8	65.3	71.0	63.8	57.5	60.3	46.6	45.5	49.9	−41.1%
$7,500–$14,999	56.4	60.7	49.8	52.1	51.2	49.3	44.5	37.8	36.9	31.5	30.8	−45.4
$15,000–$24,999	49.0	50.7	48.9	44.1	40.1	39.4	35.3	31.8	31.8	30.0	26.3	−46.3
$25,000–$34,999	51.0	47.3	47.1	43.0	40.2	42.0	37.9	29.8	29.1	27.0	24.9	−51.2
$35,000–$49,999	45.6	47.0	45.8	43.0	38.7	31.7	30.3	28.5	26.3	25.6	21.4	−53.1
$50,000–$74,999	44.0	48.0	44.6	37.5	33.9	32.0	33.3	23.7	21.0	18.7	22.9	−48.0
$75,000 or more	41.3	39.5	37.3	30.5	30.7	33.1	22.9	22.3	18.5	19.0	17.5	−57.6

Note: Annual rates are based on interviews conducted during the calendar year. For 2003 the racial categories are white/black/other "only" and "two or more races." The collection of racial and ethnic categories in 2003 changed from that of previous years; however, because about 0.9% of survey respondents identified two or more races, the impact on the victimization rates for each race is small. The population estimates for 2003 incorporate controls based on the 2000 decennial Census.
— Not available.

SOURCE: Shannan M. Catalano, "Table 4. Violent Victimization Rates of Selected Demographic Categories, 1993–2003," in *Criminal Victimization, 2003*, U.S. Department of Justice, Bureau of Justice Statistics National Crime Victimization Survey, September 2004, http://www.ojp.usdoj.gov/bjs/pub/pdf/cv03.pdf (accessed September 19, 2004)

For these and many other feminists, violence is an issue of power, and in both society and marriage, power is held almost exclusively by men. They caution that approaching the issue of spousal abuse using a family violence model may have negative repercussions for women, because this model reinforces the notion that women become victims of abuse by provoking their partners. They also argue that research and analyses based on the family violence model often lead to policy decisions that are harmful to women, such as reduced funding for women's shelters or testimony against battered women in court. Furthermore, they argue that the family violence model encourages mental health workers and counselors to propose interventions and actions that focus on a client's personal problems without identifying the social, political, and economic inequalities between men and women that feminists contend form the basis for battering.

A CRITIQUE OF THE CONFLICT TACTICS SCALE. Kurz and Yllöo observed that when women were asked about the context of their use of violence, most reported that they used violence in self-defense. Other feminist scholars contend that researchers exclude the context of the situation when they ask who initiated the violence, and fail to take into account that violence is often preceded by name-calling and other psychological abuse. Women's advocates argue that women, viewing these behaviors as early warning signs of future violence, may hit first in the

hope of preventing physical abuse. Even when women initiate violence, they conclude, it may very well be an act of self-defense. Research revealing that wives often report their use of violence as self-defense or retaliation supports this theory. Violent men, on the other hand, attribute their aggression to external causes.

Michael S. Kimmel has criticized the Conflict Tactics Scale (CTS), a measure that is widely used in surveys of domestic violence ("'Gender Symmetry' in Domestic Violence: A Substantive and Methodological Research Review," *Violence against Women*, vol. 8, November 2002). He questions whether violence can or should be measured as a conflict tactic, arguing that "such framing assumes that domestic violence … has more to do with being tired or in a bad mood than it does with an effort to control another person." He also argues that the CTS needs to take into account the context of violence. The fact that it does not evaluate context leads to a skewing of results. "Thus," he wrote, "if she pushes him back after being severely beaten, it would be scored one conflict tactic for each. And if she punches him to get him to stop beating their children or pushes him away after he has sexually assaulted her, it would count as one for her and none for him."

Russell P. Dobash and colleagues also question the findings that result from use of the Conflict Tactics Scale. In "Separate and Intersecting Realities: A Comparison of

Men's and Women's Accounts of Violence against Women" (*Violence against Women*, vol. 4, no. 4, August 1998), the researchers disputed the assumption that the CTS accounts of violence, whether from men or women, are unbiased and reliable. Comparing men's accounts of their violence with accounts given by women, Dobash et al. found an overall pattern of inconsistency between the reports of men and women. An even greater discrepancy was seen in the reported frequency of violent acts.

CAUSES AND PREVENTION OF ABUSE BY WOMEN. The difficulty with these feminist viewpoints, Straus and Gelles argue, is that they explain wife abuse in terms of patriarchy, which focuses on the power and control men exert over women and overlooks other important variables. Furthermore, patriarchy does not explain many other types of domestic violence, such as child abuse, sibling abuse, elder abuse, and violence by women.

Straus and Gelles claim that in some cases data on assaults by women have intentionally been suppressed. The *Survey of Spousal Violence against Women in Kentucky* by Mark A. Schulman (Washington, DC: U.S. Government Printing Office, 1979) was one of the first issue-defining studies, yet it did not publish the data gathered on violence committed by women. When other researchers obtained the survey data set, they reported that among violent couples, 38% of attacks were committed by women who had not been attacked first by their male partners.

Straus and Gelles do believe that the generally greater size, strength, and aggressiveness of men means that the same action taken by a man is likely to inflict more pain or injury than a comparable act committed by a woman. They also allow that some violence inflicted by women against men is in retaliation or self-defense. Still, they argue, violence by women cannot be ignored, and efforts to prevent it are needed for several reasons. A fundamental reason is the intrinsic moral incorrectness of attacking a spouse, whether woman or man. Other reasons to prevent female-initiated or -instigated abuse include the danger of escalation, the model of violence as perceived by children, and the validation of any type of violence between spouses. When women hit, they legitimize the abuse they receive from men. If a woman slaps her partner, she gives him justification to hit her when he does not like her behavior.

Straus offers three reasons why injury should not be used as a criterion for defining abuse in "Conceptualization and Measurement of Battering: Implications for Public Policy" (*Women Battering: Policy Responses*, Michael Steinman, ed. [Cincinnati, OH: Anderson Publishing, 1991]). First, the effect on legislation would be detrimental to women who must rely on police ability and authority to make arrests without visible evidence of injury. Second, injury-based rates would eliminate from the data 97% of assaults by men that did not result in injury but are still serious and harmful. Finally, focusing exclusively on injury rates would make it easier to ignore the abuse by women because physical violence inflicted by women frequently does not result in significant injury.

Violence Reexamined

The National Youth Survey, a self-reported longitudinal study following selected participants over time, measured problem behavior in a national sample of young people. It began in 1976 when the respondents were eleven to seventeen years old and followed the participants for sixteen years into adulthood in 1992, when they were twenty-seven to thirty-three years old. Analyzing data from the 1983, 1986, 1989, and 1992 surveys, researcher Barbara Morse determined the level of violence between married or cohabiting partners and described her conclusions in "Beyond the Conflict Tactics Scale: Assessing Gender Differences in Partner Violence" (*Violence and Victims*, vol. 10, Winter 1995).

The surveys found high levels of violence in many relationships—54.5% of partners reported some violence in 1983, declining to 32.4% by 1992. About one-quarter reported severe violence in the first survey, compared to 15.8% in 1992. These high rates, three to four times the rate reported by Straus, were attributed to the youth of the National Youth Survey respondents.

About 10% of the couples reported at least one incidence of severe male-to-female violence in the year that preceded both the 1983 and 1989 surveys; however, the rate dropped to 5.7% in 1992. The youth survey rates of female-to-male violence were remarkably high. About 48% of youth survey respondents reported one or more female-to-male assaults in their relationships in 1983. The rate declined sharply to 27.9% in 1992, but was still higher than rates reported by other researchers.

WHO WAS RESPONSIBLE? Morse conceded that the National Youth Survey rates were higher than rates found in most other studies and that they contradict common beliefs as well as police and hospital records. One explanation of the contradictory findings may be that men tend to underreport violence while women are more likely to be accurate reporters. Morse, however, found that both genders underreported violence when their accounts were compared to their partners' reports.

Morse found that women were significantly more likely than men to slap or throw something at their partners, as well as to kick, bite, or hit their partners with a fist or an object. On the other hand, males were much more likely than females to "beat up" their partners. Among men who beat their partners, the reported frequency of battering averaged three to four times per year. That was at least three times as often as women who engaged in similar behavior.

TABLE 2.8

Percent of all murders by intimates by age, 1976–2002

	Male victims	Female victims
Under 18	1%	6%
18–24	2	29
25–29	5	37
30–34	7	41
35–39	8	43
40–44	10	41
45–49	10	40
50–59	10	32
60+	7	20

SOURCE: James Alan Fox and Marianne W. Zawitz, "Percent of All Murders by Intimates, 1976–2002," in *Homicide Trends in the United States*, U.S. Department of Justice, Bureau of Justice Statistics National Crime Victimization Survey, September 28, 2004, http://www.ojp.usdoj.gov/bjs/homicide/intimates.htm (accessed December 9, 2004)

TABLE 2.9

Homicides by relationship and weapon type, 1990–2002

Relationship of victim to offender	Total	Gun	Knife	Blunt object	Force	Other weapon
Husband	100%	70%	26%	2%	1%	2%
Ex-husband	100	87	9	1	0	2
Wife	100	68	14	5	9	4
Ex-wife	100	78	12	2	6	2
Boyfriend	100	46	45	3	3	3
Girlfriend	100	57	19	5	14	5

SOURCE: James Alan Fox and Marianne W. Zawitz, "Homicides by Relationship and Weapon Type, 1990–2002," in *Homicide Trends in the United States*, U.S. Department of Justice, Bureau of Justice Statistics National Crime Victimization Survey, September 28, 2004, http://www.ojp.usdoj.gov/bjs/homicide/intimates.htm (accessed December 9, 2004)

Morse also found that the violence was mutual in about half the cases. In the remaining half, women accounted for about two-thirds of the nonreciprocal violence. This finding was supported by reports from both men and women. When asked who started the fight that led to the violence, men claimed that both parties were responsible 44% of the time, that 26% of the time they started it, and that 30% of the time their partners initiated it. In comparison, women blamed their partners 46% of the time, took equal responsibility 36% of the time, and took full blame 18% of the time.

Women were also more likely to receive medical treatment for their injuries. About 20% of the female respondents in each survey reported that the violence led to personal injury. In contrast, only 10% of the men reported injuries in 1989 and 14% in 1992.

ABUSED TO DEATH

According to the FBI, between 1976 and 2000, 11% of homicide victims had been killed by intimates. In 2000, 26.1% of the 1,700 victims were men. James Alan Fox and Marianne W. Zawitz reported their findings in *Homicide Trends in the United States* (Washington, DC: U.S. Department of Justice, Bureau of Justice Statistics National Crime Victimization Survey, September, 2004.)

Although these statistics sound alarming, they reflect a positive trend in domestic homicides. Since 1976, when the FBI first began keeping statistics on intimate murders, the number of men and women killed by an intimate partner has dropped significantly. The number of men killed by an intimate declined by 67.6% between 1976 and 2000, and the number of women killed was stable until 1993 when it began to decline. The peak for intimate murders occurred in 1976, when 2,957 men and women were killed.

Although the number of white females killed by an intimate increased during the 1980s, it declined after 1987. In 1997, it reached its lowest point in two decades. Nevertheless, in 2000 the percentage of all female homicide victims killed by an intimate was roughly comparable with rates reported twenty-five years earlier.

According to the same research, the number of intimate homicides for all other race and gender groups declined over the same period, with a drop of 77.3% for black males killed by an intimate and a 53.4% decrease for black females. The number of white males killed by an intimate declined 53.5% during the same span of time.

Women of every age are substantially more likely to be killed by an intimate partner than men. (See Table 2.8.) Every year, about one-third of all females murdered in the United States are killed by an intimate (33.5% in 2000). In comparison, only 3.7% of all male murder victims were killed by an intimate in 2000.

Women are also more likely to be killed by their spouses, although this rate has declined substantially in the years since the survey was first conducted. The intimate homicide rate declined for blacks of both genders in every relationship category but was actually higher for white girlfriends in 2000 than it had been in 1976. (See Figure 2.4.)

Of all intimate homicides committed during this period, guns were used in a majority of the murders, although such other weapons as knives were also used. In the period between 1990 and 2000, more than two-thirds of all victims of murder at the hands of spouses and former spouses were killed by guns. However, almost half of the boyfriends murdered by their partners (45%) and one in five of the girlfriends murdered by their partners (19%) were killed with knives. Intimate homicides were more likely to involve knives than murders by nonintimates. (See Figure 2.5 and Table 2.9.)

One researcher has investigated what factors present in abusive relationships might indicate a threat of the violence escalating to homicide. Carolyn Rebecca Block found that certain types of past violence directed against

FIGURE 2.4

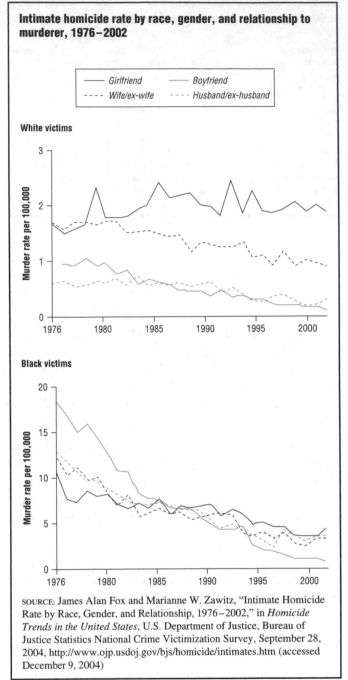

Intimate homicide rate by race, gender, and relationship to murderer, 1976–2002

Legend:
— Girlfriend
— Boyfriend
--- Wife/ex-wife
--- Husband/ex-husband

White victims

Black victims

SOURCE: James Alan Fox and Marianne W. Zawitz, "Intimate Homicide Rate by Race, Gender, and Relationship, 1976–2002," in *Homicide Trends in the United States*, U.S. Department of Justice, Bureau of Justice Statistics National Crime Victimization Survey, September 28, 2004, http://www.ojp.usdoj.gov/bjs/homicide/intimates.htm (accessed December 9, 2004)

FIGURE 2.5

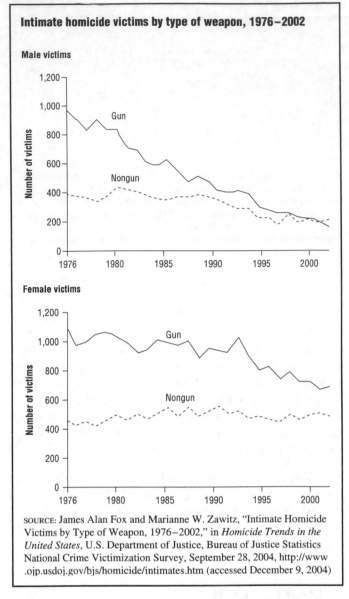

Intimate homicide victims by type of weapon, 1976–2002

Male victims

Female victims

SOURCE: James Alan Fox and Marianne W. Zawitz, "Intimate Homicide Victims by Type of Weapon, 1976–2002," in *Homicide Trends in the United States*, U.S. Department of Justice, Bureau of Justice Statistics National Crime Victimization Survey, September 28, 2004, http://www.ojp.usdoj.gov/bjs/homicide/intimates.htm (accessed December 9, 2004)

female intimates indicate an increased risk of homicide, especially choking ("How Can Practitioners Help an Abused Woman Lower Her Risk of Death?" *National Institute of Justice Journal*, no. 250, November 2003). She also found that recently abused women were more likely to be killed—half of women who were killed by their partners had experienced violence in the previous thirty days. She also found that increasingly frequent violent incidents posed a higher risk of homicide.

DOMESTIC ABUSE AMONG SAME-SEX COUPLES

One aspect of domestic abuse that often has been overlooked is violence between men or women in same-

sex relationships. There are few published studies about this subject, but investigator Vernon R. Wiehe in *Understanding Family Violence* (Thousand Oaks, CA: Sage, 1998) finds that comparable forms of physical, emotional, and sexual abuse occur between partners in same-sex relationships as heterosexual partners with one difference: emotional abuse may also include threats to disclose a partner's homosexuality.

Researchers have difficulty comparing the prevalence of partner abuse in same-sex relationships to abuse rates in heterosexual relationships because they must rely on nonrandom, self-selected samples. These studies consider persons who identify themselves as homosexuals and agree to participate in a research study as opposed to randomly selected persons representative of the population to be studied. As with other forms of abuse, same-sex partners may underreport violence in their relationships. Most of the published studies examining same-sex domestic violence indicate that abuse rates are about the same as for male and female same-sex couples. including one by Michelle Aulivola titled "Outing Domestic Violence: Affording Appropriate Protections to Gay and Lesbian Victims" (*Family Court Review*, vol. 42, January 2004).

How Abusive Are Women in Same-Sex Relationships?

There are some survey data about women in same-sex relationships that indicate that lesbians endure considerable levels of physical and sexual violence. Linda A. Bernhard, in "Physical and Sexual Violence Experienced by Lesbian and Heterosexual Women" (*Violence against Women*, vol. 6, no. 1, January 2000), observes that while lesbians, like other women, are at risk of abuse from past and present male partners, they also risk being victimized by their female partners. In addition, because lesbians are also at greater risk for hate crimes than their heterosexual counterparts, they may experience more violence than heterosexual women.

Based on the limited research done on lesbian violence, it appears the risk factors for abuse are similar to those of heterosexual women. Dependency and jealousy, both of which may precipitate abuse in heterosexual relationships, have been identified as the main contributors of lesbian battering. The literature about this subject also contains clinical case studies and anecdotal reports indicating that lesbian batterers may also abuse alcohol or drugs, feel powerless, and suffer from low self-esteem.

Battered lesbians are among the most underserved population of battered women, often facing denial from other lesbians and homophobia from health and social service providers. Many states have narrow definitions of family that deny gay and lesbian victims of domestic violence the possibility of seeking family court orders of protection or other civil redress. Complicating the issue are the myths that same-sex violence is mutual and the abuse is not as dangerous or destructive as heterosexual abuse. In fact, according to health care providers, the abuse is rarely mutual and can be just as harmful as abuse in heterosexual relationships.

Gender Issues in Same-Sex Relationships

In a study of gender issues in male and female same-sex relationships, Linda M. Waldner-Haugrud and colleagues interviewed 165 gays and 118 lesbians, all of them white and highly educated. In "Victimization and Perpetration Rates of Violence in Gay and Lesbian Relationships: Gender Issues Explored" (*Violence and Victims*, vol. 12, no. 2, 1997), Waldner-Haugrud et al. found that 47.5% of lesbians and 29.7% of gay men reported being involved in violent relationships at some point in their lives. Pushing and threatening were the most frequent methods of abuse, while use of a weapon ranked lowest.

Among lesbian respondents, 38% reported perpetrating the violence, primarily by pushing, slapping, or threatening. Victimization and perpetration rates were higher for lesbians than for gay men, with the exception of violence inflicted with a weapon. Lesbians were far more likely to report pushing or being pushed than were gay men.

Waldner-Haugrud et al. concluded that several factors may increase the likelihood of violence in lesbian couples. Among these factors are "prejudice-encouraged" social isolation, overdependency of one partner on the other, the tendency of lesbians to create "closed" relationships, and sexual-orientation identity issues. The researchers acknowledged it was probable that gay men underreported partner abuse. They also noted the limitations of findings from an exclusive, nonrepresentative sample such as theirs. Still, the implications of the findings may indicate a need to move beyond theories that use gender to define victim and perpetrator.

EMOTIONAL AND PSYCHOLOGICAL ABUSE

Most definitions of abuse focus on situations where physical violence was either threatened or used. Official definitions used by the courts and police do not include emotional or psychological abuse, although it can cause as much long-term damage as acts of physical violence.

Emotional and psychological abuse is usually harder to define than physical abuse, where bruises and scars are clearly evident. Almost all couples scream and shout at one another at some point. But abuse is distinguished from the heated arguments that may ensue in the course of otherwise healthy relationships because the abuser uses words to project power over a mate in a demeaning way. This can produce serious and often debilitating emotional or psychological consequences.

Some domestic violence researchers and counselors equate emotional abuse with the Amnesty International definition of psychological torture, which includes verbal degradation, denial of power, isolation, monopolizing perceptions, and threats to kill. Health and social service workers who counsel victims cite emotional violence as one of several factors that may paralyze women, preventing them from fleeing dangerous and abusive relationships.

Table 2.10 is a checklist prepared by the National Coalition against Domestic Violence to help identify characteristics and patterns of emotional abuse. The coalition and many researchers believe that early identification of and effective intervention to end emotional abuse may prevent this emotional violence from escalating to physical abuse. Table 2.11 is a list of characteristics, attitudes, and actions presented by the coalition in the form of ten questions that may help predict whether a partner will become violent.

A Landmark Study of Verbal Aggression

Renowned researchers Murray Straus and Stephen Sweet returned to the 1985 National Family Violence Sur-

TABLE 2.10

Abusive relationship checklist

Look over the following questions. Think about how you are being treated and how you treat your partner. Remember, when one person scares, hurts or continually puts down the other person, it's abuse.

Does your partner...

____ Embarrass or make fun of you in front of your friends or family?
____ Put down your accomplishments or goals?
____ Make you feel like you are unable to make decisions?
____ Use intimidation or threats to gain compliance?
____ Tell you that you are nothing without them?
____ Treat you roughly—grab, push, pinch, shove or hit you?
____ Call you several times a night or show up to make sure you are where you said you would be?
____ Use drugs or alcohol as an excuse for saying hurtful things or abusing you?
____ Blame you for how they feel or act?
____ Pressure you sexually for things you aren't ready for?
____ Make you feel like there "is no way out" of the relationship?
____ Prevent you from doing things you want—like spending time with your friends or family?
____ Try to keep you from leaving after a fight or leave you somewhere after a fight to "teach you a lesson"?

Do you...

____ Sometimes feel scared of how your partner will act?
____ Constantly make excuses to other people for your partner's behavior?
____ Believe that you can help your partner change if only you changed something about yourself?
____ Try not to do anything that would cause conflict or make your partner angry?
____ Feel like no matter what you do, your partner is never happy with you?
____ Always do what your partner wants you to do instead of what you want?
____ Stay with your partner because you are afraid of what your partner would do if you broke up?

If any of these are happening in your relationship, talk to someone. Without some help, the abuse will continue.

SOURCE: "Checklist," *The Problem*, National Coalition against Domestic Violence, http://www.ncadv.org/problem/checklist.htm (accessed September 19, 2004)

veys data to examine verbal aggression in their study "Verbal/Symbolic Aggression in Couples: Incidence Rates and Relationships to Personal Characteristics" (*Journal of Marriage and the Family*, vol. 54, 1992). Straus and Sweet found no significant differences between man-to-woman and woman-to-man verbal aggression. They also found that when one partner engaged in verbal aggression, the other responded in similar fashion. Women reported more abuse regardless of who initiated the aggression, but the researchers were unable to determine whether men minimized the incidence of verbal abuse or women exaggerated it.

Straus and Sweet's study found no correlation between race or socioeconomic status and verbal aggression, although other studies have reported increased frequency of verbal aggression among black couples. They did find, however, a link between age and levels of abuse, indicating that verbal aggression declines with age regardless of how much conflict there is in a relationship. Straus and Sweet's analysis also revealed a direct connection between alcohol consumption and verbal aggression—the more often men drank excessively, the more likely they were to be verbally abusive. Similarly, the more women used drugs, the greater the probability of verbal abuse. For men, however, drug use did not significantly affect the use of verbal abuse. Straus and Sweet cautioned that their research reveals a correlation between these two variables, but not causation—in other words, it demonstrated a relationship between alcohol consumption and abuse, but did not show whether men and women drink to provide themselves with excuses for abusive behavior or whether drinking causes their aggression.

ABUSE OF IMMIGRANT WOMEN

Luke J. Larsen reported in "The Foreign-Born Population in the United States: 2003" that the total foreign-born population in March 2003 was 33.5 million people, or 11.7% of the U.S. population (*Current Population Reports* [Washington, DC: U.S. Government Printing Office, 2004]). Abuse of immigrant women remains a problem in the United States. Immigrant women may be at increased risk for various reasons, including a cultural background that teaches them to defer to their husbands. Many foreign-born women cannot speak English and do not know their rights in the United States. Others fear they will be deported or have no resources or support systems to turn to for help.

In March 2003, Asian immigrants accounted for 25% of all immigrants in the United States. Along with other immigrant groups, the Asian immigrant community has become increasingly aware of domestic abuse. Some Asian women have been sent to this country as the result of arranged marriages to live with men they barely know. In some cases, the husband takes his immigrant bride's money, jewelry, and passport, leaving her completely dependent on him. The abusive husband often tells his immigrant wife that if she leaves him, she will be deported. For some abused immigrant women, it would be worse to return home and bring shame on their family than to stay with the abusive partner. In some cultures, divorced women are outcasts with no place in society.

U.S. immigration laws have unintentionally contributed to the problem of abuse among immigrant

TABLE 2.11

Predictors of domestic violence

The following signs often occur before actual abuse and may serve as clues to potential abuse:

1. Did he grow up in a violent family? People who grow up in families where they have been abused as children, or where one parent beats the other, have grown up learning that violence is normal behavior.
2. Does he tend to use force or violence to "solve" his problems? A young man who has a criminal record for violence, who gets into fights, or who likes to act tough is likely to act the same way with his wife and children. Does he have a quick temper? Does he over-react to little problems and frustration? Is he cruel to animals? Does he punch walls or throw things when he's upset? Any of these behaviors may be a sign of a person who will work out bad feelings with violence.
3. Does he abuse alcohol or other drugs? There is a strong link between violence and problems with drugs and alcohol. Be alert to his possible drinking/drug problems, particulary if he refuses to admit that he has a problem, or refuses to get help. Do not think that you can change him.
4. Does he have strong traditional ideas about what a man should be and what a woman should be? Does he think a woman should stay at home, take care of her husband, and follow his wishes and orders?
5. Is he jealous of your other relationships—not just with other men that you may know—but also with your women friends and your family? Does he keep tabs on you? Does he want to know where you are at all times? Does he want you with him all of the time?
6. Does he have access to guns, knives, or other lethal instruments? Does he talk of using them against people, or threaten to use them to get even?
7. Does he expect you to follow his orders or advice? Does he become angry if you do not fulfill his wishes or if you cannot anticipate what he wants?
8. Does he go through extreme highs and lows, almost as though he is two different people? Is he extremely kind one time, and extremely cruel at another time?
9. When he gets angry, do you fear him? Do you find that not making him angry has become a major part of your life? Do you do what he wants you to do, rather than what you want to do?
10. Does he treat you roughly? Does he physically force you to do what you do not want to do?

SOURCE: "Predictors of Domestic Violence," *The Problem*, National Coalition against Domestic Violence, http://www.ncadv.org/problem/predictors.htm (accessed September 19, 2004)

women. The Immigration Marriage Fraud Amendments were passed in 1986 in an attempt to prevent immigrants from illegally obtaining resident status through a sham marriage to a U.S. citizen. The amendments require that spouses, usually husbands, petition for conditional resident status for an undocumented mate. Conditional status lasts a minimum of two years during which time the couple must remain married. If the marriage dissolves, the immigrant loses conditional status and may be deported. As a result, some wives become prisoners of abusive husbands for as long as the husbands control their conditional resident status.

The law was amended under the Immigration Act of 1990 to permit a waiver of conditional status if the immigrant could prove battery or extreme cruelty. While the new law attempts to provide relief for battered brides, the initial filing for conditional status is still in the hands of the husband; if the abuse begins before he chooses to file the petition, the woman has no legal recourse.

In addition, a proposed implementation of the Medicare Modernization Act of 2003, an aid package meant to defray the costs of providing health care to immigrants, will harm battered immigrant women, according to a Family Violence Prevention Fund "Newsflash" online article, "Hospital Reg-

ulation Would Threaten Battered Immigrant Women, Experts Warn" (http://endabuse.org, September 1, 2004). Under the proposal, hospitals wanting aid will be required ask uninsured patients intimidating questions about their immigration status. These regulations may keep battered women from seeking medical care.

The Diversity of Different Cultures

Many immigrants come from cultures that are radically different from the predominant American society. Among the Asian-American community, including Chinese, Vietnamese, Indians, Koreans, Thai, and Cambodians, there is widespread acceptance of male dominance and a belief that the community and the family take priority over the individual. Asian women are generally raised to accept their husbands' dominance and are more reluctant to complain or to leave than their American counterparts. Complicating the problem of domestic abuse in this community are strong family ties, economic dependency, the stigma of divorce, and fear of bringing shame to the family.

Still, researchers have found that rates of domestic abuse in immigrant communities are no higher than among the native population. Cecilia Menjivar and Olivia Salcido wrote, "the experiences of immigrant women in domestic violence situations are often exacerbated by their specific position as immigrants, including limited host-language skills, lack of access to dignified jobs, uncertain legal statuses, and experiences in their home countries, and thus their alternatives to living with their abusers are very limited" ("Immigrant Women and Domestic Violence: Common Experiences in Different Countries," *Gender & Society*, vol. 16, December 2002).

There is documented evidence of abuse in practically every immigrant community in the United States. For example, research conducted during the 1990s by the Immigrant Woman's Task Force of the Northern California Coalition for Immigrant Rights found that 34% of Latinas and 25% of Filipinas surveyed had experienced domestic violence. Findings were reported by Deena L. Jang et al. in *Domestic Violence in Immigrant and Refugee Communities: Asserting the Rights of Battered Women* (San Francisco: Family Violence Prevention Fund, 1997).

The report by Jang et al. also noted that language barriers compound immigrant women's problem, often making it difficult for women to seek and obtain help. Women who do not speak English generally do not know how to find help, have difficulties in availing themselves of the help that does exist, and do not know their rights in the United States. Social workers report that interpreters, often male, do not always translate correctly, preferring to maintain community values rather than support the battered wife. In addition, many Asian women do not know the law and are misinformed by their husbands that they will be deported or lose their children if they report the abuse.

FIGURE 2.6

Power and control wheel indicating how battered immigrant women are abused

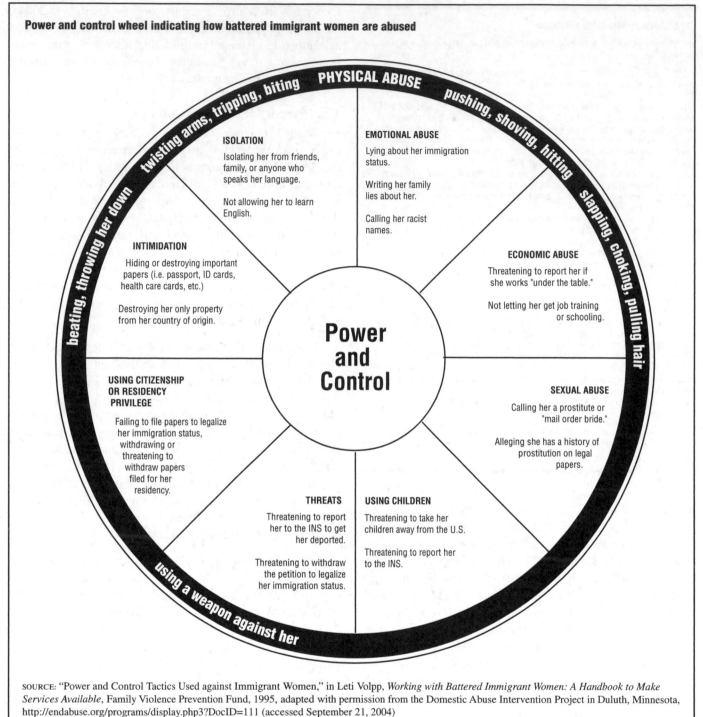

SOURCE: "Power and Control Tactics Used against Immigrant Women," in Leti Volpp, *Working with Battered Immigrant Women: A Handbook to Make Services Available*, Family Violence Prevention Fund, 1995, adapted with permission from the Domestic Abuse Intervention Project in Duluth, Minnesota, http://endabuse.org/programs/display.php3?DocID=111 (accessed September 21, 2004)

Figure 2.6 shows some of the distinctive ways that battered immigrant women are abused. Threatening to report a woman to the Immigration and Naturalization Service, have her deported, or to withdraw her petition to legalize her immigration status are among the actions an abusive husband may take to control his immigrant wife.

In September 1994 President Bill Clinton signed the Violence against Women Act as part of the Violent Crime Control and Law Enforcement Act of 1994. The Violence against Women Act permitted undocumented battered women to obtain lawful permanent resident status by petitioning for that status or through the suspension of deportation. In order to take advantage of this law, however, immigrant women must hire a lawyer and enter a system many of them misunderstand and mistrust.

New policies and programs for recent immigrant victims have emerged across the country, especially in cities with large immigrant populations. To improve the communication between immigrants and the criminal justice system, authorities have made special efforts to reach immigrant victims by hiring multicultural criminal justice staffs and providing informational materials in a variety of languages. Police representatives also attend meetings of immigrant groups, and members of the immigrant community are encouraged to serve as representatives on citizen police committees.

The most effective programs to assist immigrant women acknowledge the multiple pressures these women face during their efforts to become oriented and to assimilate themselves into American culture and society. Along with cultural shock and language barriers, many immigrant women confront racism, class prejudice, and sexism. Fear of authority and the absence of social networks and support services compound the problem. Finally, recognizing that many women are brought to the United States in circumstances that increase the likelihood of victimization—as mail-order brides, child-care workers, or prostitutes—is an important step in stemming the crisis and addressing the crime of domestic violence.

CHAPTER 3
THE CAUSES OF WIFE ABUSE

Although researchers have studied wife abuse for about thirty years, scholars from different intellectual traditions often disagree on its origins and the actions required to prevent and address the problem. Sociologists and anthropologists interpret data differently from economists and political scientists. Psychologists and other therapists perceive different facets of the problem, as do social service and shelter workers. Abused women have their own perspectives on the problem.

WHO IS ABUSED?

In the past, domestic violence was viewed as a phenomenon exclusively affecting the lower classes. But when researchers began investigating the causes of family violence in the 1970s, they noticed that although lower-class women at first appeared to make up the majority of victims, domestic violence, in reality, spanned all social and economic groups.

Middle- and upper-class women were also abused, the researchers found, but they often did not turn to hospital emergency rooms and shelters for help. Instead, they utilized private facilities and remained largely unknown, unreported, and uncounted by the public agencies that attempt to measure the rates of domestic violence and aid victims.

While women of any social class may be victims of abuse, general population studies find that women with lower incomes and less education, as well as minority women, are more likely to be the primary victims of domestic violence. Still, researchers note, classification is not exclusive. Just about anyone, rich or poor, male or female, may be a victim of domestic violence.

The Bureau of Justice Statistics defines an intimate partner as a spouse, former spouse, or a current or former boyfriend or girlfriend, either of the same sex or the opposite sex. (See Table 3.1.) The National Crime Victimization Surveys found that in 2001 an estimated 588,490 violent

crimes—rape, sexual assault, aggravated assault (assault with a weapon), and simple assault victimizations (assault without a weapon and resulting in minor injuries)—were committed against women by their intimate partners. (See Table 3.2.) About 85.1% of all intimate partner violent crimes were committed against women.

TABLE 3.1

Definitions of an intimate partner

Intimate partner relationships involve current spouses, former spouses, current boy/girlfriends, or former boy/girlfriends. Individuals involved in an intimate partner relationship may be of the same gender. The FBI does not report former boy/girlfriends in categories separate from current boy/girlfriends. Rather, they are included in the boy/girlfriend category during the data collection process.

The FBI, through the Supplementary Homicide Reports (SHR), and BJS, using the NCVS gather information about the victim's and offender's relationship, using different relationship categories. In this report responses to the victim-offender question from both data sets are collapsed into four relationship groups: intimate, friend/acquaintance, other family, and stranger. These groups are created from the following original response categories:

	NCVS categories	SHR categories
Intimate	Spouse	Husband/wife
	Ex-spouse	Common-law husband or wife
	Boyfriend/girlfriend	Ex-husband/ex-wife
	Ex-girlfriend/ex-boyfriend	Boyfriend/girlfriend
		Homosexual relationship
Friend/ acquaintance	Friend/ex-friend	Acquaintance
	Roommate/boarder	Friend
	Schoolmate	Neighbor
	Neighbor	Employee
	Someone at work/customer	Employer
	Other non-relative	Other known
Other family	Parent or step parent	Mother/father
	Own child or stepchild	Son/daughter
	Brother/sister	Brother/sister
	Other relative	In-law
		Stepfather/stepmother
		Stepson/stepdaughter
		Other family
Stranger	Stranger	Stranger
	Known by sight only	

SOURCE: "Definitions of *Intimate Partner*," in *Intimate Partner Violence*, U.S. Department of Justice, Bureau of Justice Statistics, May 2000, http://www.ojp.usdoj.gov/bjs/pub/pdf/ipv.pdf (accessed September 23, 2004)

TABLE 3.2

Violence against women by intimate partners, 2001

	Intimate partner violence					
	Total		Female		Male	
	Number	Rate per 1,000 persons	Number	Rate per 1,000 females	Number	Rate per 1,000 males
Overall violent crime	691,710	3.0	588,490	5.0	103,220	0.9
Rape/sexual assault	41,740	0.2	41,740	0.4	—	—
Robbery	60,630	0.3	44,060	0.4	16,570	0.1
Aggravated assault	117,480	0.5	81,140	0.7	36,350	0.3
Simple assault	471,860	2.1	421,550	3.6	50,310	0.5

— Based on 10 or fewer sample cases.

SOURCE: Callie Marie Rennison, "Table 1. Violence by Intimate Partners, by Type of Crime and Gender of Victims, 2001," in "Intimate Partner Violence, 1993–2001," Bureau of Justice Statistics Crime Data Brief, February 2003, NCJ 197838, http://www.ojp.usdoj.gov/bjs/pub/pdf/ipv01.pdf (accessed September 22, 2004)

WHO ARE THE OFFENDERS?

Like victims of domestic abuse, batterers come from all socioeconomic groups and all ethnic backgrounds. They may be male or female, young or old. They share a common characteristic—they all have personal relationships with their victims.

In the Bureau of Justice Statistics report *Criminal Victimization* (Washington, DC, September 2004), statistician Shannan M. Catalano analyzed general crime trends and confirmed that most female violent crime victims in 2003 knew their offenders, while most men were victimized by strangers. Rape and sexual assault victims were the most likely victims to know their assailants. Of the 5.4 million violent crimes that took place in 2003, Catalano found that intimates were offenders in 19% of the violent assaults on females; intimates were involved in only 3% of violent assaults on males. (See Table 2.5 in Chapter 2.)

Marital status was a factor in much of the violence. Never married, divorced, and separated men and women experienced higher rates of victimization than persons who were married or widowed. (See Table 3.3.) In addition, rates of violent victimization by an intimate partner toward women increase as household incomes go down, according to Callie Marie Rennison and Sarah Welchans in "Intimate Partner Violence" (U.S. Department of Justice, Bureau of Justice Statistics, May 2000, NCJ 178247).

The Effects of Poverty

Murray Straus, a highly regarded researcher and codirector of the Family Research Laboratory at the University of New Hampshire, found that serious physical acts of wife abuse are more likely to occur in poorer homes. His research shows that for lower levels of violence, such as shoving or slapping, the differences in socioeconomic status are small. For more serious types of violence, the rates increase dramatically as the socioeconomic status drops.

University of Massachusetts researchers Gerald T. Hotaling and David B. Sugarman found that in eight of eleven studies of socioeconomic status, low socioeconomic status was consistently related to wife assault ("A Risk Marker Analysis of Assaulted Wives," *Journal of Family Violence,* vol. 5, 1990). Hotaling and Sugarman proposed two interpretations of this finding. First, men of lower socioeconomic status are exposed to greater stress and possess fewer resources to cope with it, such as economic security or education. Second, the relationship between lower socioeconomic status and wife abuse is a response to a subculture of violence that makes these individuals more likely to hold values permitting the abuse of women.

The 1985 National Family Violence Survey, based on 6,002 households, provided researchers with the primary data to test their observations against a database large enough to produce statistically significant, valid findings. In the survey, families living at or below the poverty level had a rate of marital violence 500% greater than more affluent families.

More recent research funded by the National Institutes of Health offered additional support for the relationship between socioeconomic status and abuse. Deborah Pearlman et al. presented the findings of an analysis of police-reported domestic violence in relation to variables including socioeconomic conditions, age, race, and ethnicity (*Neighborhood Environment, Racial Position and Domestic Violence Risk: Contextual Analysis,* Academy for Health Service Research and Health Policy, Annual Meeting, June 24, 2002). Researchers found a complex but strong relationship between poverty and domestic violence. They speculated that one explanation for the increased risk of domestic violence in poorer neighborhoods might be differences in law enforcement availability and practices—economically deprived communities might have less police notification, attention, and documentation.

TABLE 3.3

Rates of violent crime and personal theft, by household income, marital status, region, and location of residence of victims, 2003

		Victimizations per 1,000 persons age 12 or older						
		Violent crimes						
					Assault			
Characteristic of victim	Population	All	Rape/sexual assault	Robbery	Total	Aggravated	Simple	Personal theft
Household income								
Less than $7,500	8,335,120	49.9	1.6*	9.0	39.3	10.8	28.5	1.2*
$7,500–$14,999	15,893,630	30.8	1.8*	4.0	25.0	7.9	17.0	1.1*
$15,000–$24,999	24,560,390	26.3	0.8*	4.0	21.5	4.5	17.0	0.7*
$25,000–$34,999	24,252,930	24.9	0.9*	2.2	21.8	5.0	16.9	0.8*
$35,000–$49,999	32,082,950	21.4	0.9*	2.1	18.3	4.8	13.5	0.7*
$50,000–$74,999	35,174,290	22.9	0.5*	2.0	20.4	5.2	15.2	0.5*
$75,000 or more	47,855,860	17.5	0.5*	1.7	15.4	2.7	12.6	1.0
Marital status								
Never married	76,429,290	41.6	1.6	5.2	34.8	8.7	26.1	1.4
Married	120,862,960	10.2	0.2*	0.8	9.2	1.8	7.4	0.3
Divorced/separated	25,907,600	35.1	1.9	3.5	29.7	7.8	21.9	0.7*
Widowed	14,297,780	3.5	0.0*	1.1*	2.5	0.1*	2.3	0.8*
Region								
Northeast	44,525,430	21.0	0.2*	2.7	18.1	3.9	14.2	1.1
Midwest	55,886,090	23.6	1.5	2.7	19.4	4.6	14.8	1.0
South	86,489,420	21.1	0.9	2.5	17.8	4.4	13.4	0.5
West	52,405,050	25.2	0.6*	2.1	22.5	5.6	16.9	0.6
Residence								
Urban	66,466,630	28.2	0.8	3.7	23.8	5.4	18.3	1.3
Suburban	115,814,150	21.3	1.0	2.3	18.1	4.3	13.7	0.7
Rural	57,025,210	18.6	0.6	1.6	16.4	4.2	12.2	0.3*

Note: The National Crime Victimization Survey includes as violent crime rape, sexual assault, robbery, and assault. Because the NCVS interviews persons about their victimizations, murder and manslaughter cannot be included.
*Based on 10 or fewer sample cases.

SOURCE: Shannan M. Catalano, "Table 7. Rates of Violent Crime and Personal Theft, by Household Income, Marital Status, Region, and Location of Residence of Victims, 2003," in *Criminal Victimization, 2003*, U.S. Department of Justice, Bureau of Justice Statistics National Crime Victimization Survey, September 2004, http://www.ojp.usdoj.gov/bjs/pub/pdf/cv03.pdf (accessed September 19, 2004)

A QUESTION OF POWER

The struggle for power in a relationship appears to play a significant role in battering. Some researchers suggest that the need to exert control over one's partner begins long before marriage.

In a study by Diane R. Follingstad et al. titled "Risk Factors and Correlates of Dating Violence: The Relevance of Examining Frequency and Severity Levels in a College Sample" (*Violence and Victims,* vol. 14, no. 4, Winter 1999), 290 male and 327 female college students were questioned about violence in their dating relationships. The authors found that students who used physical force in dating relationships often did so in order to exercise greater control over their dating partners. Compared to students who did not use violence in their dating relationships, respondents who reported using force were more likely to express anger, experience higher levels of jealousy, have poorer communication skills, report more daily stressors, display more irrational behavior and beliefs, and have more difficulty controlling their anger. These same respondents also reported more problems with alcohol, more verbal aggressiveness, and more efforts to control their dating partners than the students who never used force. The researchers concluded that intervention in the

area of dating violence should focus specifically on an individual's need to control his or her dating partner and the motivations for the need to control.

Dissatisfaction with the amount of power a dating partner felt in a relationship was associated with the use of violence for both men and women, according to "Power and Dating Violence Perpetration by Men and Women," a study of 352 male and 296 female undergraduate college students by Shelby A. Kaura and Craig M. Allen. They found, however, that witnessing parental violence was a stronger predictor (*Journal of Interpersonal Violence,* vol. 19, May 2004). The study also found that women reported they were the perpetrators of significantly more dating violence than did men. The authors concluded that "dissatisfaction with power in relationships is important for both genders."

The Balance of Power

The desire to dominate one's partner may be manifested using methods other than violence, such as attempts at financial, social, and decision-making control. Some researchers theorize that men of lower socioeconomic status are more likely to batter because they do it to assert the power that they lack economically. Violence becomes the tactic that compensates for the control, power, independence, and self-sufficiency these men lack in other areas.

In "Marital Power, Conflict, and Violence in a Nationally Representative Sample of American Couples," Diane Coleman and Murray Straus analyzed data from the 1975 National Family Violence Survey to determine the characteristics of families most prone to violence (*Violence and Victims,* vol. 1, no. 2, 1986). They asked respondents to indicate "who has the financial say" when it came to buying a car, having children, choosing a house or apartment, the type of job either partner should take, whether a partner should work, and how much money to spend each week for food. The response options were divided into "husband only," "husband more than wife," "husband and wife exactly the same," "wife more than husband," and "wife only."

Coleman and Straus arranged the responses to create four categories: male-dominant, female-dominant, equal, and divided power. The difference between the equal and divided-power types was that in the former the wife and husband made most decisions jointly, while in the latter they divided responsibility for decisions, with each having the final say for different decisions. The highest likelihood of violence occurred in relationships where one partner was dominant. Equal and divided-power relationships, in contrast, had the lowest likelihood of violence. Coleman and Straus also found that equal relationships could tolerate more conflict before violence erupted than other power relationships. Inequality, they posited, inevitably leads to attempts to even out the relationship, which in turn causes conflicts and perhaps violence. However, the researchers observed, male- or female-dominant relationships in which the partners accepted their status in the relationship usually experienced lower levels of conflict and violence.

Learned Gender Roles

Pointing to history, some researchers see wife abuse as a natural consequence of women's second-class status in society. Among the first to express this viewpoint were Emerson Dobash and Russell Dobash in *Violence against Wives* (New York: Free Press, 1979). Dobash and Dobash argued that men who assaulted their wives were actually living up to roles and qualities expected and cherished in Western society—aggressiveness, male dominance, and female subordination—and that they used physical force as a means to enforce these roles. Many sociologists and anthropologists believe that men are socialized to exert power and control over women. Some men may use both physical and emotional abuse to attain the position of dominance in the spousal relationship.

Other researchers agree. Violence often grows out of inequality within an intimate relationship and reinforces male dominance and female subordination, according to Kersti Yllöo, in "Through a Feminist Lens: Gender, Power, and Violence," from the book *Current Controversies on Family Violence* (Newbury Park, CA: Sage, 1994). For Yllöo, violence against women in all of its forms, including sexual harassment and date rape, is a tactic of male control, and domestic violence is not just a conflict of interests, it is domination by men. In their study of thirty-three male batterers titled "Gendering Violence: Masculinity and Power in Men's Accounts of Domestic Violence," Kristin L. Anderson and Debra Umberson wrote: "violence is . . . an effective means by which batterers reconstruct men as masculine and women as feminine" (*Gender & Society,* vol. 15, June 2001).

Murray Straus compared data on wife battering with indices to measure gender equality, income, and social disorganization variables as part of his research work in "State-to-State Differences in Social Inequality and Social Bonds in Relation to Assaults on Wives in the United States" (*Journal of Comparative Family Studies,* vol. 25, no. 1, Spring 1994). Straus evaluated gender equality by measuring twenty-four indicators to determine the extent to which women have parity with men in economic, political, and legal arenas. Income inequality was assessed using census data on family income. Social disorganization measures the level of societal instability, such as geographic mobility, divorce, lack of religious affiliation, female- or male-headed households, and the ratio of tourists to residents in each state.

In all fifty states studied, Straus found that gender equality was the variable most closely related to the rate of wife assault—states where the status of women was higher were less likely to report high rates of wife abuse. Social disorganization was also related to abuse—the higher degree of social disorganization, the greater the probability that the state would have a high rate of wife assault. Straus found that economic inequality did not appear to be related to wife abuse rates.

Attitudes toward Violence

Some researchers believe attitudes about violence are shaped early in life, long before the first punch is thrown in a relationship. In "The Attitudes Towards Violence Scale: A Measure for Adolescents" (*Journal of Interpersonal Violence,* vol. 14, no. 11, November 1999), Susan B. Funk et al. asked junior high and high school students attending an inner-city public school in a Midwestern city about their attitudes toward violence. Some students identified themselves as victims of violence and others completed the survey before and after participating in a violence awareness program.

Using the responses of 638 students who took the survey prior to the violence awareness program, the researchers examined the correlation of violence with gender, grade-level, and ethnicity. They found that males endorsed more pro-violence attitudes independent of age, grade-level, and ethnicity, as did those students who identified themselves as victims of violence. African-American teenagers endorsed "reactive violence," or violence used in response to actual or perceived threats, at higher levels than other groups. Endorsement of reactive violence was linked to having violent behaviors in one's repertoire, willingness to act in a violent manner, and supporting the actual choice of a violent response. Hispanic Americans endorsed "culture of violence" measures, reflecting a pervasive identification with violence as a valued activity, at slightly higher levels than the teenagers as a group. "Culture of violence" measures included the conviction that the world is a dangerous place where the best way to ensure survival is to be vigilant and prepared to take the offensive. European Americans scored lower on measures of "reactive violence" as well as "total pro-violence attitudes."

The study found that gender, ethnicity, and self-identification as a victim of violence were all related to pro-violence attitudes. Males, regardless of cultural background, were more likely than females to endorse pro-violence attitudes. The researchers concluded that a combination of biological, environmental, and social influences were responsible for these findings.

Does a Patriarchal Society Breed Violence?

Donald Dutton, a professor of psychology and director of a treatment program for batterers, questioned the role of male domination in wife battering and offered alternative explanations for violence in "Patriarchy and Wife Assault: The Ecological Fallacy" (*Violence and Victims,* vol. 9, no. 2, 1994). According to the patriarchal model, societies that place a high value on male dominance should have high rates of abuse. But Dutton and other investigators cite studies that contradict this premise. For example, Coleman and Straus found that in marriages where spouses agreed that the husband should be dominant, violence levels were low.

Other research discounts the weight of the patriarchal theory of abuse. David B. Sugarman and Susan Frankel, in "Patriarchal Ideology and Wife-Assault: A Meta-Analytical Review" (*Journal of Family Violence,* vol. 11, no. 1, 1996), examined studies for evidence of a relationship between patriarchy and violence. They measured whether violent husbands had a higher acceptance of violence than nonviolent men and whether they believed that women should exhibit traditional gender roles of obedience, loyalty, and deference. The researchers also measured whether assaultive men were more likely to possess a traditional "gender schema," an internal perception of an individual's own levels of masculinity, femininity, or androgyny. They also considered whether assaulted wives held more traditional gender attitudes than wives who

were not battered and whether battered wives held more traditional feminine gender schemas.

Overall, their analysis found support for only two of the five hypotheses. Predictably, assaultive husbands found marital violence more acceptable than nonviolent husbands, and battered wives were more likely to be classified as having "traditional" feminine gender schemas than wives who were not assaulted. Sugarman and Frankel concluded that their findings offered only partial support for the patriarchy theory.

Mark Totten, however, found another link between patriarchy and violence. He concluded in a study of thirty male adolescents, primarily gang members, that underprivileged males in society use violence toward women in response to their lack of access to the traditional benefits of patriarchy ("Girlfriend Abuse as a Form of Masculinity Construction among Violent, Marginal Male Youth," *Men and Masculinities,* vol. 6, July 2003). Totten posited that the ideals of patriarchy—and the inability of these disenfranchised boys to wield any patriarchal power outside of their gangs or family groups—led them to be violent toward their girlfriends as one way to define their masculinity. "Violence," he wrote, "was one of the few resources over which they had control." On the other hand, he wrote, "Men with more resources can commit different, less visible forms of abuse."

PSYCHOLOGICAL EXPLANATIONS OF ABUSE

Most sociologists and psychologists agree that lower levels of aggression, such as slapping and shoving, can escalate over time into more severe forms of abuse, such as battering and weapon use. However, while most relationships characterized by severe violence begin with milder forms of abuse, many partners limit their aggressive physical behavior to pushing and slapping. K. Daniel O'Leary, in "Through a Psychological Lens: Personality Traits, Personality Disorders, and Levels of Violence" (*Current Controversies on Family Violence* [Newbury Park, CA: Sage, 1994]) argued that the different levels of aggression—verbal, mild physical aggression, and severe physical violence—are three distinct but related behaviors. Although they exist along a continuum, he contends that men who engage in the milder forms of aggression are not motivated by the same impulses as men who commit severe abuse.

As further evidence of the differences in levels of abuse, O'Leary observed that in marriages with low levels of physical violence, the abuse is often mutual, and that women do not describe their use of force as self-defense. In severely violent relationships, however, women often claim that they use violence in self-defense. O'Leary maintained that this difference is important because while marital therapy may be appropriate and effective treatment for low-level violence, it is neither appropriate nor effective for relationships characterized by severe abuse.

O'Leary found that mildly abusive men scored high on personality tests for impulsiveness, a readiness to defend oneself, aggression, suspicion of others, and a tendency to take offense easily. Men in treatment programs for abuse—generally extremely abusive men—usually have been diagnosed with serious psychological disorders, including schizoid/borderline, narcissistic/antisocial, and possessive/dependent/compulsive personality traits. These men were significantly different from men who were in bad marriages but were not abusive. O'Leary contended that these findings are evidence of a strong psychological component to abuse rather than a social system that promotes the domination of women.

Some feminist researchers disagree with the concept of distinguishing between types of abuse and theories that link the causes of abuse to the severity of the violence. They consider all violence against women unacceptable, and they reject the idea that the pathological personality characteristics of the perpetrators (serious mental health diagnoses) explain or excuse all of their violent behaviors. Feminist researchers and academics question psychological interpretations of violence that portray batterers as psychologically different from the rest of society because many believe that any man has the capability to become a batterer simply by virtue of living in a patriarchal society.

SOCIOLOGICAL EXPLANATIONS OF ABUSE

Richard Gelles, the chair of Child Welfare and Family Violence and interim dean of the University of Pennsylvania School of Social Work, thinks it is risky to place too much emphasis on a psychological explanation of abuse. He contended that the picture of a mentally deranged, violent abuser focuses attention on only the most extreme cases of abuse, stereotyped as a psychotic offender and an innocent victim. According to Gelles, only about 10% of abusive incidents are caused by mental illness. The rest, he asserted, cannot be explained by a psychological model. Gelles said a more complete understanding of the causes of abuse may be gained from an examination of sociological models.

General Systems Theory

The general systems theory views violence as a system rather than as a result of individual mental disturbance. It describes a system of violence that operates at the individual level, the family level, and at a societal level.

Straus developed eight concepts to illustrate the general systems theory:

- Violence between family members has many causes and roots, and personality, stress, and conflicts are only some of the causes of domestic violence.

- More family violence occurs than is reported.

- Most family violence is either denied or ignored.

- Stereotyped family-violence imagery is learned in early childhood from other family members.

- The family-violence stereotypes are continually reaffirmed through ordinary social interactions and the mass media.

- Violent acts by violent persons may generate positive feedback; that is, these acts may produce desired results.

- Use of violence, when contrary to family norms, creates additional conflict.

- Persons who are labeled violent may be encouraged to play out a violent role, either to live up to the expectations of others or to fulfill their own self-concepts of being violent or dangerous.

The Resource Theory

The second theory in sociological models is known as the resource theory. According to this theory, the more resources—social, personal, and economic—a person can command, the more force he or she can potentially call on. The individual who is rich in terms of these resources has less need to use force in an open manner. In contrast, a person with little education, low job prestige and income, or poor interpersonal skills may use violence to compensate for a real or perceived lack of resources and to maintain dominance.

The Exchange/Social Control Theory

The exchange/social control theory argues that violence can be explained by the principle of costs and rewards. The private nature of the family, the reluctance of social institutions to intervene, and the low risk of other interventions reduce the risk of negative consequences from abuse. This theory maintains that cultural sanction and approval of violence increase the potential rewards for violence.

The Subculture of Violence Theory

The fourth theory posits that there is a subculture of violence in which some groups within society hold values that permit, and even encourage, the use of violence. This theory is offered as an explanation of why some segments of society and some cultures are more violent than others. This theory is perhaps the most widely accepted theory of violence.

Feminist Theory

Feminist theories of violence against women emphasize that societal patriarchal structures of gender-based inequalities of power are at the root of the problem. The violence, rather than being an individual psychological problem, is instead an expression of male domination of females. Violence against women, in the feminist view, includes a variety of "control tactics" meant to control women.

Structure of Interpersonal Relationships Theory

A more recent theory argued that several key structural features of relationships are conducive to domestic violence. It was presented by Donald Black in "Making Sociological Sense Out of Trends in Intimate Partner Violence" (*Violence against Women,* vol. 10, June 2004). Black, like Gelles, argued that many of the insights of other theories need to be integrated into a more comprehensive theory of the impact of the structure of relationships on domestic violence. He argued that key risk factors of domestic violence included 1) social isolation of the couple, 2) separate peer support networks, 3) inequality between partners, 4) lack of relational distance, or a high degree of intimacy within a couple, 5) the centralization of authority—in other words, patriarchal dominance within a family, and 6) exposure to violence and violent networks.

SUBSTANCE ABUSE AND VIOLENCE

The role of alcohol and drug abuse in family violence is featured in many studies, and it is a factor in physical violence and stalking, according to such researchers as Pam Wilson et al. who examined the issue in their article "Severity of Violence against Women by Intimate Partners and Associated Use of Alcohol and/or Illicit Drugs by the Perpetrator" (*Journal of Interpersonal Violence,* vol. 15, September 2000.) Although researchers generally don't consider alcohol and drug use to be the cause of violence, they find that it can contribute to, accelerate, or increase aggression. A variety of data sources establish correlation (a complementary or parallel relationship) between substance abuse and violence, but correlation does not establish causation. In theory, and possibly even in practice, substance abuse may promote or provoke domestic violence, but both may also be influenced by other factors, such as environmental, biological, and situational stressors. Based on available research, it remains unclear whether substance abuse is a key factor in most domestic violence incidents.

Analyzing 2002 National Crime Victimization Survey data, authors of the 2003 Bureau of Justice Statistics report *Drugs and Crime Facts* found that 17% of victims of violent assaults believed their offenders had been using alcohol, 4.6% believed offenders had been using both alcohol and drugs, 5.6% believed offenders had been using drugs only, and 1.5% believed offenders had used either alcohol or drugs. (See Figure 3.1.) Only 27.7% of victims believed the offender had not used any drugs or alcohol, while another 43.3% reported they did not know.

While anecdotal evidence suggests that alcohol and drugs appear to be linked to violence and abuse, in controlled studies the connection is not as clear. For example,

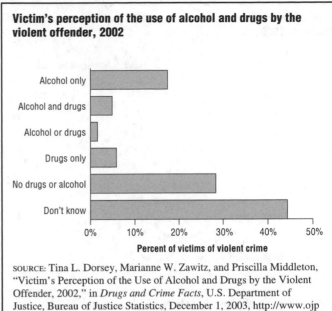

FIGURE 3.1

Victim's perception of the use of alcohol and drugs by the violent offender, 2002

SOURCE: Tina L. Dorsey, Marianne W. Zawitz, and Priscilla Middleton, "Victim's Perception of the Use of Alcohol and Drugs by the Violent Offender, 2002," in *Drugs and Crime Facts*, U.S. Department of Justice, Bureau of Justice Statistics, December 1, 2003, http://www.ojp.usdoj.gov/bjs/dcf/duc.htm (accessed September 23, 2004)

some research finds that heavy binge drinking is more predictive of abuse than daily consumption of alcohol. Other research reveals little evidence that drug use directly causes people to become aggressive or violent, and some investigators believe that the substance abuse–violence link varies across individuals, over time within an individual's life, and even in response to environmental influences, such as epidemics of drug use and changing law enforcement policies.

In "Alcohol and Other Drugs Are Key Causal Agents of Violence" (*Current Controversies on Family Violence,* [Newbury Park, CA: Sage, 1994]), Jerry Flanzer suggested that while not all alcoholics are violent, alcoholism does cause family violence. He observed that personality characteristics of alcoholics and abusers are remarkably similar, marked by behaviors such as blaming others, jealousy and possessiveness, depression, low self-esteem, and "blacking out" critical incidents. Not all alcoholic families are violent and not all violent families include alcohol abusers, but Flanzer speculated that a careful examination of family histories would reveal overlap between violence and alcohol abuse.

Alcohol acts as a disinhibitor, allowing an individual to act out emotions, including anger, that were previously held in check. It also impairs an individual's understanding of a situation, which may lead a drinker to respond inappropriately with anger. Alcohol is also frequently used to rationalize erratic behavior and violence, allowing an abuser to avoid responsibility for violent behavior by blaming it on the effects of alcohol. Finally, alcoholism distorts the family system by constantly forcing the family to accommodate the short-term demands of the alcoholic to maintain some measure of family stability. This

TABLE 3.4

Alcohol and drug use by victims and their partners in the year prior to the killing or attempted killing of women or the worst violent incident, 1996

Substance	Homicide/attempted homicide %		Abused %		Nonabused %	
	Women	Partners	Women	Partners	Women	Partners
Alcohol						
Drunk every day	—	35.1	—	11.6	—	1.2
Problem drinker	13.0	49.2	7.0	31.1	1.7	6.2
Drinks per episode						
1–2	64.6	24.4	61.4	35.1	77.7	65.8
3–4	22.9	17.1	27.9	27.2	18.2	25.5
5–6	8.9	24.8	7.9	18.2	3.8	4.8
7+	3.7	33.7	2.9	19.5	.03	3.9
Ever been in alcohol treatment	27.7	13.5	13.3	18.1	57.1	19.2
Drugs						
Use drugs	18.4	54.2	13.4	25.0	6.7	4.3
Ever been in drug treatment	20.6	11.3	3.5	12.4	14.3	21.4

SOURCE: Phyllis Sharps, Jacquelyn C. Campbell, Doris Campbell, Faye Gary, and Daniel Webster, "Table 1: Alcohol and Drug Use by Victims and Their Partners in the Year Prior to the Killing or Attempted Killing of Women or the Worst Violent Incident," in "Risky Mix: Drinking, Drug Use, and Homicide," *National Institute of Justice Journal*, no. 250, November 2003, http://ncjrs.org/pdffiles1/jr000250d.pdf (accessed September 10, 2004)

restructuring of family life establishes an atmosphere that tolerates and accommodates violence.

A 2003 study of patterns of alcohol and drug use in murders and attempted murders of women by their partners showed a relationship between substance use and violence (Phyllis Sharps, Jacquelyn C. Campbell, Doris Campbell, Faye Gary, and Daniel Webster, "Risky Mix: Drinking, Drug Use, and Homicide," *National Institute of Justice Journal*, no. 250, November 2003). Researchers found that in the year before the violent incident, female victims used alcohol and drugs less frequently and consumed smaller amounts than did their male partners. (See Table 3.4.) Researchers also found that during the homicide or attempted homicide, 31.3% of perpetrators consumed alcohol, 12.6% of perpetrators used drugs, and 26.2% used both. Less than one in three perpetrators (29.9%) used neither alcohol nor drugs. (See Table 3.5.) On the other hand, perpetrators who abused their partners without attempting to kill them consumed alcohol 21% of the time, drugs 6.7% of the time, and both drugs and alcohol 5.8% of the time. These perpetrators had not used substances almost two-thirds of the time (65.8%). Researchers concluded that increased substance use results in more serious violence.

An Excuse, Not a Cause

Gelles disagreed with Flanzer and others who have presented substance abuse as a cause of family violence in "Alcohol and Other Drugs Are Not the Cause of Violence" (*Current Controversies on Family Violence* [Newbury Park, CA: Sage, 1994]). Gelles argued that although substantial evidence has linked alcohol and drug use to violence, there is little scientific evidence that alcohol or other drugs, such as cocaine, have pharmacological prop-

erties that produce violent and abusive behavior. Although amphetamines have been proven to generate increased aggression, there is no evidence that such aggression is routinely expressed as family or intimate partner violence. Gelles maintained that although alcoholism may be associated with intimate violence, it is not a primary cause of the violence.

If alcohol had the pharmacological property of inducing violence, it would do so in all cultures, Gelles argued. Cross-cultural studies of alcohol consumption and violence, however, do not support this correlation between alcohol and violence. In some cultures individuals who drink become passive; in others they become aggressive. In U.S. culture, Gelles noted, drinking disinhibits, permitting violent behavior without responsibility. Social expectations about drinking and drinking behavior exacerbate the problem, teaching people that if they want to avoid accountability or responsibility for their violence, alcohol consumption provides one socially acceptable justification.

Experiments using college students as subjects find that when the students thought they were consuming alcohol, they acted more aggressively than if they were told they had been given nonalcoholic drinks. According to Gelles, it is the expectation of the effects of alcohol that influences behavior, not the actual liquor consumed. He also observed that although abusive families may also abuse alcohol, an analysis of the drinking behavior at the time of the abuse finds that alcohol was not used immediately prior to the abuse in a majority of cases.

The "Drunken Bum" Theory of Wife Beating

Glenda Kaufman Kantor and Murray Straus have tested three commonly held beliefs: that alcohol and wife

TABLE 3.5

Substance use during the killing or attempted killing of women or the worst violent incident, 1996

	Homicide/attempted homicide		Abuse	
	Victims (N=456) %	Perpetrators (N=456) %	Victims (N=427) %	Perpetrators (N=427) %
Substance use				
Alcohol	14.6	31.3	8.9	21
Drugs	3.3	12.6	1.6	6.7
Both	4.7	26.2	0.9	5.8
None	77.4	29.9	88.5	65.8

SOURCE: Phyllis Sharps, Jacquelyn C. Campbell, Doris Campbell, Faye Gary, and Daniel Webster, "Table 2: Substance Use During the Killing or Attempted Killing of Women or the Worst Violent Incident," in "Risky Mix: Drinking, Drug Use, and Homicide," *National Institute of Justice Journal*, no. 250, November 2003, http://ncjrs.org/pdffiles1/jr000250d.pdf (accessed September 10, 2004)

abuse are related, that wife abuse is more common in blue-collar than white-collar families, and that the acceptance of violence contributes to spousal abuse. In "The 'Drunken Bum' Theory of Wife Beating" (*Physical Violence in American Families* [Piscataway, NJ: Transaction, 1990]), Kantor and Straus found that the combination of blue-collar work status, drinking, and approval of violence were associated with the highest likelihood of wife abuse. Men with these characteristics had a rate of abuse that was 7.8 times greater than the rate of white-collar men who drank little and disapproved of violence.

Kantor and Straus emphasized that in three-quarters of the cases (76%), alcohol was not consumed immediately prior to the instance of wife abuse. In about 14% of the instances, only the male was drinking, in 2% only the female was drinking, and in 8% both the male and female were drinking. The researchers found a definite correlation between the amount of alcohol consumed and violence. Approximately 6.8% of those who abstained from alcohol abused their wives, while almost three times as many binge drinkers (19.2%) used violence. Kantor and Straus, however, underscored the importance of not overlooking the considerable amount of wife abuse perpetrated by nondrinkers and moderate drinkers.

The researchers also found that the major factor determining wife abuse was whether the individual approved of the use of violence against women. Not surprisingly, men who approved of a man hitting his wife were far more likely to have hit their wives than men who disapproved.

The Relationship Is Complex

Glenda Kaufman Kantor warned that considering alcohol as simply a disinhibitor of violence understates the complexity of the problem in her study "Refining the Brushstrokes in Portraits of Alcohol and Wife Assaults" (*Alcohol and Interpersonal Violence: Fostering Multidis-*

ciplinary Perspectives [Rockville, MD: National Institute on Alcohol Abuse and Alcoholism Research, 1993]). She proposed that the finding that heavy drinking by wives can increase their risk of being abused may be because intoxicated women violate what is considered to be the normal gender role. Furthermore, if women become verbally or physically aggressive under the influence of alcohol, they risk being beaten. Alcoholic women are also more likely to suffer abuse from their partners than nonalcoholic women. However, this finding does not imply that the wife has brought on the abuse by her drinking. Kantor emphasized that violence is initiated by the aggressor, not the victim.

In their study "When Women Are under the Influence: Does Drinking or Drug Use by Women Provoke Beatings by Men?" (*Recent Developments in Alcoholism* [New York: Plenum, 1997]), Glenda Kaufman Kantor and Nancy Asdigian found little evidence that women's drinking provoked or preceded aggression by husbands. The authors theorized that women drink or use drugs as a means of coping with violent partners. In households where the husband is a substance abuser and abuses his wife, the wife is also more likely to be a substance abuser. The authors proposed that both excessive drinking and spousal abuse have common roots in childhood experiences of physical and/or sexual abuse.

Does Treatment Help?

Timothy O'Farrell and Christopher Murphy, in "Marital Violence before and after Alcoholism Treatment" (*Journal of Consulting and Clinical Psychology*, vol. 63, no. 2, 1995), examined whether behavioral marital therapy was helpful in reducing violence in abusive relationships. The researchers found the percentage of couples who experienced violent acts decreased from about 65% before treatment to about 25% after treatment. Severe violence dropped from between 30% and 35% before to about 10% after treatment.

Following treatment, recovering alcoholics no longer had elevated violence levels, but alcoholics who relapsed did. Based on women's reports of their partners' violence, 2.5% of nondrinking alcoholics, compared to 12.8% of the nonalcoholic sample, were violent. In contrast, 34.7% of the relapsed alcoholics were violent. O'Farrell and Murphy warned that the data do not permit drawing the conclusion that drinking caused the continued violence since other factors may have influenced behavior. They did conclude, however, that their findings support the premise that recovery from alcoholism can reduce the risk of marital violence.

A more recent study supported these findings. After intensive inpatient treatment of male batterers for alcoholism, both alcohol consumption and levels of violence within families decreased, according to Gregory L. Stuart, et al. in "Reductions in Marital Violence Following Treatment for Alcohol Dependence" (*Journal of Interpersonal Violence,* vol. 18, October 2003). Not only did the frequency of husband-to-wife physical and psychological abuse decrease, but the frequency of wife-to-husband marital violence also decreased significantly.

ABUSE OF PREGNANT WOMEN

Research about intimate partner violence reveals that violence does not stop when women become pregnant. The Centers for Disease Control and Prevention's Division of Reproductive Health gathers data about the health of expectant mothers using its Pregnancy Risk Assessment Monitoring System (PRAMS). An analysis of PRAMS data revealed that between 2.9% to 5.7% of women reported being abused by their husbands or partners in the year before they gave birth. Author Jana L. Jasinski believed this estimate too low, since the PRAMS asks limited questions about domestic violence and asks about abuse rather than about particular behaviors ("Pregnancy and Domestic Violence: A Review of the Literature," *Trauma, Violence, & Abuse,* vol. 5, January 2004). Still, she argued, pregnancy does not appear to increase the risk of domestic violence, although more research into that question is needed.

Studies estimating higher rates of abuse of pregnant women—as many as 324,000 women per year and rates as high as 20% of pregnant women—have been reported (Julie Gazmararian et al., "Prevalence of Violence against Pregnant Women," *Journal of the American Medical Association,* vol. 275, no. 24, 1996; and Julie Gazmararian et al., "Violence and Reproductive Health: Current Knowledge and Future Research Directions," *Maternal and Child Health Journal,* vol. 4, no. 2, 2000). Higher abuse rates were reported later in pregnancy, with 7.4% to 20% of that violence occurring in the third trimester. The lowest rates were reported in a study of women with higher socioeconomic status who were treated in a private clinic. The assailants were mainly intimate or former intimate partners, parents, or other family members. Two studies that also examined violence in the period after birth found that violence was more prevalent after birth than during pregnancy.

Jana L. Jasinski's research, cited above, suggested that violence directed toward pregnant women is usually part of an ongoing pattern of domestic violence. Some factors, however, do seem to increase the risk of violence for pregnant women. Julie Gazmararian et al. found that women with unwanted pregnancies had 4.1 times the risk of experiencing physical violence by a husband or boyfriend during the months prior to delivery than did women with desired pregnancies. Researchers have found higher rates of violence during pregnancy for women who are young, have fewer than twelve years of education, are unmarried, are of low socioeconomic status, have postponed or foregone prenatal care, or have an unintended pregnancy. Other studies have found more reported violence when the partner is unhappy about the pregnancy.

INTERGENERATIONAL ABUSE

Research demonstrates a relationship between having been a victim of violence and becoming violent in future relationships. In fact, a 1996 report prepared by the American Psychological Association Task Force on Violence and the Family concludes that children's exposure to their father abusing their mother is the single strongest risk factor for passing violence down from one generation to the next. A study of 352 male and 296 female undergraduate college students found that witnessing parental violence was the strongest predictor of perpetrating dating violence (Shelby A. Kaura and Craig M. Allen, "Power and Dating Violence Perpetration by Men and Women," *Journal of Interpersonal Violence,* vol. 19, May 2004). Straus, however, cautioned against jumping to the conclusion that once violence occurs in a family, it will inevitably or automatically be transmitted to the next generation. Not all men who grow up in violent families end up abusing their spouses, and not all abused children or abused wives will abuse others. Conversely, some violent individuals grow up in nonviolent families.

Richard Gelles and Murray Straus, in *Intimate Violence* (New York: Simon and Schuster, 1989), reported that the experience of children seeing their parents strike one another teaches three lessons:

- Those who love you are also those who hit you and those you love are people you can hit.

- Seeing and experiencing violence in your home establishes the moral rightness of hitting those you love.

- If other means of getting your way, dealing with stress, or expressing yourself do not work, violence is permissible.

Gerald T. Hotaling and David B. Sugarman, in "An Analysis of Risk Markers in Husband-to-Wife Violence: The Current State of Knowledge" (*Violence and Victims,* vol. 2, no. 2, 1989), considered fifty-two studies of domestic violence for ninety-seven potential risk markers, defined as attributes or characteristics associated with an increased risk of either the use of husband-to-wife violence or of being victimized by husband-to-wife violence. They found only one consistent risk for the victims in the relevant literature: women who have experienced physical spousal abuse are more likely to have witnessed violence between parents or caregivers during their childhoods. Experiencing violence was a weaker predictor of severe husband-to-wife violence than is witnessing violence.

Shame

Donald Dutton et al. in "The Role of Shame and Guilt in the Intergenerational Transmission of Abusiveness" (*Violence and Victims,* vol. 10, no. 2, Summer 1995), tested their theory that being shamed in childhood leads to an assaultive adulthood. The distinction between shame and guilt is that shame produces disturbances in self-identity, while guilt produces bad feelings and remorse about the condemned behavior but not the self. Using a series of psychological tests with 130 battering men, researchers concluded that shaming experiences in childhood contribute to the formation of a borderline personality disorder, including identity disturbances, temporary psychotic experiences, and the use of defenses such as projecting blame on someone else or the "splitting" of an individual's personality. According to the authors, shaming experiences result in personality disturbances, while parental abuse contributes the model behavior for expressing anger.

Beaten Child, Beaten Wife

Ronald Simons et al. in "Explaining Women's Double Jeopardy: Factors that Mediate the Association between Harsh Treatment as a Child and Violence by a Husband" (*Journal of Marriage and the Family,* vol. 55, 1993), examined the link between women who received harsh treatment in childhood and later married abusive husbands. Researchers asserted that women who were abused in childhood marry abusive husbands—not because they have learned that violence is permissible, but because they are apt to marry men from similar backgrounds. Children raised in violent environments are often noncompliant, defiant, aggressive, and perform poorly in school. Researchers found that the abusive behavior by adults who were abused in childhood was part of a long-standing pattern of interpersonal difficulties and antisocial behavior.

The researchers did not find a connection between abuse and traditional gender beliefs that men are supposed to be dominant. Nor did they find a connection between the level of control the women felt they had in their lives and the incidence of abuse. On the contrary, the women in abusive marriages were not submissive; they tended to have a history of aggressive, deviant behavior. Simons et al. theorized that rebellious girls are more likely to date and marry equally antisocial, rebellious young men and end up in abusive relationships.

STRESS AND SPOUSE ABUSE

Straus and Gelles have found that selected variables, including employment status, income, and number of children, are often associated with domestic violence in a given family. Families with the lowest incomes, the most children, and the lowest level of employment of the husband tend to be at greater risk for spouse abuse.

In *Behind Closed Doors: Violence in the American Family* (Garden City, NY: Anchor Books, 1980), Murray Straus, Richard Gelles, and Suzanne Steinmetz constructed a scale to measure overall family stress and applied it to National Family Violence Surveys data. In addition to income, number of children, and employment, they included other stressors: illness or death in the family, arrest or conviction of a family member, relocation, sexual difficulties, and problems with in-laws. They found a strong correlation between the number of stressful events experienced during the past year and the rates of family violence and abuse. The greater the stress, the greater the likelihood of abuse.

Other studies have also found a relationship between domestic abuse and stress. "Frequency and Correlates of Intimate Partner Violence by Type: Physical, Sexual, and Psychological Battering" (*American Journal of Public Health,* 2000) revealed that stressors, such as a male partner's unemployment and alcohol and/or drug use, were associated with an increased risk for physical, sexual, and emotional abuse.

INTIMATE PARTNER VIOLENCE DECLINES WITH INCREASING AGE

Jill Suitor, Karl Pillemer, and Murray Straus in "Marital Violence in a Life Course Perspective" (*Physical Violence in American Families,* [Piscataway, NJ: Transaction, 1990]), found that both marital conflict and verbal aggression consistently decline with age over every ten-year period. Analysis of the National Family Violence Surveys data from 1975 and 1985 revealed that the rate of violence in the eighteen- to twenty-nine-year-old group dropped when its members entered the thirty- to thirty-nine-year-old group. The rate dropped even further when the older group became the forty- to forty-nine-year-old group. The consistent decline applied to both men and women in all age groups between eighteen and sixty-five.

Suitor, Pillemer, and Straus concluded that marital conflict and verbal aggression decrease with age. They considered several different possible explanations for this observation, including greater pressure to conform (perhaps because of a greater stake in society), the greater cost of deviating from accepted patterns—having "more to lose"—and greater expectations.

Subsequent studies confirm that intimate partner violence declines with advancing age. Analyzing National Crime Victimization Survey data, Rennison found married women aged twenty to twenty-four had eight victimizations per one thousand women, compared to just one per one thousand among married women aged fifty or older (*Intimate Partner Violence and Age of Victim, 1993–99,* [Washington, DC: Bureau of Justice Statistics, 2001]). Callie Rennison and Michael Rand also found lower rates of intimate partner violence in women over age fifty-four in their study "Nonlethal Intimate Partner Violence against Women" (*Violence against Women,* vol. 9, December

2003). They believed lower rates might be due to several factors, such as homicides of younger women, earlier divorces from abusive partners, or the turning of older perpetrators to other forms of victimization, such as psychological abuse or economic domination.

Spousal Abuse among Older Adults

Spouse abuse is a known form of elder abuse, but there is little known about its precise causes or frequency. The rate of spouse abuse among older adults is estimated to be less than 20% of all elder abuse reported by the *National Elder Abuse Incidence Study* (Washington, DC: National Center on Elder Abuse, 1998). Researchers speculate that an abusive relationship between older adults may simply be a continuation of abuse that began earlier in a marriage or may begin in response to age-related stresses, such as retirement, failing health, caregiver burdens, or increased dependency. Historically, social and support services for abused older adults have been largely health related and there is scant help available for elders trapped in abusive intimate partner relationships.

Sarah Harris, in "For Better or for Worse: Spouse Abuse Grown Old" (*Journal of Elder Abuse and Neglect,* vol. 8, no. 1, 1996), used the 1985 National Family Violence Survey data to compare respondents under sixty years old to those over age sixty. Although the incidence of spouse abuse in older couples was significantly less than that of younger couples, many of the risk factors for violence were the same. Not surprisingly, abuse occurred most often in situations where there was a high degree of conflict.

The factors associated with older partner violence included lower education levels, lower family income, verbal aggression, drug abuse, depression, perceived stress, low use of reasoning tactics, and marital conflict. Racial/ethnic group affiliation also played a part: blacks and Hispanics in the younger group and blacks in the over-sixty group were more likely to experience couple violence. When violence was reported for more than the twelve months preceding the survey, intergenerational violence and poor physical health were also found to be significant.

Rennison and Rand found that spouse abuse among their oldest cohorts was similar to that found in younger cohorts: most incidents (85%) were committed without a weapon, a substantial portion of the abusers used alcohol or drugs, and the likelihood of injuries across all age groups was similar. However, mature women were less likely to report the violence to police than younger women.

SIGNS OF POTENTIAL VIOLENCE

Predictive Characteristics and Risk Markers

Can a woman expect to see certain signs of potential violence in a man she is dating or living with before she becomes a victim of abuse? The National Coalition against Domestic Violence published a checklist of predictive behaviors in men that signal violence. (See Table 2.11 in Chapter 2.) Along with the predictors described in the checklist, there are other indicators, known as risk markers, which may indicate an increased propensity for violence. These include:

- an unemployed male
- a male who uses illegal drugs
- males and females with different religious backgrounds
- a male who saw his father hit his mother
- male and female unmarried cohabitants
- males with blue-collar occupations
- males who did not graduate from high school
- males between eighteen and thirty years of age
- males or females who use severe violence toward children in the home
- total family income below the poverty level

In "Men Who Batter: The Risk-Markers," Richard Gelles, Regina Lackner, and Glen Wolfner found that in families where two risk markers were present, there was twice as much violence as those with none (*Violence Update,* vol. 4, no. 12, 1994). In homes with seven or more of those factors, the violence rate was a staggering forty times higher.

A separate analysis by Hotaling and Sugarman surveyed risk markers present in more than four hundred studies. In "A Risk Marker Analysis of Assaulted Wives" (*Journal of Family Violence,* vol. 5, no. 1, 1990) and in "Prevention of Wife Assault" (*Treatment of Family Violence* [New York: Wiley, 1990]), the researchers found that abused women do not differ in specific personality traits from women who are not abused in terms of age, educational level, race, occupational status, length of time in the relationship, or number of children. Furthermore, a woman's poor self-esteem did not appear to be a risk factor but rather a consequence of abuse.

Contrary to other researchers, Hotaling and Sugarman found that being an abused child or seeing a parent being abused does not necessarily mean a woman has a greater chance of becoming a battered wife. Instead, severe male batterers can be distinguished from nonassaultive and verbally abusive men, as well as men who commit minor abuse, by the greater likelihood of having witnessed violence between their parents. In addition, men who engage in minor physical aggression are more likely to have experienced violence in the past than are men who were verbally abusive.

Hotaling and Sugarman also concluded that the only factor that differentiates abused wives from wives who are not abused is the level of marital conflict. Obviously, if a marriage has very little or no conflict, there is no reason or provocation for violence. The researchers maintained that while there is some level of conflict in every relationship, it does not necessarily result in violence. Individuals in adequately functioning relationships negotiate their way through disagreements, while individuals in violent relationships lack these skills and resort to violence.

Hotaling and Sugarman concentrated on four factors most often associated with abuse: marital conflict, the frequency of the husband's drinking, expectations about the division of labor in the relationship, and a measure of educational incompatibility. Hotaling and Sugarman concluded that to understand wife abuse, researchers are better served by consideration of the perpetrators' behavior rather than the characteristics of the victims.

RISK MARKERS AND A CONTINUUM OF AGGRESSION. Sugarman et al. used the analysis of risk markers to test the theory that there is a continuum of aggression in husband-to-wife violence that is linked to some of the risk markers. The risk markers considered were marital conflict, depressive symptoms, alcohol use, attitude toward interpersonal violence, violence in the family in which the individuals grew up, nonfamily violence level, and socioeconomic status. The researchers found that an increase in the severity of husband-to-wife violence was associated with an increase in depressive symptoms in the husband, along with his greater acceptance of marital violence and a higher likelihood that he experienced and witnessed violence in his family as a child. In addition, greater alcohol use and higher levels of nonfamily violence by the couple were linked to more severe violence.

Consistent with other research, Sugarman et al. concluded that persons who engage in minor violence do not necessarily progress to severe violence, but those who use severe violence almost always began with minor violence. The most important implication of this finding is that early intervention may prevent more severe abuse. Most treatment programs are only initiated after a woman has suffered severe battering. Prevention programs that emphasize the importance of seeking treatment for low-level abuse before it escalates to serious violence might encourage women to escape abuse before it claims their health or their lives.

A study by Jacquelyn C. Campbell et al. titled "Assessing Risk Factors for Intimate Partner Homicide," evaluated the risk factors among abused women for being killed by their intimate partners (*National Institute of Justice Journal*, no. 250, November 2003). The researchers found that abused women whose abusers owned guns and who had threatened to kill them were at high risk of being killed by their intimate partners. (See Figure 3.2.) Other

FIGURE 3.2

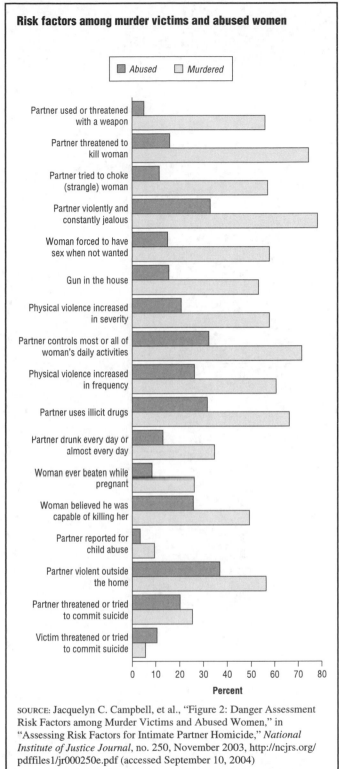

Risk factors among murder victims and abused women

SOURCE: Jacquelyn C. Campbell, et al., "Figure 2: Danger Assessment Risk Factors among Murder Victims and Abused Women," in "Assessing Risk Factors for Intimate Partner Homicide," *National Institute of Justice Journal*, no. 250, November 2003, http://ncjrs.org/pdffiles1/jr000250e.pdf (accessed September 10, 2004)

high risk factors for homicide included extreme jealousy, attempts to choke, and marital rape. The study authors hope that the "danger assessment" tool they used may assist women and advocates for battered women to better assess the level of risk in abusive relationships.

CHAPTER 4
THE EFFECTS OF ABUSE—WHY DOES SHE STAY?

Why don't battered women leave? This question does not have a single answer but, rather, many answers. Even the question has many connotations. For battered women, the question is not uniformly, "How can I leave him?" but "How can I get the violence to stop?" or "How can I get my relationship to be happy and fulfilling?" For women who want to leave, the question may become "Can I support myself and the children by myself?" "How can I escape?" "Will he kill me if I try?" or "How will my children fare without a father?" For clinicians working with battered women, the question might be "How can she make any decisions when she is so emotionally traumatized?"

—Ola W. Barnett, "Why Battered Women Do Not Leave, Part 1, " *Trauma, Violence, and Abuse*, vol. 1, no. 4, October 2000

One of the most frequently asked questions about abused women is: Why do they stay? Some authors and advocates argue that the relevant questions for battered women themselves are very different. They believe that the very question implies there is something wrong with the woman for staying, rather than placing the blame where it belongs—on the batterer. Better questions, Barnett argues, might be: "Why does he beat her?" or "Why does society let him get away with it?" or "What can be done to stop him?"

But not all women stay in abusive relationships. Many leave abusive relationships and situations without turning to the police or support organizations. While their number is unknown, most who leave without asking for help usually have strong personal support systems of friends and family or employment and earnings that enable them to live economically independent of their abusive partners. Yet, there can be little question that a large percentage of women remain with their abusers. There are as many reasons why women stay as there are consequences and outcomes of abusive relationships.

REASONS TO STAY

Women stay in abusive relationships for a variety of reasons. A major reason women stay is their economic dependency on their batterers. Many women feel they are better off with a violent husband than facing the challenge of raising children on their own. Some harbor deep feelings for their abusive partners and believe that over time they can change their partners' behavior. Others mistakenly interpret their abusers' efforts to control their life as expressions of love. Other frequently reported considerations include:

- Most women have at least one dependent child who must be cared for.
- Many are unemployed.
- Their parents are either distant, unable, or unwilling to help.
- The women may fear losing mutual friends and the support of family, especially in-laws.
- Many have no property that is solely their own.
- Some lack access to cash, credit, or any financial resources.
- If the woman leaves, then she risks being charged with desertion and losing her children and joint assets.
- She may face a decline in living standards for herself and her children, and the children, especially older ones, may resent this reduced living standard.
- The woman and/or children may be in poor health.
- The abuser may have threatened or harmed her pets, as noted by Catherine A. Faver and Elizabeth B. Strand in "To Leave or To Stay? Battered Women's Concern for Vulnerable Pets" (*Journal of Interpersonal Violence*, vol. 18, no. 12, December 2003).

Some battered women hold values and beliefs that experts term "traditional ideology." These patriarchal beliefs, often reinforced by clergy, mental health professionals, and physicians, tend to normalize violence against women. This ideology may include:

- a belief that divorce is not a viable alternative and that marriage is a permanent commitment

- a belief that having both a mother and father is crucial for children

- an emotional dependence on her husband, and a feeling she needs someone to take care of her

- feelings of helplessness and a belief that she is dependent on a man and unable to take the initiative to escape her situation

- a belief that a "successful marriage" depends on her, leading her to assume responsibility or to blame herself for the abuse

- feelings of low self-esteem and self-worth

- the rationalization that her situation is caused by heavy stress, alcohol, problems at work, or unemployment

- a cycle of abuse that includes periods when her husband is exceedingly romantic, leading her to believe that she still loves him or that he is basically good

- a feeling of isolation from friends and family that may have been forced on her by a jealous and possessive husband who did not allow her any freedom

Some social isolation may be self-imposed by a woman who is ashamed and neither wishes to admit that the person she loves is an abuser, nor wants visible signs of beating to be seen by friends or family.

Leaving an abusive partner is a process some therapists and counselors have termed an "evolution of separation," because many victimized women have to make several attempts before they depart from and remain parted from their abusive husbands. In order to separate from their abusers, women must first acknowledge that their relationship is unhealthy and will not get better, experience a catalyst for leaving (for example, a particularly severe beating), give up their dreams for the relationship, and accept that some aspects of the relationship will continue (for example, child-visitation arrangements). On average, women leave and return five times before separating for a final time (see Barnett citation at the head of this chapter).

Whether a separated woman will permanently leave her battering spouse largely depends on whether she has the economic resources to survive without him. Women who are economically dependent on their husbands are more likely to be battered, and also less likely to leave. Leaving will expose these women to the hazards of poverty: crime, violence, lack of health care, lack of affordable housing and quality child care. Batterers also often interfere with their partners' ability to find and keep employ-

ment, according to Ola W. Barnett in "Why Battered Women Do Not Leave, Part I" (*Trauma, Violence, & Abuse*, vol. 1, October 2000).

The Most Prevalent Reasons Women Stay in Abusive Relationships

A 1999 research project in Maricopa County, Arizona, considered intimate partner violence and asked women who participated why they remained in emotionally and physically abusive situations. Although nearly half of the study participants said they fought weekly or even daily with their abusive partners, 62% felt they would be unlikely to leave their current partners. The reasons they offered for remaining in dangerous and destructive relationships included:

- Income—Sixty percent of participants said they earned less than $20,000 per year and 32% said they had no money of their own.

- Hope—Fifty-five percent felt they would be able to repair the relationship.

- Fear—Forty-five percent worried that they could not take their children with them if they left their abusers.

- Opportunity—Forty-four percent could not see any way they could earn enough money to support themselves and their children.

- Education—Forty percent reported no education beyond high school.

- Lack of information—Thirty-six percent of respondents said they did not know where to go to escape an abusive relationship.

More than 30% of the participants said they had been abused as children and more than half had grown up watching their parents in abusive relationships. Analyzing these data, Jude Miller-Burke concluded that along with the stated economic reasons and practical logistical considerations involved in ending abusive relationships, many women remain because they mistakenly believe they either cause or deserve the abuse.

How Will Abusive Men Respond When Women Try to Leave?

A battered woman's fear of reprisal is very real and well founded. As Lenore Walker explained in *Terrifying Love: Why Battered Women Kill and How Society Responds* (New York: Harper and Row, 1989), batterers often panic when they think women are going to end the relationship. In the personal stories women told Walker, they repeatedly related that after calling the police or asking for a divorce, their partners' violence escalated.

Walker observed that in an abusive relationship it is often the man who is desperately dependent on the relationship. Battered women are likely to feel that the batterers' sanity and emotional stability is their responsibility—that they are their men's only link to the normal world. Walker alleged that almost 10% of abandoned batterers committed suicide when their women left them.

It appears, however, that more batterers become homicidal than suicidal. Angela Browne, the author of *When Battered Women Kill,* and Kirk Williams, of the Family Research Laboratory, in "Resource Availability for Women at Risk and Partner Homicide" (both published in *Law and Society* [Durham, NH: University of New Hampshire, 1989]), found that more than 50% of all female homicide victims were murdered by former abusive male partners. Ola W. Barnett emphasized that evidence consistently demonstrates that after women leave abusive partners they often continue to be assaulted, stalked, and threatened, and that leaving provokes some batterers to kill their partners (see citation at the head of this chapter). Carolyn Rebecca Block concurred that an attempt to leave can escalate domestic violence; she found that 45% of homicides of a woman by a man were in response to women trying to leave abusive partners ("How Can Practitioners Help an Abused Woman Lower Her Risk of Death?" *National Institute of Justice Journal,* no. 250, November 2003).

MULTIPLE VICTIMIZATION ARGUMENTS

In order to mobilize an effective and widespread protest against intimate partner violence, the battered women's movement that emerged in the 1970s had to satisfactorily answer the question, "Why do women stay in abusive relationships?" In response, a variety of theorists emerged who explained that women were victimized and coerced into staying in violent relationships by a variety of factors. Among these theorists is Bess Rothenberg who listed several factors in "'We Don't Have Time for Social Change': Cultural Compromise and the Battered Woman Syndrome" (*Gender & Society,* vol. 17, October 2003). According to Rothenberg, women were victimized first and foremost by violent abusers; second, by a society that sanctioned the right of men to hit women and socialized women into staying in abusive relationships; third, by representatives of institutions who were in a position to help but who instead ignored the plight of battered women (for example, doctors, police, the criminal justice system, clergy, and therapists); and finally, by the everyday realities of being a woman in a patriarchal system that expects women to raise children and denies them access to education, job skills, and good employment.

Do Women Learn to Be Helpless from Their Life Experience?

Among the best known of the multiple victimization arguments is Lenore Walker's concept of "battered woman syndrome," based in part on the research of Martin Seligman.

Seligman, in *Helplessness: On Depression, Development and Death* (1975), describes how he came to discover the phenomenon he calls learned helplessness. Seligman conducted an experiment in which he attempted to teach dogs to fear the sound of a bell. He did so by restraining a dog, ringing the bell, and then subjecting the dog to a painful (but not dangerous) shock. This process was repeated many times.

Next, to test the effectiveness of the training, Seligman placed the dog in a cage with a floor that could be electrified. One wall of the cage was low enough that the dog could jump over it if it wished. Seligman then rang the bell. He expected that the dog would jump out of the cage. But most of the dogs did not. Their earlier experience, where they had been shocked with no possibility of escape, had taught them that they were helpless. And so even though they were clearly afraid of the bell and found the shocks painful, they made no attempt to escape. On closer observation Seligman found that some dogs developed coping skills, such as using their own excrement to insulate themselves from the floor.

Seligman and other psychologists have theorized that learned helplessness also occurs in humans, with similar effects. Lenore Walker, the author of several well-regarded books about intimate partner violence, theorized that victimized people tend to stop trusting their instinctive responses that protect them after they have experienced inescapable pain in apparently random and variable circumstances. When a person no longer controls his or her own life and does not know what to expect, the individual becomes helpless and develops coping skills to try to minimize the pain. Walker contends that battered women have learned that they are helpless. Although outsiders may not understand why they do not leave their abusers, battered women become conditioned to believe that they cannot predict their safety and that nothing can be done to fundamentally change their situations.

Based on her research, much of which focused on severely abused women who killed their husbands, Walker identifies five factors in childhood and seven factors in adulthood that contribute to learned helplessness. The childhood factors include physical or sexual abuse, the learning of traditional sex roles, health problems, and episodes during childhood when a child loses control of events, such as in frequent moves or the death of a family member. Adult factors include patterns of physical and sexual abuse, jealousy and threats of death from a batterer, psychological torture, seeing other abuse committed by the batterer, and drug or alcohol abuse by either partner.

Battered Woman Syndrome

In *The Battered Woman* (New York: Harper & Row, 1979) Walker argues that abused women suffer from a constellation of symptoms—"the battered woman syndrome"—that keeps them from leaving abusive partners. Walker argues that learned helplessness and a cycle of violence make it extremely difficult for women to leave abusive partners. When women fail to escape from violence, she argues, they become passive, submissive, depressed, overwhelmingly fearful, and psychologically paralyzed. While Walker recognizes, as did other multiple victimization theorists, that women were victims of a patriarchal society and institutions that failed to advocate for abused women, she emphasizes the psychological problems women develop in response to abuse.

In Walker's article "The Battered Woman Syndrome Is a Psychological Consequence of Abuse" (*Current Controversies on Family Violence* [Thousand Oaks, CA: Sage, 1994]), Walker claims that battered woman syndrome is common among severely abused women and that it is part of the recognized pattern of psychological symptoms called post–traumatic stress disorder (PTSD). Women suffering from battered woman syndrome learn that they cannot predict the outcomes of their actions because they cannot reliably determine if a particular response will bring them safety. Walker emphasizes that although they do not respond with total helplessness, they narrow their choices, choosing the ones that seem to have the greatest likelihood of success.

Normally, fear and the responses to fear abate once the feared object or circumstance is removed. People who have suffered a traumatic event, however, often continue to respond to the fear with flashbacks and violent thoughts long after the event has passed. Symptoms of PTSD can afflict individuals regardless of whether they suffer from other psychological problems. Otherwise mentally healthy, and emotionally stable people can develop these symptoms as an adaptive mechanism—a coping strategy to survive abnormal or unusually frightening experiences.

Symptoms of PTSD involve cognitive, psychological, and emotional changes that occur in response to severe trauma. Symptoms may include difficulty in thinking clearly and a pessimistic outlook. The disorder can also produce two distinct forms of memory distortions:

- Unwanted, intrusive memories of the trauma may magnify the terror.

- Partial amnesia may cause an affected individual to suppress and forget many of the painful experiences.

Other symptoms of PTSD include sleep and eating disorders and medical problems associated with persistent high levels of stress. Symptoms described under the PTSD diagnosis cover nearly every possible—and seemingly contradictory—response to battering, including chronic alertness, flashbacks, floods of emotion, detached calm, anger, inability to concentrate, sleep disturbances,

indifference, profound passivity, and depression. Over time, the more aggressive symptoms diminish and are replaced by more passive, constrictive symptoms, making the affected women appear helpless. The abused woman's outlook often improves, however, when she regains some degree of power and control in her life.

Women Are Not Helpless

Beginning in the 1980s, a number of critics emerged who argued that the emphasis on psychological problems of abuse victims was an inadequate explanation of domestic violence. Lee Bowker argued in "A Battered Woman's Problems Are Social, Not Psychological" (*Current Controversies on Family Violence* [Thousand Oaks, CA: Sage, 1994]) that women remain trapped in violent marriages because of conditions in the social system rather than because they suffer from psychological problems. According to the author, battered women are not as passive as they are portrayed in abuse literature and routinely take steps to make their lives safer or to escape abuse. Bowker viewed husbands' unwillingness to stop being dominant and a lack of support from traditional social institutions as the factors that delay battered women in escaping from abuse.

To support these findings, Bowker analyzed survey questionnaires completed by one thousand women and found that women used several major strategies to end abuse. They tried to extract promises from their partners that the battering would stop, threatened to call police or file for divorce, avoided their partners or certain topics of conversations, hid or ran away, tried to talk the men out of violent behavior, covered their bodies to deflect the blows, and, in some cases, tried to hit back. Of these strategies, extracting a promise to change helped most often (54% of the time), while self-defense proved the least effective strategy.

Because the effectiveness of these strategies was limited, most women turned to outside sources for help. First, they contacted family or friends. However, for most women, family and friends did not help stop the violence. Generally, these women then turned to organized or institutional sources of aid, such as police, physicians, clergy, lawyers, counselors, women's groups, and shelters. Calling a lawyer or prosecutor proved the most effective way to end the battering, followed by seeking assistance from women's groups and social service agencies offering referral to shelters or counselors.

Bowker did not find that loss of self-esteem inevitably paralyzes women, leading them to remain in abusive relationships. While battered women do lose self-esteem for a time, many still escape from their abusers. This suggests that when all seems hopeless, an innate need to save themselves propels abused women to escape from their situations. Bowker theorized that the reason women's groups and shelters are effective is that they counter the effects of abuse by supporting personal growth and nurturing the women's strength.

Bowker concluded that because women recover from their feelings of helplessness as they gain strength, battered woman syndrome symptoms are fundamentally different from the long-lasting symptoms that characterize most psychiatric disorders. In Bowker's interpretation, battered woman syndrome refers to the social, economic, psychological, and physical circumstances that keep women in abusive relationships for long periods. The abusive relationship engenders feelings of learned helplessness that are difficult to escape. Conditioned by their batterers to feel helpless, such women have not yet learned how to resist this type of brainwashing and how to compel their abusers to retreat without having to leave or kill the batterer.

Exploration of External Barriers to Leaving

In "Why Battered Women Do Not Leave, Part 1" (see previous citation), Ola W. Barnett argued that battered women face many obstacles to leaving abusive relationships. She argued that many of these barriers are external—in other words, not due to an individual or psychological problem with the abused woman. Barnett outlined many external obstacles to an abused woman's quest to leave her partner, including:

- The patriarchal structure of society—When men control all of a family's resources, women may be economically powerless. In addition, the political and legal system of the United States—particularly in areas of income, employment, and child support—have codified sexist practices that sabotage women's attempts to become economically independent of their abusers.

- Problems with the criminal justice system—The criminal justice system in the United States is underfunded and tends not to enforce legislation prohibiting the abuse of women. The lack of adequate funding keeps battered women from getting legal assistance. Police decisions to arrest or not arrest batterers tend to be inconsistent; when police don't arrest, it impedes women's attempts to leave as well as leaving them vulnerable to further abuse. Only one quarter of batterers are arrested, about one-third of those arrested are prosecuted, and only 1% of those prosecuted serve jail time beyond the time served at arrest. Orders of protection are ineffective because most judges will not enforce them.

- Child custody and visitation—Women fear losing their children if they report intimate partner violence. A report of domestic violence can trigger an investigation by child protective services. When women do retain custody of their children, judges usually do not take intimate partner violence into account when writing visitation orders. Court-ordered visitation is often used by abusers as an opportunity for further battering.

Internal and Psychological Barriers to Leaving

Barnett also outlined several internalized socialization beliefs—normal, learned beliefs about how society and relationships work—as well as psychological factors induced by trauma that serve as obstacles to battered women leaving their abusers ("Why Battered Women Do Not Leave, Part 2," *Trauma, Violence, & Abuse,* vol. 2, no. 1, January 2001). Barnett emphasized that many of these beliefs are detrimental to all women—but battered women are particularly vulnerable. Among them are:

- Gender-role socialization—Society values male traits more than female traits and often devalues female gender roles. As girls age into adolescents, they begin to lose self-confidence as they turn to romantic relationships for a sense of self-worth. When an adult woman values her ability to form a relationship with a male partner over other characteristics, losing the relationship may seem worse than staying and enduring the abuse.

- Distorted beliefs and perceptions—Battered women tend to hold some distorted beliefs that keep them in abusive relationships. Common distorted thought patterns among battered women include a belief that violence is commonplace and not abusive, a belief that they caused the abuse, a lack of recognition that children are harmed more by witnessing intimate partner violence than by living with a single parent, and a belief that she can and should help the abuser to change.

- Post–traumatic stress disorder—PTSD is a prolonged psychological reaction to a traumatic event. Its symptoms include difficulty sleeping, reliving trauma in flashbacks, and numbing of emotional responses. The level of psychological distress abused women experience can keep them from being able to escape the violence.

- Impaired problem-solving abilities—Many factors can impede the problem-solving abilities of battered women, including post-concussion syndrome resulting from head injuries as well as the cognitive distortions of PTSD.

- Prior victimization effects—Women who have been abused during their childhoods have an increased risk of becoming involved with an abusive intimate partner in adulthood. This may be because these women have difficulty judging how trustworthy people are, or they hold a distorted belief that they cannot escape violence.

A LARGER CONTEXT

Evan Stark and Anne Flitcraft, best known for their research about battered women who seek help in medical emergency rooms, explored the question of traumatization in a larger context in their book *Women at Risk* (Thousand Oaks, CA: Sage, 1996). Stark and Flitcraft questioned whether the severe psychological symptoms caused by post–traumatic stress disorder are a result of violence. They believe that the damage is done by the coercive control exercised by the abuser and that the damage may be compounded when law enforcement, health, and social service institutions ignore a woman's attempts to get help; traditional mental health treatment contributes to the coercion by assigning mutual responsibility or defining the issue in terms of the victim's behavioral problems, including her apparent helplessness. Stark and Flitcraft point out that often women's attempts to leave are undervalued because of the pervasiveness of the "learned helplessness" theory. The view of an abused woman as a passive victim is often easier for therapists, doctors, police officers and others to sympathize with than the view of the abused woman as a sometimes aggressive woman with a history of persistent (but failed) attempts to seek help.

In "Affect, Verbal Content and Psychophysiology in the Arguments of Couples with a Violent Husband" (*Journal of Consulting and Clinical Psychology,* vol. 62, no. 5, 1994), Neil S. Jacobson, a pioneering researcher in the area of marital violence, also questioned the view of the abused woman as a helpless and submissive victim. He theorized that a woman's intense anger, combined with fear and sadness, may be a part of her apparent helplessness. According to him, these women are hostile to their husbands and are by no means beaten into submission, but because of the physical abuse they are also afraid. Jacobson believes there is an intense need for more services and public policies to meet the needs of battered women.

DIFFERENT PERCEPTIONS OF REALITY

Some researchers have found that battered women often hold distorted beliefs and perceptions that tend to keep them in an abusive relationship. Some women blame themselves for the violence; others see the abuse as normal and rationalize the violence as "not that bad."

Self-Blame

Researchers find that women who return to abusive relationships have higher levels of self-blame than women who permanently leave their abusers. Women who blame themselves believe that they cause the abuse, and they should be able to prevent it by changing their own behavior. In "The Relationship between Violence, Social Support and Self-Blame in Battered Women" (*Journal of Interpersonal Violence,* vol. 11, no. 2, June 1996), Ola W. Barnett et al. found that battered women have higher levels of self-blame and perceive less availability of social support than women who are not battered.

Escalating levels of violence in a relationship often lead to greater use of violence by the woman as a means of self-defense or retaliation. This can result in still more self-blame, since the woman feels she is at fault for the violence. It also may deter her from seeking help and prompt her to believe no help is available. External sources of support may be less inclined to help the woman who presents the problem as her fault; as a result, the self-blaming woman may receive less assistance from health and social service agencies and organizations. To break this vicious cycle requires counselors or advisors who can help the woman shift the blame to her abusive mate. In fact, some researchers suggest that while women may blame themselves when the abuse begins, as the frequency and severity of violence increases, they do eventually begin to assign the blame to the perpetrators (see Kate Cavanagh, "Understanding Women's Responses to Domestic Violence," *Qualitative Social Work,* vol. 2, no. 2, September 2003).

"It's Not That Bad"

In "Coping with an Abusive Relationship: How and Why Do Women Stay?" (*Journal of Marriage and the Family,* vol. 53, 1991), Tracy Herbert et al. compared the perceptual differences of women who leave abusive relationships and those who stay. They theorized that all relationships are a mixture of good and bad elements, but as long as a partner perceives that the good outweighs the bad, he or she will maintain the relationship.

The researchers interviewed 130 women to find out how they viewed their relationships. They suspected that the women who stayed would emphasize the positive aspects of their marriages and minimize the negative, because as long as they could maintain positive images, they would remain. Studies find that women are often finally driven to go to shelters when their husbands' abuse suddenly becomes more severe or when kindness after beatings diminishes, thereby forcing a change in the women's perceived reality.

The women reported that the frequency of abuse was, on average, once a month or less; 78% reported verbal and physical abuse. Of these, 77% felt the verbal abuse was as difficult, or more difficult, to deal with than the physical abuse. The more frequently the woman was verbally abused, the less capable she was of seeing her relationship as positive. One woman wrote, "Bruises, cuts, etc., heal within a short time. When you listen to someone tell you how rotten you are and how nobody wants you day after day, you begin to believe it. Verbal abuse takes years to heal but before that happens, it can ruin every part of your life."

Herbert et al. did not find evidence that the women were trapped by low self-esteem or the length of the relationship. The three variables they found most closely related to the decision to stay were:

- The women perceived more positive aspects to their relationship.

- They saw little or no change in the frequency or intensity of the battering or love that their husbands expressed.

- They felt their relationship was not as bad as it could be.

WHAT CAN A WOMAN DO?

Cavanagh gathered qualitative data from interviews with the female partners of violent men to illustrate that battered women try to end the violence in their relationships in many ways, even if they stay—complicating the notion of the battered woman as passive and helpless. She found that women worked to stop the violence by talking with their partners about the violence, developing strategies for avoiding the violence (for example, being affectionate or feigning agreement with the abuser), challenging the violence (for example, fighting back, verbally or physically), telling other people about the violence, and leaving (usually temporarily) the relationship. Cavanagh argued that abused women almost always actively fight the abuse: "At some points in time the struggle to change took second place to the struggle to survive but not even women subjected to the extremes of abuse totally 'gave up.'"

Richard Gelles and Murray Straus found that only 13% of the severely abused women in the 1985 National Family Violence Survey felt their situations were completely hopeless and out of their control. In *Intimate Violence: The Definitive Study of the Causes and Consequences of Abuse in the American Family* (New York: Simon and Schuster, 1988), Gelles and Straus argued that women who experienced more severe violence and grew up in more violent homes were more likely to stay. Predictably, women who were less educated, had fewer job skills, and thus were more likely to be unemployed were also more likely to stay, as were women with young children.

Avoidance

Gelles and Straus interviewed 192 women who suffered minor violence and 140 who suffered severe violence, and asked which long-range strategies they used to avoid violence. Fifty-three percent of the minor-violence victims and 69% of the severe-violence victims learned to avoid issues they thought would anger their partners. Others learned to read a change in their partners' facial expressions as one of the first signs of impending abuse. "I have learned what gets him mad. I also know just by looking at him, when he gets that kind of weird, screwed-up expression on his face, that he is getting ready to be mad. Most of the time I figure I just have to walk on eggshells," one woman said. Avoidance worked for about 68% of those women who suffered minor abuse, but for less than one-third of the more severely abused victims.

Leaving

Some battered women do leave their husbands. Straus and Gelles found that 70% had left their spouses in the year preceding the interview. Only about half of those who left, however, reported that this was a "very effective" method of ending the abuse. In fact, for one out of eight women it only made things worse. Batterers put incredible pressure on their partners to return. Often, when the women returned they were abused more severely than before—as revenge or because the men learned that, once again, they could get away with this behavior. Women who returned also risked losing the aid of personal and public support systems, because these people perceived that their help or advice was useless or ignored.

Just Say "No"

Many researchers believe that there is real truth to the statement that men abuse because they can. A wife who will not permit herself to be beaten from the very first act of minor abuse, like a slap or push, is the most successful in stopping it. Straus and Gelles found that simply eliciting a promise to stop was by far the most effective strategy women could undertake—especially in cases of minor violence. Threatening to divorce or leave the home worked in about 40% of the minor-abuse cases, but in less than 5% of the severe-abuse situations. Physically fighting back was the most unsuccessful method. It worked in fewer than 2% of the minor abuse cases and in less than 1% of the severe-abuse cases.

Coping Strategies

Many battered women remain in abusive relationships out of fear, but it is not always fear of their husbands that causes them to stay. Some women fear they may lose custody of their children if they walk out on an abusive partner. Others fear they will lose their homes or their social status. For other women, religious or cultural pressures to hold the family together at all costs trap them in bad marriages, even as the abuse worsens.

Maria Eugenia Fernandez-Esquer and Laura Ann McCloskey studied a group of Mexican American and Anglo women to learn about the ethnic and social influences that pressured them to remain in or leave abusive relationships. In "Coping with Partner Abuse among Mexican American and Anglo Women: Ethnic and Socioeconomic Influences" (*Violence and Victims,* vol. 14, no. 3, Fall 1999), they recounted their interviews with fifty-one Mexican American and forty-one Anglo women, all of whom had violent confrontations with their spouses in the year prior to the interview. All the women had been victims of verbal abuse. About half the women reported being beaten for several minutes, choked, raped, or threatened with murder if they left. About 25% were threatened with a gun or knife or forced to engage in sex against their will.

At least 25% of respondents in both ethnic groups reported coping tactics that included verbally aggressive intervention, "thinking through" the situation, and physical separation. In addition, more than 25% of the Anglo women reported physically aggressive intervention and avoidance tactics.

Fernandez-Esquer and McCloskey found that the socioeconomic status of battered women, as defined by education and employment, affected the way they coped. As socioeconomic levels rose, abuse victims tended to report more types of internal focus-coping tactics to deal with partner abuse. The researchers theorized that women who "think through" the situation might feel more self-reliant and capable of handling the violence without police intervention. However, internal coping also involved crying spells, angry outbursts, suicidal feelings, and self-blame.

Fernandez-Esquer and McCloskey did not find support for their hypothesis that ethnicity influences coping strategies of battered women. They concluded that the study illustrated similarities between ethnic groups, especially when faced with an abusive partner.

Injuries and Medical Care

There are often urgent and long-term physical and health consequences of domestic violence. Short-term physical consequences include mild to moderate injuries, such as broken bones, bruises, and cuts. More serious medical problems include sexually transmitted diseases, miscarriages, premature labor, and injury to unborn children, as well as damage to the central nervous system sustained as a result of blows to the head, including traumatic brain injuries, chronic headaches, and loss of vision and hearing. The medical consequences of abuse are often unreported or underreported because women are reluctant to disclose abuse as the cause of their injuries, and health professionals are uncomfortable inquiring about it.

A report titled "Violence against Women" found that while more than half of abused women are physically injured by their abusers, only four out of ten seek professional medical care (*The Women's Health Data Book* [Washington, DC: Jacobs Institute of Women's Health and the Henry J. Kaiser Family Foundation, 2001]).

Abused women also are at risk for health problems not directly caused by the abuse. In "Intimate Partner Violence and Physical Health Consequences" (*Archives of Internal Medicine,* vol. 162, no. 10, May 2002), investigators from several medical centers and schools of public health compared the physical health problems of abused women to a control group of women who had never suffered abuse. The investigators found that abused women suffered from 50% to 70% more gynecological, central nervous system, and stress-related problems. Examples of stress-related problems included chronic fear, headaches, back pain, gastrointestinal disorders, appetite loss, increased incidence of

such viral infections as colds, and such cardiac problems as hypertension and chest pain. Although women who most recently suffered physical abuse reported the most health problems, the researchers found evidence that abused women remain less healthy over time.

SCREENING FOR DOMESTIC VIOLENCE. Although women have about a 30% to 44% chance of experiencing intimate partner violence at some point during their lives, health professionals detect as few as one out of twenty are victims of physical abuse. Lorrie Elliot et al. conducted a national survey of physicians to identify factors associated with the documented low screening rates for domestic violence. In "Barriers to Screening for Domestic Violence" (*Journal of General Internal Medicine,* vol. 17, no. 2, February 2002), researchers reported the responses of physicians in four medical specialties likely to encounter abused women—internal medicine, family practice, obstetrics-gynecology, and emergency medicine.

The vast majority of physician respondents (88%) said they knew patients in their practices who had experienced domestic violence, but physicians in all specialties except emergency medicine underestimated the prevalence of the problem in their states. The physicians were questioned about the percentage of their patients they screened, i.e., specifically asked about their experience with domestic violence. Overall, just 10% of respondents screened their female patients for domestic violence and of this group, just 6% screened all female patients. Of the specialties, obstetrician-gynecologists screened the highest proportion of their patients.

Although most respondents felt they should be screening for domestic violence in their practices, most did not fulfill this responsibility. Along with unrealistically low estimates of the prevalence of the problems in their communities, physicians also cited lack of training, lack of confidence in their abilities, fear of offending patients, and the mistaken belief that women will volunteer a history of abuse without being questioned. The researchers concluded that mandatory training on intimate partner violence, reminders in patients' medical charts, and physician interaction and involvement with victim service providers might all serve to increase physicians' confidence and competence to screen patients for intimate partner violence and abuse.

Hospitalization of Battered Women

The National Crime Victimization Surveys estimate that of the more than half of women battered by an intimate partner who are injured, 30% to 40% require medical treatment and 15% require hospitalization. The hospital emergency department is often the first contact the health care system has with battered women and offers the first opportunity to identify victims, refer them to support services and safe shelters, and otherwise intervene to improve their situations.

Researchers at the University of Washington reported on hospitals and battered women in "Rates and Relative Risk of Hospital Admission among Women in Violent Intimate Partner Relationships" (*American Journal of Public Health,* vol. 90, no. 9, September 2000). They found that women who had filed for protection orders against male intimate partners had an overall increased risk for earlier hospitalization than women who had not been abused. Abused women had a 50% increase in hospitalization rates for any diagnosis, compared to nonabused women, and the risk of hospitalization was highest in the younger age groups of abused women. Abused women were hospitalized much more frequently for injuries resulting from assaults, suicide attempts, poisonings, and digestive system disorders than the nonabused women and were almost four times as likely to be hospitalized with a psychiatric diagnosis. The researchers reaffirmed the observation that intimate partner violence has a significant impact on women's health and their utilization of health care services.

Improving Health Professionals' Responses to Victims of Domestic Violence

In 2001, the National Academy of Sciences Institute of Medicine released the report *Confronting Chronic Neglect: The Education and Training of Health Professionals on Family Violence* (Washington, DC: National Academy Press, 2001), which was mandated by the Health Professions Education Partnerships Act of 1998 (PL 105-392) and sponsored by the Centers for Disease Control and Prevention. The study involved fifteen professionals from a variety of disciplines, including health sciences, mental health, law, and the study or aid of victims of child maltreatment, domestic violence, and elder abuse. They reviewed available research about the training of health professionals and others who come into contact with victims; the effectiveness of training and programs to screen, identify, and refer victims of family violence in health care settings; and the outcomes of available interventions.

The report described family violence as a serious public health problem and societal tragedy, cited inadequate training of health professionals as a major problem, and called for vigorous efforts to improve health professionals' abilities to screen, diagnose, treat, and refer victims of abuse. The Institute of Medicine report recommended:

- Family violence centers should conduct research on the impact of family violence on the health care system and to evaluate and test training and education programs for health professionals. The report suggested that centers be established by the Department of Health and Human Services and modeled after similar multidisciplinary centers in fields such as injury control research, Alzheimer's disease, and geriatric education.

To lay the foundation for the centers' coordinating role, the report suggested that the U.S. General Accounting Office analyze the level and adequacy of existing investments in family violence research and training.

- Health professional organizations and educators—including academic health-center faculty—should address core competency areas for health professional curricula on family violence, including effective teaching strategies, approaches to overcoming barriers to training, and approaches to promoting and sustaining behavior changes by health professionals in dealing with family violence.

- Health care delivery systems and training settings, particularly academic health care centers and federally qualified health clinics and community health centers, should assume greater responsibility for developing, testing, and evaluating innovative training models or programs.

- Federal agencies and other funders of education programs should create expectations and provide support and incentives for evaluating curricula on family violence for health professionals. Evaluations should focus on the impact of training on the practices of health professionals and the effects on family violence victims.

Empowerment of Battered Women

Researchers and advocates have found that one of the most effective ways to deal with partner violence is by giving the victim the power, encouragement, and support to stop it. In "Estrangement, Interventions and Male Violence Toward Female Partners" (*Violence and Victims,* vol. 12, no. 1, Spring 1997), Desmond Ellis and Lori Wight asserted that abused women want the violence to stop and most, if not all, attempt to do something to stop it. They found evidence showing that empowerment of abused women is related to a decrease in the likelihood of further violence. The interventions Ellis and Wight recommended to promote gender equality include:

- social service agencies such as counselors or shelters to provide information and support

- mediation to facilitate a woman's control over the process

- prosecution with an option to drop the charges, which also facilitates control by female victims

- separation, which indicates the woman's strength in decision making

Ellis and Wight found that separation or divorce is one of the most effective strategies for ending abuse. Levels of violence after separation, according to these researchers, varies with the type of legal separation or divorce proceedings. Women who participate in mediation prior to separation are less likely to be harmed, either physically or emotionally, than women whose separation is negotiated by lawyers. Ellis and Wight found that other legal proceedings, such as restraining orders and protection orders, were relatively ineffective in protecting female abuse victims.

Interventions to Help Battered Women

Throughout the United States, voluntary health and social service agencies and institutions, such as hospitals, mental health centers, clinics, and shelters, have developed programs that aim to help abused women break free physically, economically, and emotionally from their violent partners. Still, many abused women do not seek help from these specialized programs and services as a result of fear, shame, or lack of knowledge about how to gain access to available services. Instead, many injured women seek medical care from physicians, nurses, and other health professionals. For this reason, medical professional organizations, such as the American Medical Association and the American College of Obstetricians and Gynecologists, exhort physicians to advocate on behalf of abused women. They offer guidelines to help professionals detect and intervene in cases of domestic violence.

Despite the ambitious objectives of professional societies and the widespread distribution of guidelines, many health professionals most likely to encounter victims of abuse remain untrained, fearful, and unable even to question patients about domestic violence. Barbara Gerbert et al. interviewed physicians to determine how they have overcome these and other barriers to help patients who are victims of domestic violence. Their findings were published in "Interventions That Help Victims of Domestic Violence: A Quantitative Analysis of Physicians' Experiences" (*Journal of Family Practice,* vol. 49, no. 10, October 2000).

Although physician respondents reported feeling overwhelmed, frustrated, and often ill-prepared to tackle these problems, they nonetheless felt it was their responsibility to help battered women improve their situations. The technique they believed most effective was validation—expressing concern by compassionately communicating to the woman that the abuse was undeserved. Other strategies they considered effective were:

- Overcome denial and plant seeds of change—Physicians helped the women to appreciate the seriousness of their situations and to understand that the abusers' actions were wrong and criminal. Some physicians used photographs of injuries to remind patients who denied the extent of their abuse about the severity of the injuries they had sustained.

- Nonjudgmental listening—To build trust, physicians listened without rushing to judgment or criticizing women for not fleeing their abusers.

- Document, refer, and help prepare a plan—Physicians documented abuse with photographs and detailed descriptions in the patients' medical records for use in medical and mental health treatment as well as in court proceedings. They offered ongoing, confidential referrals to hot lines, shelters, and other community resources; advised patients about when to call police; and assisted them to develop escape plans.

- Use a team approach—Physicians felt it was valuable to be able to immediately refer abused women to on-site professionals, such as counselors, nurses, social workers, or psychologists, who were able to take advantage of the medical visit as a "window of opportunity," that is, an occasion to detect and intervene to stop abuse.

- Make domestic violence a priority—Given time constraints of busy medical practices, many physicians advocated forgoing all but the most urgent medical treatment and instead used the appointment time to address the issue of abuse. They also encouraged colleagues and personnel in their practices to obtain continuing education about domestic violence, child, and elder abuse.

Carolyn Rebecca Block has made recommendations to nurses, doctors, and other service professionals likely to come in contact with battered women on what to look for as indications that the violence may soon escalate to deadly violence in "How Can Practitioners Help an Abused Woman Lower Her Risk of Death?" (*NIJ Journal,* no. 250). She found that practitioners should evaluate three aspects of the violence:

- The type of past violence—Women who had experienced at least one serious or life-threatening incident, for example, being choked, burned, or threatened with weapons in the past year were at the greatest risk of being killed by their partners. Being choked, burned, or threatened with weapons also indicated a higher risk.

- The number of days since the last incident—No matter how severe the incident of past abuse, women who have been abused within the past thirty days are at greatest risk for being killed.

- The frequency, or increasing frequency, of violence— If violent episodes are increasing, women are at high risk of deadly violence.

AN INNOVATIVE PROGRAM TO HELP BATTERED WOMEN. Collaboration between law enforcement and hospital emergency department personnel produced a novel program to prevent and intervene in domestic violence. This program was developed in Richmond, Virginia, in response to a challenge issued by Mark Rosenberg, the director of the National Center for Injury Prevention and Control at the Centers for Disease Control and Prevention. The program, called "Cops and Docs," involves participation of emergency and trauma nurses working "handcuff in glove" with law enforcement personnel. The program was described and praised in the *Journal of Emergency Nursing* (vol. 27, no. 6, December 2001).

Program personnel are trained together in a variety of techniques, including interviewing victims, collecting and preserving forensic evidence, and gathering and documenting information. In addition to helping to safeguard victims and apprehend and prosecute offenders, the program offers other health benefits to the community it serves. For example, shared emergency department data about substance abuse gives law enforcement personnel additional information to use in efforts to combat drug-related violence and crime.

CHAPTER 5
RAPE AND SEXUAL HARASSMENT AROUND THE WORLD

It went on for hours. I don't know how many policemen came through the room. It could have been fifty. I will never forget their laughter, their shouting. I cried, I prayed, I asked God why me, a respectable woman, a grandmother, who had never known any man's body except my husband's.

—Ahmedi Begum, a Pakistani woman

Historically, because women have been viewed as the possessions of their fathers and husbands, sexual abuse of a woman has been considered a violation of a man's property rights rather than a violation of a woman's human rights. However, primarily through the efforts of women's advocacy groups worldwide, rape is no longer viewed as a violation of family honor but as an abuse and violation of women. In most countries, rape is now considered a crime. In 1993, the United Nations' (UN) Declaration of the Eradication of Violence against Women (UN Resolution 49/104, December 1993) specifically named marital rape, sexual abuse of female children, selling women into slavery or prostitution, and other acts of sexual violence against women in its condemnation of "any act of gender-based violence that results in or is likely to result in physical, sexual, or psychological harm or suffering to women, including threats of such acts, coercion, or arbitrary deprivation of liberty, whether occurring in public or private life."

In many countries, only women of "good character" can demand protection from rape. In some Latin American countries, the law only recognizes rape of chaste women. These attitudes are generally based on the definition of rape as the defilement of a virgin. In the past, the traditional legal recourse required the offender to compensate the girl's father for her lost value in the marriage market.

Pakistan has perhaps the harshest attitudes toward rape in the world. The country's Hudood Ordinances, passed in 1979 as part of an Islamic overhaul of the country's law to deal with a range of sins, effectively equate

rape with adultery. Any sex outside of marriage, known as *zina*, is against the law. This view often results in the arrest of raped women rather than their rapists. In a Karachi court, about 15% of the rape trials result in women facing charges and imprisonment. In one case, a patient and his two friends raped a staff nurse in a Karachi prison. Although she did not go to police, the men reported her for engaging in sex outside marriage. The judge found that if she were a "decent" woman she would not work at night and sentenced her to five years in prison, five lashes, and a fine equivalent to a year's salary.

According to Majida Rizvi, head of the Pakistani National Commission on the Status of Women, up to 80% of all women in Pakistani jails are there on charges of violating the Hudood Ordinances—many because they were raped. Once in police custody, about 72% are raped again, this time by the police. Human Rights Watch, an independent, nongovernmental organization dedicated to investigating and exposing human rights violations worldwide, estimates that at least 1,500 Pakistani women are in prison on charges of *zina*.

Under the Hudood Ordinances, four Muslim men must witness penetration and testify to rape; if no witnesses are produced, the women are subject to prosecution for *zina*. In 2002, Zafran Bibi was convicted of *zina* and sentenced to stoning to death under the ordinances, despite her claims that her brother-in-law had raped her. She was acquitted many months later by a higher Pakistani court after an international outcry.

The Pakistani patriarchal system sometimes leads to government-sanctioned abuses of women. On June 22, 2002, during a tribal council in Punjab, Pakistan, Salma Bibi, a thirty-year-old woman, was gang raped by four men in front of local villagers as punishment for her brother's sexual misconduct. Bibi claimed that her brother was also raped and that police demanded a bribe to release him from custody.

In a letter to Pakistani president Pervez Musharraf urging closer scrutiny of the role of tribal councils in the abuse of women, LaShawn R. Jefferson, the executive director of the Women's Rights Division of Human Rights Watch, wrote: "We also remain concerned about the broader role of tribal councils in Pakistan and the authority they effectively enjoy to mete out punishments properly reserved to the state. Human Rights Watch believes that it is imperative that government authorities ensure that tribal councils act in accordance with the law and in a manner that respects women's rights, and do not usurp the proper judicial authority of the state. We request that you identify mechanisms by which local administrations in Pakistan can monitor the conduct of tribal councils, and intervene in instances where they have exercised jurisdiction belonging to the state."

PURPOSES OF RAPE

Punitive rape is sometimes practiced in countries where men resent women taking initiative or assuming positions of authority or power. In Latin America, feminists contend that women are raped as a way to force them back into the traditional sphere of home and children. In India, a leader of the Women's Development Program, an organization that helps women start businesses, was gang-raped in front of her husband by men who disapproved of her campaign against child marriages.

Rape is also practiced as a weapon of war or as a right of victorious forces—"spoils of war," as noted by Nancy Farwell in her "War Rape: New Conceptualizations and Responses" (*Affilia*, vol. 19, Winter 2004). Combatants and their sympathizers have raped women in wartime with near complete impunity. In 1993, for the first time, the UN passed a resolution identifying rape as a war crime. Documented cases of wartime rape have occurred in Sierra Leone, Kosovo, the Democratic Republic of the Congo, Afghanistan, Liberia, Rwanda, El Salvador, Guatemala, Kuwait, Bangladesh, the former Yugoslavia, and by U.S. troops in the Vietnam War. In Darfur, Sudan, rape has been used as a weapon of war by government-sponsored militia known as Janjawid since 2003 ("Darfur: Rape as a Weapon of War: Sexual Violence and Its Consequences," Amnesty International, July 19, 2004, http://web.amnesty.org/library/Index/ENGAFR540762004?open&of=ENG-373, accessed November 22, 2004).

There is little accurate information on rates of rape and sexual assault, especially in developing countries. The challenge of defining rape across cultures makes data collection difficult, and underreporting raises suspicion about the actual number of incidents. For example, a 1999 UN Children's Fund study found that from 1989 to 1997 reported rapes declined in all but three of the twelve countries for which data were available. This decline seems unlikely since during the same years there were sharp increases in all other crime statistics.

The Seventh United Nations Survey on Crime Trends and the Operations of Criminal Justice Systems (1998–2000) indicated that rapes were being reported as readily as other crimes. The survey is a major worldwide study conducted periodically by the United Nations Office on Drugs and Crime (http://www.unodc.org/unodc/en/crime_cicp_survey_seventh.html, accessed November 22, 2004). It revealed that the total number of recorded rapes in the ninety-two countries that participated in the survey dropped 30% between 1999 and 2000. The total number of recorded crimes reported by those countries also dropped by 30% during the same period. In comparison, the total number of recorded rapes actually increased slightly, by 0.2% between 1998 and 1999, and the total number of recorded crimes similarly rose by 0.4%. This possibly indicates changes in the way countries defined and recorded crimes from one year to the next.

It also may reflect an unwillingness of governments and victims to report rape. The authors of *Not a Minute More: Ending Violence against Women* (The United Nations Women's Development Fund, 2003, http://www.unifem.org/filesconfirmed/207/312_book_complete_eng.pdf, accessed November 22, 2004) notes that reporting a rape is seen as a danger by victims, who may suffer further at the hands of police or their own families:

> The stigma, disbelief, ridicule or retribution attached to speaking out makes it nearly impossible to obtain accurate national statistics on rape in many countries. Having suffered one trauma, many women do not want to undergo additional emotional pain at the hands of the police. According to the Philippines National Police, approximately two in ten rapes are reported. The rest are kept hidden; in many cases a woman's family discourages her from reporting the incident.

Rape and gender-based sexual assault are closely linked to suicide, prostitution, trafficking for sex, substance abuse, murder, high-risk and unintended pregnancy, HIV/AIDS, other sexually transmitted diseases (STDs), and disability. Having suffered rape and sexual assault also increase an individual's utilization of health care services. One U.S. study found a history of rape or sexual assault to be a stronger predictor of using health care than any other factor—rape victims used two-and-a-half times more services than women who had not been raped.

MARITAL RAPE

It was very clear to me. He raped me. He ripped off my pajamas, he beat me up. I mean, some scumbag down the street would do that to me. So to me, it wasn't any different because I was married to him, it was rape—real clear what it was. It emotionally hurt worse. I mean you can compartmentalize it as stranger rape—you were at the wrong place at the wrong time. You can manage to get over it differently. But here, you're at home with your husband and you don't expect that. I was under constant terror even if he didn't do it.

—A victim of marital rape

Rape has little to do with the sexual relations associated with love and marriage. Rape is an act of violence by one person against another. It is an act of power that aims to hurt at the most intimate level. Rape is a violation, whether it occurs at the hands of a stranger or within the home at the hands of an abusive husband or partner.

In the United States, state laws on marital rape vary. On July 5, 1993, marital rape became a crime in all fifty states. In thirty-three states, however, there are exemptions from prosecution if, for example, the husband did not use force or if the woman is legally unable to consent because of a severe disability. There is still a tendency in the legal system to consider marital rape far less serious than either stranger or acquaintance rape.

An analysis of data from the National Violence against Women Survey, sponsored jointly by the U.S. Departments of Justice and Health and Human Services and the Centers for Disease Control and Prevention, estimated that 1.5 million women and 834,700 men are raped and/or physically assaulted by an intimate partner each year. Of all surveyed women age eighteen and older, 1.5% said they were raped and/or physically assaulted by a current or former spouse, cohabiting partner, or date in the year preceding the interview, compared to 0.9% of all surveyed men. Of the women, 7.7% reported being raped by an intimate partner at some point in their lives. Although these estimates were developed in 1998, most researchers agree that these statistics are likely to remain unchanged until improved methods to respond to violence against women are instituted.

As previous reports have consistently shown, the National Violence against Women Survey reconfirms that violence against women is primarily intimate partner violence. More than three-quarters of women who were raped and/or physically assaulted from the age of eighteen were assaulted by a current or former husband, cohabiting partner, or date. Nine percent were assaulted by a relative other than a husband, and 17% were assaulted by an acquaintance, such as a friend, neighbor, or coworker. Rape or assault by a stranger accounted for only 14% of the incidents. By comparison, men were primarily raped and physically assaulted by strangers and acquaintances rather than by intimate partners.

Some researchers estimate that nearly two million marital rapes occur each year and that this form of rape is more common than both stranger and acquaintance rape. Although the legal definition varies from state to state, marital rape is generally defined as any sexual activity coerced from a wife unwilling to perform it. Research on marital rape indicates that 10% to 14% of married women

have been raped by their partners and that marital rape accounts for about 25% of all rapes.

It is vitally important to recognize the limitations of available data about marital rape and intimate partner violence in general. In *Intimate Partner Violence and Age of Victim, 1993–99* (Washington, DC: Bureau of Justice Statistics, October 2001), Callie Rennison cautioned that marital status may relate directly to a survey respondent's willingness to reveal violence at the hands of an intimate partner or spouse. For example, a married woman may be afraid to report her husband as the offender or she may be in a state of denial—unable to admit to herself or others that her husband has victimized her.

In her landmark study *Rape and Marriage* (Bloomington, IN: Indiana University Press, 1990), Diana Russell reported on interviews with a random sample of 930 women in the San Francisco area. Of all the women who had been married, 14% had been raped by their spouses at least once. Of this number, one-third reported being raped once; one-third reported between two and twenty incidents; and one-third said they had been raped by their spouses more than twenty times.

According to Russell, the first incident of rape usually occurred in the first year of marriage. Although marital rape occurred more frequently in spousal relationships where emotional and physical abuse were present, it could also happen in marriages where there was little other violence.

Raquel Kennedy Bergen in her book *Wife Rape* (Thousand Oaks, CA: Sage, 1996) reported data collected from detailed interviews with forty wife-rape victims. Fifty-five percent had been raped twenty times or more during their marriages, while 17% had experienced this abuse only once. Most of the women in the sample reported that their husbands felt a sense of ownership that granted them sexual rights to their bodies. Because of this perceived entitlement, the men did not interpret their behavior as rape. Several women also believed that the abuse was an attempt to punish them and that the rape was an attempt to control and assert power.

Marital Rape Categories

Louis J. Shiro and Kersti Yllöo, in the *Maine State Bar Association Bar Bulletin* (vol. 19, no. 5, September 1985), observed that there is no single accurate depiction of marital rape—it is no more accurate to assume that marital rape is always a savage attack than to assume it is just a sexual tiff. Both scenarios are part of a spectrum. The researchers developed three broad categories based on their interviews with fifty assault victims: battering rapes, force-only rapes, and obsessive rapes.

About 45% of the women in this study suffered battering rapes. In these rapes, the batterer used sexual assault as another brutal form of abuse against his wife.

Because of the particularly demeaning and degrading nature of some of the acts, this violent behavior appeared more brutal than other violence the abuser may have perpetrated on his wife. The battering rapist was characterized as often angry and suffering from alcohol abuse or another substance abuse problem.

Nonbattering, force-only rape, which involved about 45% of the cases, generally occurred in middle-class marriages where there was much less history of violence and abuse. The immediate reason for the rape was often a specifically sexual reason—for example, how often to have sex and the kind of sex the husband desired. The force used was much more restrained; it was enough to force intercourse but not enough to cause severe injury. This type of rape, Shiro and Yllöo observed, is not so much an instrument of anger as a tool to establish power or control or to "teach a lesson."

About 10% of the women interviewed described rapes the researchers categorized as obsessive marital rape. In these instances, the husband had very unusual, often deviant sexual demands that sometimes involved other men or violence that the wife was refusing to fulfill. This type of rapist was frequently found to be heavily involved in pornography.

How Is Aggression Related to Marital Rape?

Since marital rape frequently occurs in relationships plagued by other types of abusive behavior, some researchers view it as just another expression of intimate partner violence. Support for this idea comes from research documenting high rates of forced sex, ranging from 34% to 57%, reported by married women in battered women's shelters. Still, research has not conclusively demonstrated whether husbands who engage in physical and psychological violence will be more likely to use threatened or forced sex.

Amy Marshall and Amy Holtzworth-Munroe investigated the relationship between two forms of sexual aggression—coerced and threatened/forced sex—and husbands' physical and psychological aggressiveness. They reported their findings in "Varying Forms of Husband Sexual Aggression: Predictors and Subgroup Differences" (*Journal of Family Psychology,* vol. 16, no. 3, September 2002).

Marshall and Holtzworth-Munroe interviewed 164 couples and evaluated husbands using their own self-reports and their wives' reports on three measures: the revised Conflict Tactics Scale, a questionnaire called the Sexual Experiences Survey, and the Psychological Maltreatment of Women Inventory, a fifty-eight-item measure of psychological abuse. The researchers found that the most severely physically violent men most often used sexual coercion, while physical aggression was most predic-

tive of threatened/forced sex. Husbands who were rated as generally violent/antisocial engaged in the most threatened/forced sex. Interestingly, even the subtype of physically nonviolent men was found to have engaged in some sexual coercion in the year preceding the study.

Marshall and Holtzworth-Munroe concluded that their findings underscore the need to consider sexual aggression as a form of intimate partner abuse. They also called for research to determine the extent to which sexual coercion precedes and predicts threatened/forced sex and whether this association holds true for all relationships or only for those relationships in which there are other forms of marital violence.

The Effects of Marital Rape

Contrary to the traditional belief that victims of marital rape suffer few or no consequences, research reveals that women may suffer serious long-term medical and psychological consequences from this form of abuse. In her review of the relevant research *Marital Rape* (Applied Research Forum, National Electronic Network on Violence against Women, http://www.vawnet.org/DomesticViolence/Research/VAWnetDocs/AR_mrape.php, March 1999), Raquel Kennedy Bergen reported rape-related genital injuries, such as lacerations (tears), soreness, bruising, torn muscles, fatigue, vomiting, unintended pregnancy, and infection with sexually transmitted diseases. Victims who had been battered before, during, or after the rape suffered broken bones, black eyes, bloody noses, and knife wounds, as well as injuries sustained when they were kicked, punched, or burned.

The short-term psychological effects are similar to those experienced by other victims of sexual assault and include anxiety, shock, intense fear, suicidal thinking, depression, and post–traumatic stress disorder. But marital rape victims reportedly suffer higher rates of anger and depression than women raped by strangers, perhaps because the violence was perpetrated by a person they had loved and trusted to not harm them. Long-term consequences include serious depression, sexual problems, and emotional pain that lasts years after the abuse. And J. A. Bennice et al. found that marital rape survivors were more likely than other battered women to suffer the debilitating effects of post–traumatic stress disorder (PTSD), even when controlling for the severity of the beatings. They reported their findings in "The Relative Effects of Intimate Partner Physical and Sexual Violence on PTSD Symptomatology" (*Violence and Victims,* vol. 18, no. 1, 2003).

As is true with other violent acts, marital rape prompts some women to leave their rapist husbands. Kennedy Bergen reported that women from selected ethnic groups, such as Latinas, appeared less likely to characterize forced sex as rape and consequently less likely to accuse or flee their spouses. The fact that married women do leave their abusers, however, was confirmed by an analysis of National Crime Victimization Surveys data that compared marital status of survey respondents from one survey to the next. Table 5.1 shows that 30% of the female victims of intimate partner violence who were married during the previous survey interview when they had reported being victimized had separated by the next year, and an additional 8% had divorced their husbands.

Attitudes about Wife Rape

Historically, wives were considered the property of the husband, and therefore, rape of a wife was viewed as impossible. No husband still living with his wife was prosecuted for marital rape in the United States until 1978—and at that time, marital rape was a crime in only five states, as reported by Jennifer A. Bennice and Patricia A. Resick in "Marital Rape: History, Research, and Practice" (*Trauma, Violence, & Abuse,* vol. 4, no. 3, July 2003). By 1993, marital rape under some conditions was recognized in all fifty states.

However, public attitudes toward rape in marriage have been slow to change, with many people believing that marital rape is not "real rape." Researcher Kathleen Basile of Georgia State University in Atlanta sought to examine variables that might predict specific attitudes about wife rape: beliefs about the occurrence and frequency of forced sex by a husband on his wife and whether respondents would classify various scenarios as constituting rape. She reported her findings in "Attitudes Toward Wife Rape: Effects of Social Background and Victim Status" (*Violence and Victims,* vol. 17, no. 3, June 2002).

Nearly all previous attitudinal research had focused on limited populations, such as college students, and could not be generalized to the public at large. Basile chose to analyze data from a nationally representative telephone survey of 1,108 adults to produce more widely applicable findings.

Basile hypothesized that social background variables and victim status would predict how survey respondents felt about marital rape. Based on earlier research, she believed that males, blacks, and other racial minorities would express opinions more supportive of wife rape. Similarly, Basile expected that supportive attitudes would increase with age. She felt that victims and persons with higher educational attainment would hold less supportive views of wife rape.

Survey respondents were asked whether they "think husbands ever use force, like hitting, holding down, or using a weapon, to make their wives have sex when the wife doesn't want to" to find out if they thought wife rape occurs. Respondents who answered "yes" to this question were asked how often they thought this occurs to gauge their perceptions of the frequency of wife rape. They also

TABLE 5.1

Change in marital status among married female victims who experienced a violent act by an intimate, 1993–99

Marital status over 6 months	Women married at the time of the earlier interview	
	Experienced intimate violence	Experienced non-intimate violence
Total	**100%**	**100%**
Still married	62	97
Divorced	8	1
Separated	30	1

Note: Percentages may not add to 100% due to rounding. Percentages exclude women who did not complete two consecutive interviews. Among married female respondents reporting having experienced a violent victimization, those who reported that an intimate had victimized them were substantially more likely to also report a change in their marital status.

SOURCE: Callie Marie Rennison, "Among Married Female Respondents Reporting Having Experienced a Violent Victimization, Those Who Reported That an Intimate Had Victimized Them Were Substantially More Likely to Also Report a Change in Their Marital Status," in *Intimate Partner Violence and Age of Victim, 1993–1999*, U.S. Department of Justice, Bureau of Justice Statistics, NCJ 187635, October 2001, http://www.ojp.usdoj.gov/bjs/pub/pdf/ipva99.pdf (accessed October 15, 2004)

listened to descriptions of three scenarios of forced sex: two scenarios involved forced sex between husband and wife and the other was a woman forced to have sex with someone with whom she was previously intimate. The respondents were asked whether they considered each scenario to be an instance of rape.

Basile found that nearly three-quarters (73%) of respondents believed that wife rape occurs, 18% thought it does not occur, and 5% were unsure. Among those who thought wife rape occurs, 38% said it happens often, and an additional 40% felt it happens somewhat often. Fifteen percent felt wife rape is infrequent and 4% said it is a rare occurrence.

Basile found support for nearly all her of hypotheses. The older the respondents, the less likely they were to believe that wife rape occurs, and white respondents were 2.5 times more likely to believe that wife rape occurs than blacks and other minorities. Women thought wife rape occurs more frequently than did men and, predictably, victims were more than twice as likely as nonvictims to feel that wife rape occurs.

The most surprising finding was that more education was associated with the belief that wife rape is less frequent. Basile observed that this finding might simply indicate that even persons with higher educational attainment remain ignorant about the frequency of wife rape.

Although Basile found that overall national attitudes about wife rape are less supportive than she would have predicted prior to her study, the variations in attitudes toward the two marital rape scenarios prompted her to observe that many Americans still feel victims play some part in their own victimization.

ACQUAINTANCE RAPE

According to a number of widely publicized studies, young women are at high risk of sexual assault by acquaintances or boyfriends. Studies have found rates ranging from a low of 15% for rape to a high of 78% for unwanted sexual aggression. Researchers surmise that acquaintance rape is especially underreported because the victims believe that nothing can or will be done, feel unsure about how to define the occurrence, or are uncertain about whether the action qualified as abuse.

Date rape is considered a form of acquaintance rape, especially if the perpetrator and victim have not known one another for long and the abuse begins early in the relationship. In "Adolescent Dating Violence and Date Rape" (*Current Opinion in Obstetrics and Gynecology,* vol. 14, no. 5, October 2002), a review of the current research and literature about date rape, Vaughn I. Rickert, Roger D. Vaughan, and Constance M. Wiemann observed that female teens aged sixteen to nineteen years old and young adult women aged twenty to twenty-four are not only four times as likely to be raped as women of other ages, but also that teens who have experienced rape or attempted rape during adolescence are twice as likely to experience an additional assault when they are college aged.

Rickert, Vaughan, and Wiemann also focused on high-risk subgroups of adolescents that, although less often studied, appear to experience high rates of date rape and other dating violence. They cited academically underperforming teens as at high risk, with 67% of female students and 33% of male students in a high school dropout prevention program admitting to having perpetrated dating violence, including sexual abuse and rape.

Acts of Aggression

David Riggs and K. Daniel O'Leary, in their study "Aggression between Heterosexual Dating Partners" (*Journal of Interpersonal Violence,* vol. 11, no. 4, December 1996), analyzed questionnaires from 345 undergraduates and found that overall rates of aggression by men and women are quite similar. About one-third of both men and women report engaging in physical aggression in their current relationships, and nearly all have used at least one form of verbal aggression.

Men are somewhat more likely to use serious forms of aggression, while women are twice as likely to slap a partner and more than five times as likely to kick, hit, or bite. Women are more likely to engage in nearly all forms of verbal aggression. Riggs and O'Leary acknowledged that their research does not reveal how much of the aggression reported by women was in self-defense.

The Influence of Alcohol on Sexual Assault

Alcohol reduces inhibitions and, in some cases, enhances aggression, so it is not surprising that researchers examine the link between alcohol and sexual assault. In "Alcohol and Sexual Assault in a National Sample of College Women" (*Journal of Interpersonal Violence,* vol. 14, no. 6, June 1999), Sarah E. Ullman, George Karabatsos, and Mary P. Koss examined how drinking prior to an assault influenced the severity of the attack.

The researchers administered a questionnaire to 3,187 college-age women, more than half of whom had been victims of rape, attempted rape, unwanted sexual contact, or sexual coercion. They measured the participants' alcohol use, the severity of the sexual attack, the social context in which the assault occurred, and the victims' familiarity with the offenders. As expected, victims who reported getting drunk more often also reported more severe assaults than those who were drunk less often. Neither the victim's family income nor how well the victim knew the offender was related to the severity of the attack, although older women experienced more severe victimization.

The researchers also found that alcohol's role in predicting the severity of an attack did not vary according to how well the victim knew her attacker or whether a social situation, such as a party, was the setting for the assault—with one exception. Unplanned social situations were associated with more severe assaults when offenders were not drinking prior to the assault than when they were drinking. The victim's use of alcohol was related to the severity of the attack in cases where the rapist was not drinking. According to Ullman, Karabatsos, and Koss, this finding suggests that intoxicated victims may be targeted by offenders, who perceive an opportunity to engage in sex without using coercive behaviors.

As anticipated, the study found that victims who abused alcohol or offenders and victims who used alcohol prior to the attack suffered higher rates of severe assaults. The study also found that offender drinking was related to more aggressive offender behavior and more severe victimization, suggesting that more violent assaults occurred when assailants had been drinking. Conversely, victim drinking was related to less offender aggression, possibly because force was not needed to complete the rape of intoxicated victims.

Not all researchers agree that the use of alcohol by offenders increases the severity of sexual assaults. Leanne R. Brecklin and Sarah E. Ullman found that alcohol use of offenders did not affect victim physical injury or need for medical attention. They reported their findings in "The Role of Offender Alcohol Use in Rape Attacks: An Analysis of National Crime Victimization Survey Data" (*Journal of Interpersonal Violence,* vol. 16, no. 1, January 2001). They also found that alcohol use was related to less completed rape. They suggested, however, that alcohol use might be indirectly associated with injury outcomes, because offenders using alcohol were more likely to assault in more dangerous situations (assaulting at night and outdoors, and attacking strangers).

Sexual Coercion

Sexual coercion is any situation where one person uses verbal or physical methods to obtain sex or sexual activity without consent of the other. Two studies examining the frequency of sexual coercion in dating relationships were published in *Violence and Victims*, vol. 10, nos. 3–4, 1995.

The first, "Male and Female Sexual Victimization in Dating Relationships: Gender Differences in Coercion Techniques and Outcomes," by Lisa Waldner-Haugrud and Brian Magruder, found that a "phenomenal" amount of sexual coercion was reported by 422 college students. Only 17% of the females and 27% of the males reported never experienced any coercion. The most common coercion techniques experienced by both sexes were persistent touching and the use of alcohol and drugs. Together, these methods comprised more than half the reported incidents of coercion. Women were more likely to experience unwanted detainment, persistent touching, lies, and being held down.

In the second study, Michele Poitras and Francine Lavoie questioned 644 adolescents between fifteen and nineteen years of age. Their results were published as "A Study of Prevalence of Sexual Coercion in Adolescent Heterosexual Dating Relationships in a Quebec Sample." The most frequently occurring unwanted sexual experiences reported by the adolescents were kissing, petting, and fondling. Verbal coercion was the most frequently used technique. Two in five girls reported sexual contact resulting from verbal coercion, and one in five reported intercourse resulting from verbal coercion. Approximately one out of ten females reported intercourse resulting from the use of force, alcohol, or drugs. Boys rarely reported the use of force, although 2.3% reported that they had had sex after giving their partners drugs or alcohol, and 2.9% reported intercourse as a result of verbal coercion. Poitras and Lavoie speculated that some of the differences in the reported rates of girls as the recipients of coercion and boys inflicting it may be attributed to the fact that adolescent girls frequently date older men, who may be more likely than boys to engage in coercive behaviors.

Leah E. Adams-Curtis and Gordon B. Forbes complicate the view of sexual coercion in their review of research, "College Women's Experiences of Sexual Coercion" (*Trauma, Violence, & Abuse*, vol. 5, no. 2, April 2004). They argued that coercive sexual behavior must be understood within prevalent sexual values on college campuses, including attitudes toward women, beliefs about sexual behavior, rape-supporting beliefs, coercion-

TABLE 5.2

Extent of rape among women college students, by number of victims, and number of incidents by type of victimization incident, 1996

Type of victimization	Victims			Incidents	
	Number of victims in sample	Percentage of sample	Rate per 1,000 female students	Number of incidents	Rate per 1,000 female students
Completed rape	74	1.7	16.6	86	19.3
Attempted rape	49	1.1	11.0	71	16.0
Total	**123**	**2.8**	**27.7**	**157**	**35.3**

*Total has been rounded (from 27.665 to 27.7).

SOURCE: Bonnie S. Fisher, Francis T. Cullen, and Michael G. Turner, "Exhibit 3. Extent of Rape, by Number of Victims, and Number of Incidents, by Type of Victimization Incident," in *The Sexual Victimization of College Women*, U.S. Department of Justice, Office of Justice Programs, NCJ 182369, December 2000, http://www.ncjrs.org/pdffiles1/nij/182369.pdf (accessed October 15, 2004)

supporting peer groups like fraternities and athletic teams, gender concepts of both victims and perpetrators, and sexual promiscuity and its link with alcohol.

The researchers posited that sexual coercion has its roots in traditional sex roles and expectations. Perpetrators of sexual coercion are not psychopaths, but rather, men not particularly different from other men. Instead, the authors wrote, "We view sexual coercion as a complex, multiply determined, social behavior that has its origins in normal heterosexual interactions. . . . The factors influencing the progression from normal sexual negotiations to coercive sexuality are often commonplace elements of college life." The authors recommended that work be done to change traditional concepts of masculinity and femininity that result in the large percentages of college women being coerced into unwanted sexual activity.

College Rape

The National College Women Sexual Victimization study found a disturbingly high rate of rapes among college women. The study was based on a telephone survey of randomly selected, national sample of 4,446 women attending colleges and universities in fall 1996. Respondents were asked between late February and early May 1997 if they had experienced sexual victimization "since school began in fall 1996."

The study found that in that period of almost seven months, 2.8% of the women had experienced either an attempted or completed rape. (See Table 5.2.) The authors suggested that the data show that nearly 5% of women college students are victimized in a given calendar year, and that the percentage of attempted or completed rape victimizations of college women during their college careers approaches one in four. The authors concluded that although the 2.8% figure might "seem" low, "from a policy perspec-

TABLE 5.3

Extent of sexual victimization among women college students, 1996

Type of victimization	Victims			Incidents	
	Number of victims in sample	Percentage of sample	Rate per 1,000 female students	Number of incidents	Rate per 1,000 female students
Completed or attempted					
Completed sexual coercion	74	1.7	16.6	107	24.1
Attempted sexual coercion	60	1.3	13.5	114	25.6
Completed sexual contact with force or threat of force	85	1.9	19.1	130	29.2
Completed sexual contact without force	80	1.8	18.0	132	29.7
Attempted sexual contact with force or threat of force	89	2.0	20.0	166	37.6
Attempted sexual contact without force	133	3.0	29.9	295	66.4
Threats					
Threat of rape	14	0.31	3.2	42	9.5
Threat of contact with force or threat of force	8	0.18	1.8	50	11.3
Threat of penetration without force	10	0.22	2.3	50	11.3
Threat of contact without force	15	0.34	3.4	75	16.9
Total	**568**			**1,161**	

SOURCE: Bonnie S. Fisher, Francis T. Cullen, and Michael G. Turner, "Exhibit 5. Extent of Sexual Victimization," in *The Sexual Victimization of College Women*, U.S. Department of Justice, Office of Justice Programs, NCJ 182369, December 2000, http://www.ncjrs.org/pdffiles1/nij/182369.pdf (accessed October 12, 2004)

tive, college administrators might be disturbed to learn that for every one thousand women attending their institutions, there may well be thirty-five incidents of rape in a given academic year. . . . For a campus with ten thousand women, this would mean the number of rapes would exceed 350."

Researchers also asked respondents about other types of sexual victimization. They found that 1.7% of their sample had been victims of completed sexual coercion (unwanted sexual penetration with the threat of punishment or promise of reward), 1.3% had been victims of attempted sexual coercion, 1.9% had been victims of unwanted completed sexual contact with force or the threat of force, and 1.8% had been victims of completed sexual contact without physical force. Smaller percentages of women had been sexually threatened. Table 5.3 shows these additional types of sexual victimization. Figure 5.1 displays the data slightly differently, showing that 7.7% of college women surveyed had experienced sexual victimization involving physical force, 11% had experienced sexual victimization involving nonphysical force, and 15.5% had experienced any victimization since the start of the academic year.

The National College Women Sexual Victimization study also found that fewer than 5% of the rapes and attempted rapes had been reported to police, and even lower percentages of other types of sexual victimization were reported. (See Table 5.4.) A national study of college students reported by the Centers for Disease Control backed up this result, finding that 27.5% of women said they had suffered rape or attempted rape at least once since age fourteen, but just 5% of victims reported the incidents to the police.

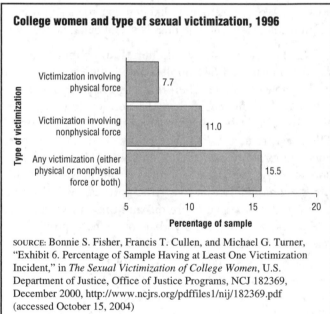

FIGURE 5.1

College women and type of sexual victimization, 1996

SOURCE: Bonnie S. Fisher, Francis T. Cullen, and Michael G. Turner, "Exhibit 6. Percentage of Sample Having at Least One Victimization Incident," in *The Sexual Victimization of College Women*, U.S. Department of Justice, Office of Justice Programs, NCJ 182369, December 2000, http://www.ncjrs.org/pdffiles1/nij/182369.pdf (accessed October 15, 2004)

These numbers confirm other researchers' findings that students overwhelmingly do not report acquaintance rapes or attempted rapes, including those of Bonnie S. Fisher et al. in "Reporting Sexual Victimization to the Police and Others: Results from a National-Level Study of College Women" (*Criminal Justice and Behavior,* vol. 30, no. 1, February 2003). According to the Centers for Disease Control, the term "hidden rape" has been used to describe this finding of widespread unreported and underreported sexual assault. Anecdotal reports from college and university administrators suggest that many female students who have been raped not only fail to report the offense, but also drop out of school.

TABLE 5.4

Reasons for not reporting incident to the police, by type of victimization, 1996

Type of incident	Incident was not reported %	Reason for not reporting incident*											
		Did not want family to know %	Did not want other people to know %	Lack of proof that incident happened %	Fear of being treated hostilely by police %	Fear of being treated hostilely by other parts of justice system %	Not clear it was a crime or that harm was intended %	Did not know how to report %	Police wouldn't think it was serious enough %	Police wouldn't want to be bothered %	Afraid of reprisal by assailant or other %	Did not think it was serious enough to report %	Other %
Completed or attempted													
Completed rape	95.2	44.4	46.9	42.0	24.7	6.2	44.4	13.6	27.2	25.9	39.5	65.4	7.4
Attempted rape	95.8	32.4	32.4	30.9	8.8	1.5	39.7	7.4	33.8	13.2	25.0	76.5	1.5
										(9)	(17)	(52)	(1)
Completed sexual coercion	100.0	41.9	43.8	33.3	8.6	1.9	58.1	14.3	24.8	21.9	31.4	71.4	1.9
Attempted sexual coercion	100.0	21.2	19.5	15.9	2.7	2.7	46.9	6.2	28.3	18.6	11.5	86.7	0
Completed sexual contact with force or threat of force	99.2	19.5	16.4	21.9	9.4	0	37.5	7.0	37.5	30.5	22.7	81.3	3.1
Completed sexual contact without force	98.5	4.7	11.7	18.0	4.7	1.6	43.0	5.5	29.7	18.8	12.5	91.4	0.8
Attempted sexual contact with force or threat of force	97.0	13.8	21.9	23.1	8.8	6.3	37.5	10.0	31.3	22.5	23.8	80.0	2.5
Attempted sexual contact without force	99.3	7.2	10.2	18.1	4.4	1.4	39.6	6.1	22.9	18.4	10.9	88.4	2.7
Threats													
Threat of rape	90.5	26.3	34.2	31.6	13.2	7.9	39.5	13.2	34.2	31.6	26.3	65.8	2.6
Threat of contact with force or threat of force	90.0	22.2	20.0	20.0	8.9	4.4	51.1	13.3	37.8	26.7	17.8	68.9	4.4
Threat of penetration without force	100.0	20.0	22.0	24.0	4.0	4.0	46.0	6.0	30.0	30.0	12.0	88.0	2.0
Threat of contact without force	98.7	6.8	8.1	21.6	8.1	6.8	31.1	2.7	21.6	9.5	13.5	83.8	0

*Percentages may be greater than 100 because a respondent could give more than one response.

SOURCE: Bonnie S. Fisher, Francis T. Cullen, and Michael G. Turner, "Exhibit 12. Reasons for Not Reporting Incident to the Police, by Type of Victimization," in *The Sexual Victimization of College Women*, U.S. Department of Justice, Office of Justice Programs, NCJ 182369, December 2000, http://www.ncjrs.org/=dffiles1/nij/182369.pdf (accessed October 15, 2004)

In "Acquaintance Rape and the College Social Scene" (*Family Relations,* vol. 40, January 1991), Sally Ward et al. surveyed 518 women and 337 men at a large university. Thirty-four percent of the female respondents had experienced unwanted sexual contact, such as attempted or actual kissing, fondling, or touching; 20% had experienced unwanted attempted sexual intercourse; and 10% had unwanted intercourse, which was defined as any form of sexual penetration, including vaginal, anal, and oral. The majority of incidents were party related, and most involved alcohol, with 75% of the males and over half the females reporting alcohol consumption at the time of the incident.

Women reported that the majority of the perpetrators initiated the acts without warning. The percentage of cases involving force by men ranged from 8% for sexual contact to 21% for completed intercourse. Most of the women verbally protested, although 20% of victims said they were too frightened to protest. Victims most frequently chose to confide in a roommate or close friend, although 41% of the women told no one about the rape. Counselors were almost never told of the incidents.

The men reported a very different picture of unwanted sexual behavior on campus. Only 9% reported committing either unwanted sexual contact or attempted intercourse, and 3% admitted to incidents of unwanted sexual intercourse. Ward et al. proposed that the reason for the different results is that men and women read sexual cues and form sexual expectations differently. A 2003 study titled "Likelihood of Acquaintance Rape as a Function of Males' Sexual Expectations, Disappointment, and Adherence to Rape-Conducive Attitudes" found that men are far more likely than women to interpret a woman's behavior as sexual and misconstrue it as an invitation to sexual intimacy. The study's authors, V. J. Willan and Paul Pollard, wrote, "In conjunction with the finding that males significantly misperceived the female's sexual intent to engage in sexual intercourse, following the initial contact, this suggests that males, in a bid to calculate the probability of obtaining sexual intercourse, overestimate the predictive value of the female's initial consent to 'attend a party together.' This consequently leads to greater goal expectation, which, combined with hostile beliefs about women, might result in a greater likelihood of nonconsensual sexual intercourse" (*Journal of Social and Personal Relationships,* vol. 20, no. 5, 2003).

Fraternities and Athletics

Fraternity members are frequently blamed as perpetrators of college rapes. Martin Schwartz and Carol Nogrady, in "Fraternity Membership, Rape Myths, and Sexual Aggression on College Campus" (*Violence against Women,* vol. 2, no. 2, June 1996), think this characterization is false. They argue that men who are most likely to rape in college are fraternity pledges, and postulate that

fraternity members are more likely to have a narrow conception of masculinity, espouse group secrecy, and sexually objectify women. Schwartz and Nogrady asserted that alcohol is the crucial variable, and because fraternity members are often heavy drinkers, researchers have mistakenly linked these men and sexually aggressive behavior.

Mary Koss and Hobart Cleveland, in "Athletic Participation, Fraternity Membership and Date Rape: The Question Remains—Self-Selection or Different Causal Processes?" (*Violence against Women,* vol. 2, no. 2, June 1996), tried to determine whether date rape is more likely to be perpetrated by athletes and fraternity members. They speculated that a fraternity-sponsored party draws acquaintances of the same social network together, while the fraternity controls the limited physical space with very little supervision. Together, these circumstances create an environment that legitimizes the actions of the members, thereby minimizing the chance of reporting as well as the credibility of women who do report sexual misconduct. Koss and Cleveland concluded that there is very low reporting of fraternity rape.

Several studies have found that peer support of violence and social ties with abusive peers are predictors of abuse against women. In addition, training for violent occupations such as athletics and the military can "spill over" into personal life. Athletic training is sex-segregated, promotes hostile attitudes toward rivals, and rewards athletes for physically dominating others. Todd Crosset et al. in "Male Student-Athletes and Violence against Women" (*Violence against Women,* vol. 2, no. 2, June 1996), gathered data from the judicial affairs offices of the ten Division I schools with the largest athletic programs. Although male student-athletes made up just 3% of the student population, they accounted for 35% of the reported perpetrators.

Crosset et al. contended that the special society of athletics promotes violent, woman-hating attitudes. In "Sports' Dirty Secret" (*Sports Illustrated,* vol 83, issue 5, July 31, 1995), Crosset explained that it is an important aspect of male athleticism to not be considered feminine, meaning a "wimp" or a "sissy." Women are despised, degraded, and not respected. In this climate, the athlete needs to "act like a man," and to be accused of acting like a woman is a grave insult.

Researchers Stephen E. Humphrey and Arnold S. Kahn have complicated the question of whether fraternity members and male athletes are more likely to perpetrate sexual assaults than other college males in "Fraternities, Athletic Teams, and Rape: Importance of Identification with a Risky Group" (*Journal of Interpersonal Violence,* vol. 15, December 2000). They argued that one reason that previous studies have yielded conflicting results is that they treat all sports teams and fraternities as the same, but that "there is evidence that fraternities vary widely in their attitudes toward women and their behavior toward them." They concluded that some "high-risk groups" had higher levels of sexual aggression and hostility toward women, as well as more support for sexual violence than did other "low-risk groups." In other words, the members of some fraternities and athletic teams *are* more likely to perpetrate sexual assault, while others are not.

Alcohol on Campus

Alcohol has been implicated in most sexual assault cases on campuses. According to the Center on Addiction and Substance Abuse, in *Rethinking Rites of Passage: Substance Abuse on America's Campuses* (New York: Columbia University, 1994), 90% of all college rapes occur when either the victim or the rapist is under the influence of alcohol. Other studies estimate that one-third to three-quarters of all rapes and sexual assaults involve the use of alcohol by one or both parties.

Antonia Abbey et al. in "Alcohol and Dating Risk Factors for Sexual Assault among College Women" (*Psychology of Women Quarterly,* vol. 20, 1996), concluded that having one's sexual intentions misperceived was directly related to experiencing sexual assault. They argued that women tend to send misperceived messages when alcohol is consumed.

Other researchers also suggest that alcohol consumption increases the likelihood of sexual assault. In men, it appears to promote the expression of traditional gender beliefs about sexual behavior and creates expectancies associated with male sexuality and aggression, providing justification or a rationale for men to commit sexual assault. Furthermore, drinking increases the likelihood that men will misread women's friendly cues as signs of sexual interest. For women, alcohol consumption limits the ability to correct men's misunderstanding of cues. Drinking also decreases women's capacity to resist sexual assault and often prompts the victims to feel responsible for assaults.

In "Alcohol and Sexual Assault in a National Sample of College Women," Sarah E. Ullman, George Karabatsos, and Mary P. Koss polled a group of 3,187 college-age women about their own alcohol abuse, sexual victimization, sexual assault experience, and the social events surrounding their experience (*Journal of Interpersonal Violence,* vol. 14, June 1999). Of the 54.2% of women who had experienced some sexual victimization, over half (53.4%) reported that their assailants were using alcohol at the time of the incident, and 42% reported that they themselves were using alcohol. Over a third of the assaults (39.7%) occurred during dates with men that the women knew well or moderately well. Most assaults were committed without weapons, although 40% of the men used physical force. More than 90% of the victims said they attempted to resist the assault.

Ullman, Karabatsos, and Koss found that the victim's propensity to abuse alcohol and the use of alcohol prior to the assault by both victim and assailant were associated with more severe sexual victimization. The research revealed that a victim's use of alcohol before the assault did not predict more severe sexual victimization, as hypothesized; instead, researchers speculated that victim drinking may have been related to less offender aggression, because force was not needed to complete the rape of an intoxicated victim. Nor did alcohol's role in predicting the severity of sexual victimization vary in relationship to how well the victim knew the offender or whether a social situation was the setting for the assault. Ullman, Karabatsos, and Koss concluded that assaults in unplanned social situations were opportunistic in nature, and therefore were not affected by offender drinking.

Overall, the study findings indicated that alcohol use by victims and offenders before an assault plays direct and indirect roles in the severity of assaults, but generally the woman's drinking behavior contributes less strongly to the outcome of the attack.

Rohypnol—The "Date Rape Pill"

While alcohol abuse remains a significant problem on college campuses, other drugs, such as Rohypnol, have made resistance to attacks practically impossible. A hypnotic sedative ten times more powerful than Valium, Rohypnol (known as "Roofies," "Roches," and "Ropies") has been used to obtain nonconsensual sex from many women. Mixed in a drink, it causes memory impairment, confusion, and drowsiness. A woman may be completely unaware of a sexual assault until she wakes up the next morning. The only way to determine if a victim has been given Rohypnol is to test for the drug within two or three days of the rape, and few hospital emergency departments routinely screen for this drug. Health educators, high school guidance counselors, resident advisors at colleges, and scores of newspaper and magazine articles advise women not to accept drinks at parties or to leave drinks sitting unattended.

Although Rohypnol is legally prescribed outside of the United States for short-term treatment of severe sleep disorders, it is neither manufactured nor approved for sale in the U.S. The importation of the drug was banned in March 1996, and the U.S. Customs Service began to seize quantities of Rohypnol at U.S. borders. In response to reported abuse, the manufacturers reformulated the drug as green tablets that can be detected in clear liquids and are visible in the bottom of a cup.

In October 1996 President Bill Clinton signed a bill amending the Controlled Substances Act to increase penalties for using drugs to disarm potential victims of violent crime. Anyone convicted of slipping a controlled substance, including Rohypnol, to an individual with intent to commit a violent act, such as rape, faces a prison term of up to twenty years and a fine as high as two million dollars. The law also increased penalties for manufacturing, distributing, or possessing Rohypnol with the intent to distribute it.

Two other drugs are also used as date rape pills. Gamma hydroxybutyric acid (GHB, also known as "Liquid Ecstasy") enhances the effects of alcohol, which reduces the drinker's inhibitions. It also causes a form of amnesia. Ketamine hydrochloride (also known as "Special K") is an animal tranquilizer used to impair a person's natural resistance impulses. During 2002, anecdotal reports about another dangerous drug surfaced—a combination of methylenedioxymethamphetamine (known as "Ecstasy," "MDMA," or "crystal methamphetamine") and Viagra (a prescription drug used to treat erectile dysfunction)—dubbed "Sextasy." According to media reports, the drugs are taken together by male teens because Viagra offsets impotence, a potential side effect of methamphetamine use. Public health officials are alarmed by this "off-label" use of Viagra and fear that it may contribute to increased rates of sexually transmitted diseases and sexual assault.

The Political Conflict: "One in Four"

The frequency of date rape has become a highly controversial subject. The most widely publicized rate of date rape, and the source of this dispute, was that "one in four" women are victims. This number originated in a study by Mary Koss, C. Gedycz, and N. Wisniewski. In "The Scope of Rape: Incidence and Prevalence of Sexual Aggression and Victimization in a National Sample of Higher Education Students" (*Journal of Consulting and Clinical Psychology,* vol. 55, 1987), Koss, Gedycz, and Wisniewski interviewed more than three thousand women nationwide about sexual violations. Among the ten questions asked by the researchers were: "Have you had sexual intercourse when you didn't want to because a man gave you alcohol or drugs? Have you had sexual intercourse when you didn't want to because a man threatened or used some degree of physical force to make you? Have you had sexual acts (anal or oral intercourse or penetration by objects other than the penis) when you didn't want to because a man threatened or used some degree of physical force to make you?"

Based on the interviews, Koss, Gedycz, and Wisniewski determined that 15.4% of the women had been raped and 12.1% had been victims of attempted rape, making the total number of women who were victims of rape or attempted rape 27.5%. The women, however, saw things differently. Only 27% of the 15.4% Koss et al. had labeled as "raped" agreed with that classification. Of the remainder, 49% said it was "miscommunication," 14% said it was a crime but not rape, and 11% said they didn't feel victimized. Furthermore, Koss, Gedycz, and Wis-

niewski found that 42% of the women they had classified as rape victims had sex again with their attackers on at least one other occasion.

Critics of this study faulted Koss, Gedycz, and Wisniewski for counting among their rape victims women who had had intercourse as a result of alcohol or drugs. If a woman passed out and her partner had intercourse with her, she had been raped, since the act was committed without her consent. But not everyone agreed that she had been raped if she had too much to drink and engaged in sex because her judgment was impaired, regardless of whether or not she regretted her actions later.

Katie Roiphe, the author of *The Morning after: Sex, Fear, and Feminism* (Boston: Back Bay, 1994), observed in a 1993 interview that date rape has become a synonym for bad sex, sex that is pressured, sex while drunk, or next-day regrets. If all these situations were called rape, she concluded, then almost everybody has been "raped" at one time or another. The Roiphe interview was conducted by Judith Stone and published as "Sex, Rape and Second Thoughts" (*Glamour,* 91, October 1993).

If the women in Koss, Gedycz, and Wisniewski's study who did not identify themselves as raped while under the influence of drugs or alcohol were removed from the total, the rate of rape and attempted rape drops from one in four to one in twenty-two and one in thirty-three, respectively. Koss, Gedycz, and Wisniewski defended their inclusion of these women, citing the Ohio law that states, "No person shall engage in sexual conduct with another person . . . when . . . for the purpose of preventing resistance the offender substantially impairs the other person's judgment or control by administering any drug or intoxicant to the other person." But the researchers later conceded that the question was ambiguously worded, because they omitted the portion of the statute that refers to "the situation where a person plies his intended partner with drink or drugs in hopes that the lowered inhibition might lead to a liaison."

Despite the firestorm of criticism that followed the widespread dissemination of the rates cited in Koss, Gedycz, and Wisniewski's study, their research continues to be cited by credible providers of health and social policy data, including the Centers for Disease Control in the *Dating Violence Fact Sheet* and *Dating Violence* (Atlanta, GA: National Center for Injury Prevention and Control, 2002).

RAPE AMONG LESBIANS AND GAY MEN

Lesbians and gay men have been victims of rape and sexual abuse at rates comparable to or higher than rates in the heterosexual community. In "Comparing Violence over the Lifespan in Samples of Same-Sex and Opposite Sex Cohabitants" (*Violence and Victims,* vol. 14, no. 4, 1999), researchers Patricia Tjaden, Nancy Thoennes, and Christine J. Allison found that cohabiting lesbians were nearly twice as likely as women living with male partners to have been forcibly raped as a minor (16.5% versus 8.7%) and nearly three times as likely to report being raped as an adult (25.3% versus 10.3%). The study also found that 15.4% of cohabiting gays were raped as minors, while 10.8% were raped as adults. The rate of rape for heterosexual men living with female partners was insignificant.

The researchers found that cohabiting gays usually had been raped by strangers and acquaintances, while cohabiting females usually had been raped by intimate partners. A vast majority of the rape victims, regardless of gender or sexual preference, were raped by men.

Gay and lesbian cohabitants were also significantly more likely to report being physically assaulted as a child by an adult caretaker. Among gays, 70.8% reported such violence, compared to 50.3% of heterosexual cohabitants. Among women, the figures were 59.5% and 37.5%, respectively. Gay and lesbian cohabitants also experienced higher levels of physical assault in adulthood.

The study also found that same-sex cohabiting partners reported significantly more intimate partner violence than did cohabiting heterosexuals. About 32% of gay respondents said they had been raped or physically assaulted by a spouse or cohabiting partner at some point in their lives, compared to just 7.7% of heterosexual men. Among lesbian cohabitants, 39.2% reported having been physically assaulted by a spouse or cohabiting partner, compared to 20.3% of women living with male partners. Tjaden, Thoennes, and Allison noted that lesbian cohabitants were also more than twice as likely to report having been victimized by male intimate partners than by female intimate partners, with 30.4% of the lesbian cohabitants raped or physically assaulted by male intimates. Only 11.4% of that group said they were raped or physically assaulted by female intimate partners. The same group reported less violence by their female partners than did heterosexual women living with males, leading the researchers to conclude that women are far more likely to be assaulted by male intimate partners than by female intimate partners.

SEXUAL HARASSMENT

Guys were encouraged to get as drunk as they could, and do whatever they could to the women. If they felt like grabbing a woman by the boob or the ass, that was okay. They would use their power and authority to make you think you didn't have a job if you didn't go along.

—A former pharmaceutical company sales representative

Sexual harassment is hardly a new phenomenon. In the early days of Hollywood, it was generally accepted that many actresses auditioned for roles on the "casting couch," finding their way into films by acquiescing to the sexual demands of directors. The businessman chasing his secretary around the desk has long been a common theme of cartoonists. Until the 1970s, remarks laced with sexual innuendo were still considered acceptable in the workplace. But as women became more prominent in the work force, behavior that had been condoned and even encouraged was redefined as sexual harassment.

Definitions

Sexual harassment is a form of sexual discrimination prohibited under Title VII of the Civil Rights Act of 1964. According to the U.S. Department of Justice, sexual harassment is "unwelcome sexual advances, requests for sexual favors, and other verbal or physical conduct that enters into employment decisions and/or conduct that unreasonably interferes with an individual's work performance or creates an intimidating, hostile, or offensive working environment." Despite the legal definition, sexual harassment allegations remain difficult to prove and hard to refute.

There are two forms of harassment: quid pro quo, the Latin term meaning "this for that," and hostile-work-environment harassment. Quid pro quo harassment occurs when an employee is pressured to choose between submitting to sexual advances or losing a job benefit, such as a promotion, raise, or the job itself. Hostile-work-environment harassment is unwelcome conduct that is so severe that it creates an intimidating or offensive work environment. For example, an employee who tells sexually explicit jokes that offend coworkers could be accused of creating a hostile work environment.

In 1986 the landmark U.S. Supreme Court case *Meritor Savings Bank v. Vinson* established the legal standard of a hostile work environment. The case originated when Michelle Vinson sued her employer, claiming her supervisor had harassed her constantly and raped her. A lower court ruled against Vinson, but the Supreme Court reversed the decision, focusing on the hostile environment clause of the law, which, the court found, "affords employees the right to work in an environment free from discriminatory intimidation, ridicule, and insult."

Cases

The Equal Employment Opportunity Commission is the federal agency responsible for investigating and resolving charges of sexual harassment. The commission received 6,127 sexual harassment cases in 1990. By 1997 that number reached its highest level, 15,889. The number dropped slightly over the subsequent four years, but had increased again to 15,792 in 2002. While the number of cases has remained about the same, the amount of money awarded to sexual harassment victims has grown steadily, from a total of $7.1 million in awards in 1990 to $50.3 million in 2002. Changes in the Civil Rights Act of 1991 gave people suing for sexual harassment the right to jury trials and permission to sue for compensatory and punitive damages, opening the door for larger monetary awards. Some critics charge that the huge awards are excessive and disproportionate to the offenses.

When considering the merits of cases, courts apply a variety of tests to distinguish merely rude behavior from true instances of harassment. They ask whether a given gesture, comment, or action was unwelcome and of a sexual nature. If it meets these criteria, courts then examine the severity and prevalence of the behavior. Generally, the more extreme the behavior, the less frequently it needs to have occurred to be deemed sexual harassment.

Some experts predicted that sexual harassment would be eliminated, or at least sharply reduced, as women became more accepted in the workplace. Instead, 1998 saw four major sexual harassment cases in the U.S. Supreme Court, three of which were brought under Title VII of the Civil Rights Act of 1964. These three cases clarified employer liability for sexual harassment in the workplace. The first involved Joseph Oncale, who was sexually assaulted by his coworkers and a supervisor on an oil rig off the coast of Louisiana. He filed a federal lawsuit alleging sexual harassment. Oncale lost to the lower court because he and his coworkers were male. But according to the unanimous ruling by the Supreme Court in *Oncale v. Sundowner Offshore Services,* same-sex sexual harassment constitutes legal discrimination.

In *Faragher v. City of Boca Raton,* Beth Faragher, who was employed for five years as a lifeguard for Boca Raton, Florida, alleged she endured repeated incidences of touching, sexual gestures, and sexual comments from two male bosses. Because Faragher feared retaliation, she did not report the abuse until after leaving her job, when she filed a sexual harassment suit against the city. The city responded that because it was never made aware of the events, it had no liability for the alleged actions of the supervisors. Although the city had a sexual harassment policy, it had not distributed that policy to Faragher or her department. The Supreme Court made it clear that any large employer must establish, distribute, and enforce a sexual harassment policy.

In *Burlington Industries v. Ellerth,* the court considered the case of Kimberly Ellerth, who claimed she was subjected to constant sexual harassment by a manager. Burlington Industries argued that Ellerth was not financially burdened by the harassment and that as a result, Burlington was not liable. The Supreme Court held that an employer could be liable when a supervisor causes a hostile work environment, even when the employee suffers no tangible job consequences and the employer is unaware of the offensive conduct. The manager's numerous alleged threats were found to constitute severe or pervasive conduct.

In both the Faragher and Ellerth cases, the Supreme Court made it clear that a worker who is harassed has a duty to report it. Employers must have a sexual harassment policy that is compliant with the law, disseminate the policy so that all employees know about it and know how to use it, ensure that employees have effective avenues to file complaints, respond promptly and effectively to complaints, and enforce the policy with appropriate actions.

The fourth case, *Gebser v. Lago Vista Independent School District,* was brought under Title IX of the Education Amendments Act of 1972. It concerned a school district's liability for a teacher's sexual involvement with a fourteen-year-old student. Alida Gebser, a student in the Lago Vista, Texas, school district, claimed her relationship with the teacher was consensual, but she also said she was afraid to tell anyone about it, fearing she would be barred from the advanced-level courses the teacher taught. The teacher pleaded guilty to charges of statutory rape, and Gebser filed a civil suit against the school district. The Supreme Court ruled that a school district could not be held liable because the student had not told a supervisor, stating that a student must prove a school district acted with "deliberate indifference" to a complaint.

Sexual Harassment in the Military

Sexual harassment in the military captured the public's attention in 1991 when eighty-three female officers claimed they were abused at a convention of naval and marine pilots, which created an uproar that became known as the Tailhook Scandal. Of about 140 charges leveled at officers as a result, not one case made it to trial. Less than half of the accused men "went to the mast," an internal disciplinary procedure that levied fines and career penalties.

In November 1996 four drill instructors and a captain at the U.S. Army's Aberdeen, Maryland, training center were charged with harassment and rape of female recruits. Within a month, more than fifty women had filed charges alleging sexual assault or rape. Sergeant Major Gene McKinney was tried on charges of coercing sexual favors from six women after they accused him of harassing or assaulting them. A month-long military trial resulted in McKinney's acquittal of all sex-related charges. He was, however, found guilty of a single count of obstructing justice and was subsequently demoted to master sergeant.

On July 7, 2000, the army inspector general confirmed charges of sexual harassment made by Lieutenant General Claudia Kennedy against Major General Larry Smith. Kennedy did not report the harassment until she learned Smith was to be selected to serve as deputy inspector general of the army, a position responsible for oversight of investigating instances of sexual harassment and directing programs to prevent and eliminate harassment. As a result of the substantiated charges, Smith did not assume the position of deputy inspector general and was issued an administrative memorandum of reprimand.

Military regulations forbid intimate relations between officers and enlisted personnel and between supervisors and their subordinates. The official army policy on sexual harassment calls for "zero tolerance" on the issue, and the edict is drilled into soldiers from their first day in the service. Nevertheless, violations continue throughout the armed services. Through the Department of Veterans Affairs, female veterans are counseled for sexual trauma. Caseloads are up sharply, from 2,090 in 1993 to more than ten thousand just nine years later. Marsha Tansey Four, Chair of the Advisory Committee on Women Veterans in the U.S. Department of Veterans Affairs, testified before the U.S. House of Representatives Veteran Affairs Committee on May 6, 2004 that a 2002 survey had found that 5% of female veterans and 1% of male veterans had experienced sexual trauma in the military.

The situation in the military is aggravated by the almost absolute power a superior has over a subordinate, especially in basic and advanced training units. From the moment recruits enter basic training, they learn that they must always obey their drill sergeants. With such absolute, unquestioned power, the drill sergeant can easily make a purposely difficult situation even worse.

Teri Spahr Nelson, a therapist and editor of *For Love of Country: Confronting Rape and Sexual Harassment in the Military* (Binghamton, NY: Haworth Maltreatment and Trauma Press, 2002), estimated that "two-thirds of female service members experience unwanted, uninvited sexual behavior in the military. The problems of sexual harassment and sexual assault in the U.S. military are epidemic." Nelson wrote that in one year alone, an estimated 9% of women in the Marines, 8% in the Army, 6% in the Navy, and 4% in the Air Force and Coast Guard have very likely been victims of rape or attempted rape.

HARASSMENT IN THE FEDERAL WORKPLACE

In the study *Sexual Harassment in the Federal Workplace* (Washington, DC: U.S. Merit Systems Protection Board, 1995), the latest report on sexual harassment in the federal work force available, workers were polled about sexual harassment in 1980, 1987, and 1994. According to these polls, rates of sexual harassment remained fairly stable over the fourteen-year period. In 1987, 14% of men and 42% of women reported harassment, compared to 19% of men and 44% of women in 1994. These rates included behavior that ranged from pressure for dates to sexual jokes to rape.

In the 1980 survey, 91% of women and 84% of men thought it was harassment for a supervisor to pressure for sexual favors. By 1994 nearly all of the respondents thought pressure for sexual favors from a supervisor was

harassment (99% of women and 97% of men). Some portion of the observed shift in thinking and apparent heightened awareness of these issues may be attributable to Anita Hill's 1991 appearance before the U.S. Senate during Clarence Thomas's Supreme Court confirmation hearing. Hill, who had worked as Thomas's assistant at the Equal Employment Opportunity Commission, alleged that Thomas had repeatedly pressured her for dates and made lurid remarks during her employment. An estimated thirty million households watched the three-day televised proceedings, which made sexual harassment one of the year's most hotly debated topics. In the year following that hearing, the Equal Employment Opportunity Commission recorded a 50% increase in sexual harassment complaints.

Different Perceptions

The Merit Systems Protection Board study revealed that men and women view sexual teasing, jokes, and remarks differently. In 1987 less than half the men, or 47%, thought this behavior was harassment when it was done by a coworker, compared with 64% of women. In 1994 these percentages rose to 64% for men and 77% for women. At least twice as many women as men reported experiencing sexual harassment throughout the period of the study.

This difference in perception is at the heart of a legal controversy about how to define sexual harassment. Normally, a court defines behavior as harassment if a "reasonable person" views the situation as harassment. Some advocates insist that harassment should be defined on a "reasonable woman" standard instead. The U.S. Court of Appeals for the 9th Circuit, in the 1991 case *Ellison v. Brady,* advocated a "reasonable woman" standard when it argued that words and actions men might consider mild harassment, women found threatening and perhaps a prelude to more serious sexual assault. The Cato Institute, a libertarian think tank in Washington, D.C., disagreed, charging that this standard would have the effect of "gutting the concept of neutrality under the law."

Differences between male and female perceptions were underscored in the Merit Systems Protection Board study. Nearly twice as many men as women thought the issue of sexual harassment had been overemphasized.

Handling Harassment

The Merit Systems Protection Board study found that the most frequent response to sexual harassment was to ignore it—44% of harassment victims did just that. The reason for some of this inaction may be related to the perceived insignificance of the offense. For some, however, the harassing behavior was quite serious, and yet they did nothing. The next most common reaction to unwanted sexual attention was to ask or tell the perpetrator to stop. About one-third of harassment victims said this was the approach they used. Another 28% responded by avoiding the harasser.

The survey found that respondents felt that the most effective methods of dealing with harassment were to ask or tell the person to stop and to report the situation to a supervisor. The strategies that survey respondents considered most effective for preventing harassment largely relied on the adequacy of communication and the organization's ability to get the word out to employees at every level. One-quarter of harassment victims filed grievances or adverse action appeals, 30% filed discrimination complaints or suits, and 42% requested an investigation by the employing organization. Less than 15% of victims requested an investigation by an outside organization, and 17% took other actions. Although some victims took more than one action to report and seek recourse against those who harassed them, others chose to take no action at all. Half of the victims who chose not to take formal action said they did not consider the offense serious enough, 40% felt other actions resolved the situation, and 29% feared that taking formal action would worsen their work situations.

There are sharp penalties for violating federal agency sexual harassment policies. Employees risk suspension, demotion, and loss of their jobs. Victims opting to sue the federal government for on-the-job harassment may seek as much as $300,000 in compensation for the abuse.

CHAPTER 6

TREATMENT FOR MALE BATTERERS

The first batterer intervention programs were established in the late 1970s. Activists working with battered women created the programs because they felt that real progress in reducing domestic violence required changing the behavior of batterers. Criminal justice agencies responded by referring an increasing number of batterers to intervention programs in an effort to deter further violence. Several hundred intervention and treatment programs for batterers now exist throughout the United States.

Studies of the effectiveness of male batterer treatment programs are inconclusive and many are discouraging about the programs' effectiveness. Some follow-up studies performed four to twenty-four months after batterers complete programs indicate nonviolence rates of between 53% 85%. Other reports find no difference in outcomes between those attending batterer programs and control groups that did not. In assessing whether these programs work, many factors must be considered, including the type of batterer and the kind of treatment that works best. Although researchers are beginning to identify different types of abusers, they have not yet definitively shown which treatment approach is most effective with each group.

STANDARDS FOR BATTERER INTERVENTION PROGRAMS

Most states have developed battering intervention programs to deal with violent batterers. But states differ over the type of batterers who must attend and the penalties they incur if they fail to attend. Critics contend that state-mandated standards for participation and program type produce inflexible programs that fail to take into account research demonstrating the need for different approaches to deal with different batterers.

Some critics charge that these standards were written by those who felt regulation was necessary to ensure that male batterers were held accountable. They believe such standards focus on domestic violence as a crime that requires criminal sanctions. Mental health professionals, however, view domestic abuse as a dysfunctional disorder that is best treated with mental health treatment and therapy. Other critics feel that the standards may result in a limited treatment approach, even though research has not yet determined the effectiveness of any one program in deterring future abuse.

In "Standards for Batterer Intervention Programs: In Whose Interest?" (*Violence against Women*, vol. 5, no. 1, 1999), Larry Bennett and Marianne Piet found that much of the conflict over program standards results from a misunderstanding about the purpose of these standards. They argued that rather than focus on program content and potentially prevent creation and implementation of innovative practices, standards should be designed to hold men accountable for their actions, hold providers accountable for their programs, and increase the safety of the victims of domestic violence.

A NATIONAL STUDY OF BATTERER INTERVENTION

In *Batterer Intervention: Program Approaches and Criminal Justice Strategies* (Washington, DC: National Institute of Justice, 1998), Kerry Healey and Christine Smith reported on their study of batterer intervention programs. The study was designed to help criminal justice personnel better understand the issues surrounding batterer intervention to enable them to make appropriate referrals to programs and to communicate effectively with program providers. Healey and Smith looked at both "mainstream" programs and innovative approaches across the country. Although many programs are structurally similar, there is considerable diversity in terms of the theoretical approaches used to treat perpetrators of intimate partner violence.

The Feminist Model

The feminist model attributes domestic violence to social values that legitimize male control. In this view, violence is a way to maintain male dominance of the family. Feminist programs attempt to raise consciousness about sex-role conditioning and how it influences men's emotions and behavior. These programs use education and skill building to resocialize batterers and help them learn to build relationships based on trust instead of fear. Most feminist approaches also support confronting men about their misuse of power and control tactics.

Detractors of this approach claim that the feminist perspective overemphasizes sociocultural factors to the exclusion of individual factors, such as growing up abused or witnessing family violence. Some observers argue that the feminist approach is too confrontational and alienates the batterer, thereby increasing his hostility.

The Family Systems Model

The family systems model is based on the theory that violent behavior stems from dysfunctional family interactions. It focuses on cultivating communication and conflict resolution skills within the family. According to this model, both partners may contribute to the escalation of conflict, with each attempting to dominate the other. Either partner may resort to violence, although the male's violence will likely have greater consequences. From this perspective, interactions produce violence; therefore, no one is considered to be a perpetrator or victim.

Critics of the family systems model contest the idea that the majority of partner abuse involves shared responsibility. They believe batterers bear full responsibility for the violence. Many also fear that counseling of the couple may place the victim at risk if the woman expresses complaints during a counseling session. This model is not widely used; in fact, couples counseling is expressly prohibited in twenty state standards.

Psychological Approaches

The psychological perspective views abuse as a symptom of underlying emotional problems. This approach emphasizes therapy and counseling to uncover and resolve a batterer's unconscious problems. Proponents of this approach believe that other interventions are superficial and only suppress violence temporarily. Critics argue that attaching psychiatric labels to batterers provides them with an excuse for their behavior.

Cognitive-behavioral group therapy is the most common psychological approach used in batterer intervention programs. This therapy is intended to help individuals function better by changing how they think and act, focusing on skills training and anger management. According to the theory underlying this approach, behaviors are learned as a result of positive and negative reinforcements, and interventions should focus on building skills and changing thought patterns. Feminists criticize this approach, however, saying it fails to explain why intimate partner batterers are not violent in other relationships and why some men continue to abuse women even when their behavior is not rewarded.

Some investigators use the psychological model to study battering behavior. In "Neuropsychological Correlates of Domestic Violence" (*Violence and Victims,* vol. 14, no. 4, Winter 1999), researchers Ronald A. Cohen et al. studied the neurological functioning of thirty-nine male abusers and sixty-three nonviolent subjects to determine whether there was any relationship between neurological functioning and domestic abuse. They divided the groups into men who suffered from head injuries and men who had not, and measured both groups for general intelligence and neurological functioning. The subjects were tested to assess their marital satisfaction and their current level of emotional distress. The subjects were also tested to diagnose antisocial personality disorders.

Cohen et al. found that the batterers had less formal education than the nonbatterers, but that neither group differed in the amount of alcohol they consumed, nor in the number of times they used illegal drugs. The batterers did, however, have past problems with aggression while under the influence of alcohol. The study also revealed a higher incidence of head injury among batterers, with 46.2% of that group reporting head injuries, compared to 20.6% of nonbatterers. In addition, batterers had a higher incidence of prior academic problems.

Batterers with head injuries also showed a higher level of frontal lobe dysfunction, which is among the clinical variables most strongly associated with violence and aggressive behavior. Researchers reported a strong relationship between neurological functioning and domestic violence.

Cohen et al. concluded that brain dysfunction may contribute to the propensity for violence and other aggressive behaviors; however, they cautioned that while dysfunction contributes to the propensity for domestic violence among some batterers, it is not involved in all cases of domestic violence, nor does it explain all types of aggression. Nonetheless, they believe that the relationship between brain dysfunction and domestic violence has significance for planning preventive and therapeutic interventions for some batterers. Patients identified with cognitive defects and with a propensity for aggression may be taught behavioral and cognitive strategies to inhibit aggressive behaviors. The results of this research also indicate the need to investigate the efficacy of biological and pharmacological (prescription drug) treatment of domestic violence.

Content of Batterer Intervention Programs

Among the batterer programs Healy and Smith studied, most combine elements of different theoretical models. They reviewed three mainstream programs. The Duluth Curriculum uses a classroom format and focuses on issues of power and control. The development of criti-

TABLE 6.1

Prevalence of criminal justice incidents involving same victim and perpetrator, 1996

	6 months after assignment[1]	12 months after assignment[2]
26-week batterer treatment (n=129)	7%	10%
8-week batterer treatment (n=61)	15%	25%
Control (community service) (n=186)	22%	26%

[1]Chi-square (2)=12.35, p=.003
[2]Chi-square (2)=13.13,p=.001

SOURCE: Shelly Jackson, Lynette Feder, David R. Forde, Robert C. Davis, Christopher D. Maxwell, and Bruce G. Taylor, "Exhibit 3. Prevalence of Criminal Justice Incidents Involving Same Victim and Perpetrator," in *Batterer Intervention Programs: Where Do We Go From Here?* National Institute of Justice, NCJ 195079, June 2003, http://www.ncjrs.org/pdffiles1/nij/195079.pdf (accessed November 12, 2004)

TABLE 6.2

Attendance in 8- versus 26-week batterers' group, 1996

	No attendance	Some attendance	Graduated
26-week format (n=129)	29%	44%	27%
8-week format (n=61)	23%	10%	67%

SOURCE: Shelly Jackson, Lynette Feder, David R. Forde, Robert C. Davis, Christopher D. Maxwell, and Bruce G. Taylor, "Exhibit 2. Attendance in 8- versus 26-Week Batterers' Group," in *Batterer Intervention Programs: Where Do We Go From Here?* National Institute of Justice, NCJ 195079, June 2003, http://www.ncjrs.org/pdffiles1/nij/195079.pdf (accessed November 12, 2004)

cal thinking skills is emphasized to help batterers understand and change their behavior. In contrast, the other two mainstream models, Emerge and AMEND, involve more in-depth counseling and are of longer duration.

THE DULUTH CURRICULUM. The Duluth model, based on the feminist idea that patriarchal ideology causes domestic violence, was developed in the early 1980s by the Domestic Abuse Intervention Project of Duluth, Minnesota. The classroom curriculum focuses on the development of critical thinking skills relating to the themes of nonviolence, nonthreatening behavior, respect, support, trust, honesty, partnership, negotiation, and fairness. Two or three sessions are devoted to exploring each theme. For example, the first session begins with a video demonstration of specific controlling behaviors. The video is followed by discussion of the actions used by the batterer in the video. Each participant contributes by describing his particular use of the controlling behavior. The group then identifies and discusses alternative behaviors that can build healthier, more equal relationships. Programs based on the Duluth model are the most commonly used batterer invention program in the country, with many states mandating its use.

The National Institute of Justice reported on evaluations of batterer intervention programs based on the Duluth model in "Do Batterer Intervention Programs Work? Two Studies" (NCJ 200331, September 2003). Two studies based in New York and Florida found that the programs had little or no effect on subsequent domestic violence, and that the programs did not change batterers' attitudes toward women and battering. The New York study, conducted in 1996, did find that men assigned to a longer, twenty-six-week program were less likely to be arrested again within twelve months than men assigned to an eight-week, accelerated program. (See Table 6.1.) However, men were much more likely to graduate from the shorter program than the longer program, illustrating the problem of high drop-out rates in implementing effective batterer intervention programs. (See Table 6.2.)

EMERGE. Emerge, a forty-eight-week batterer intervention program in Cambridge, Massachusetts, combines several different models. It begins with eight weeks of educational and skill-building sessions. Program members who complete this phase and admit to domestic violence then progress to an ongoing group that blends cognitive behavioral techniques with group therapy centered on personal accountability.

In the group, new members describe the events and actions that brought them to the program, answer questions about their behavior, and accept responsibility for their violence. Regular group members also talk about their actions during the previous week. There may also be discussion of particular incidents disclosed by members of the group.

David Adams, the president and cofounder of Emerge, considers battering any act that forces the victim to do something she does not want to do, prevents her from doing something she wants to do, or causes her to be afraid. He views violence as not simply a series of isolated blowups, but a process of deliberate intimidation intended to coerce the victim to comply with the victimizer's wishes. According to Adams, the abuser's high level of control can be seen in how agreeable he can be with police, bosses, neighbors, and others with whom it is in his best interest to appear reasonable.

Even though abusive men in the program are supposed to be working on their relationships, Emerge counselors have observed that the men devalue and denigrate their partners. Ellen Pence, who helped to develop the Duluth Curriculum, noticed that men rarely call the women they abuse by name, because they refuse to see them as people in their own right. In one group session, she counted ninety-seven references to women, many of them obscene, before someone used his partner's name. When Pence insisted program participants use the names of their partners, she reported that many could hardly speak.

Emerge focuses not only on the abusive behavior, but also on the broader relationship between the batterer and the victim. Each member formulates goals related to his control tactics, and the group helps him develop ways to address these concerns. It combines a psycho-educational curriculum, cognitive-behavioral therapy, and an assessment of the needs of the individual.

AMEND. The professionals who created AMEND (Abusive Men Exploring New Directions), a program in Denver, Colorado, share the same commitment to long-term treatment based on several treatment models as the founders of Emerge. The purpose of AMEND is to establish client accountability, increase awareness of the social context of battering, and build new social skills. AMEND group leaders serve as "moral guides" who take a firm position against violence and vigorously describe their clients' behavior as unacceptable and illegal.

The program's long-term approach has four stages. The first two stages consist of several months of education and confrontation to break through the batterer's denial and resistance. Several months of advanced group therapy follow during which the batterer identifies his own rationalizations for abusive behavior and admits the truth about his actions. This stage includes ongoing contact of program leaders with the abused partner, who can reveal relapses or more subtle forms of abuse. During this stage, the client develops a plan that includes participation in a support network to prevent future violence. The fourth stage, which is optional, consists of involvement in community service and political action to stop domestic violence.

SAN DIEGO NAVY EXPERIMENT: THE COGNITIVE-BEHAVIORAL APPROACH. In the study "The San Diego Navy Experiment: An Assessment of Interventions for Men Who Assault Their Wives" (*Journal of Consulting and Clinical Psychology,* vol. 68, no. 3, June 2000), Franklyn W. Dunford compared three different year-long interventions for men who had physically assaulted their wives. The study involved randomly assigning 861 couples to one of four groups: a men's group, a conjoint group (men and women), a rigorously monitored group, and a control group. The men's and conjoint groups received cognitive-behavioral therapy and outcomes were measured every six months.

The men's group met weekly for six months, and then monthly for the second six months. Group leaders covered a wide range of perpetrator attitudes and values and taught skills believed to be important to ending the abuse of women, such as empathy and communication skills, as well as anger and jealousy management. Along with instruction, participants practiced their newly acquired skills and developed plans to assume complete responsibility for their behavior.

Employing the same curriculum used by the men's group, the conjoint group, composed of victims and perpetrators, was a controversial treatment approach since most conventional programs do not believe it is useful or effective to treat victims and their abusers together. But the leaders were interested in finding out if couple therapy would be effective. They also anticipated some benefits from the presence of the wives, such as less "women bashing" within the context of the group and more realistic opportunities to engage participants in role-playing to help them practice more constructive behaviors.

The rigorous monitoring intervention aimed to inhibit abuse by making service members' commanding officers aware of every instance of abuse. By closely monitoring and reporting their behavior, this approach attempted to increase scrutiny of the perpetrators' lives, creating a situation Dunford called a "fishbowl" effect.

Men assigned to the control group received no treatment; however, to ensure their wives' safety, the wives were given preliminary stabilization and safety planning counseling to help prevent additional instances of abuse.

The results of the interventions were measured, controlling for demographic variables—age, rank, family size, ethnicity, education, and income—and outcome assessments. Outcomes were evaluated using self-reports and spouse reports, and the Modified Conflict Tactics Scale, which examined forty-two aspects relating to the type and frequency of abuse. Official police and court records, as well as reports of new injuries, were also considered as outcome measures.

The study found no significant differences in the prevalence or frequency of abuse, as reported by the wives or their spouses, between the treatment groups. No significant differences were found among the four groups in Modified Conflict Tactics Scale scores. The study also found no differences in terms of new arrests among the perpetrators in all four groups. These findings suggest that none of the three treatment approaches was any more effective at reducing abuse than participation in the control group.

Dunford concluded that the cognitive-behavioral model is ineffective as an intervention for spouse abuse, at least in this military setting. He called for further research to confirm his study's findings and hypothesized that the one-size-fits-all approach to treatment may be responsible for the ineffectiveness of treatment.

TREATMENT OF TYPES OF BATTERERS

Most observers conclude that a single intervention program cannot accommodate the staggering diversity of batterers. Unlike mainstream programs, innovative approaches focus on the individual profile and characteristics of a batterer, and some programs tailor their interventions to the various categories of batterers.

The criminal justice system, for example, categorizes offenders based on their potential danger, history of substance abuse, psychological problems, and risk of dropout and re-arrest. Interventions focus on the specific type of batterer and the approach that will most effectively produce results, such as linking a substance abuse treatment program with a batterer intervention program. Other program approaches focus on specific sociocultural characteristics, such as poverty, race, ethnicity, and age. Researcher Shelly Jackson argues that the effectiveness of batterer intervention programs might improve if the programs were seen as "part of a broader criminal justice and community response to domestic violence that includes arrest, restraining orders, intensive monitoring of batterers, and changes to social norms that may inadvertently tolerate partner violence." She was co-author, with Lynette Feder, David R. Forde, Robert C. Davis, Christopher D. Maxwell, and Bruce G. Taylor, of "Analyzing the Studies" (*Batterer Intervention Programs: Where Do We Go From Here?* [Washington, DC: National Institute of Justice, NCJ 195079, June 2003]).

One program that focuses on individualizing batterer treatment, currently in use in Somerset, New Jersey, is based on the Cultural Context Model, an intervention method that acknowledges a cultural basis for battering among some ethnic groups. While this treatment model requires accountability from batterers and supports the empowerment of abused spouses and their children, it also recognizes the impact that social forces have in cultures where battering is considered acceptable.

Rhea V. Ameida and Ken Dolan-Delvecchio contend that the impact of culture is often overlooked or minimized by people who work with batterers in traditional treatment programs. In "Addressing Culture in Batterers Intervention: The Asian Indian Community as an Illustrative Example" (*Violence against Women,* vol. 5, no. 6, June 1999), Ameida and Dolan-Delvecchio suggested that if program workers were trained in cultural differences, they would be better able to serve the needs of both the abuser and his family. The Cultural Context Model works by providing treatment not only to the batterer, but also to the victims of abuse, generally in a family therapy atmosphere.

As part of their therapy, participants are shown videos that illustrate abusive situations and are encouraged to talk about the video incidents and their own instances of abuse. The participants then study power and control wheel illustrations, which give them graphic, visual perspectives about how a variety of factors interact to create abusive situations. The treatment model attempts to reeducate the abused and abuser by raising their consciousness about gender, race, culture, and sexual orientation. One desired outcome of this therapy, Ameida and Dolan-Delvecchio explained, is to make participants more aware of the social impact of their actions.

Program Procedures

Regardless of an intervention program's philosophy or methods, program directors and criminal justice professionals generally monitor the offenders' behavior closely. Most batterers enter intervention programs after having been charged by the police with a specific incident of abuse. As a requirement of probation, most courts will order a batterer into an intervention program.

At the court, the batterer is first interviewed to determine the type of program that may be most effective. Known as an "intake assessment," this process may take as long as eight weeks. During this time, the batterer agrees to the terms of the program, his behavior is assessed, and he is screened for other problems, such as substance abuse or mental illness. If other problems are detected, he may be referred to a program or treatment that specifically addresses those issues. Not all batterers are accepted at intake. Some programs consider batterers inappropriate for treatment if they deny having committed violence.

Several states require that the victim be notified at various points of the intervention, and programs with a strong advocacy policy contact victims every two or three months. Victims may be asked for additional information about the relationship, given information about the program's goals and methods, and helped with safety planning. In addition, the batterer's counselor will inform the victim if further abuse appears imminent.

Batterers leave the program either because of successful completion or because they are asked to leave. Reasons for termination include failure to cooperate, nonpayment of fees, revocation of parole or probation, failure to attend group sessions regularly, or violation of program rules. Successful completion of a program means that the offender has attended the required sessions and accomplished the program's objectives. With court-mandated clients, a final report also is made to probation officials.

The Criminal Justice Response

To be successful, batterer intervention programs must have the support of the criminal justice system, which includes coordinated efforts between police, prosecutors, judges, victim advocates, and probation officers. Healey and Smith suggested that authorities can reinforce the message that battering is a crime and further support the efforts of batterer programs by taking the following steps:

- expediting domestic violence cases though the court system

- using special domestic violence prosecution and probation units and centralizing dockets where all aspects of domestic violence may be managed in one location in order to improve services to victims and better coordinate prosecution, sentencing, and supervision

- gathering offender information quickly, including previous arrests and convictions, substance abuse history, child welfare contacts, and victim information

- taking advantage of culturally competent or specialized interventions and finding appropriate interventions for batterers who are indigent, high-risk, or mentally ill

- coordinating batterer intervention with substance abuse treatment and mandate treatment where appropriate, making sure it is monitored intensively

- being alert to the risks to children in abusive households by coordinating with child protective services to ensure that the batterer's children are safe and receiving appropriate services

- creating a continuum of support and protection for victims by using victim advocates to assist victims with the criminal justice system and to monitor their safety while their batterers are sentenced to treatment programs

- encouraging interagency cooperation by organizing formal committees of probation officers, prosecutors, battered women advocates, child protection workers, and batterer intervention providers to discuss referral and monitoring policies

Post-traumatic Stress Disorder and Shame

Donald Dutton, a psychology professor and author of *The Batterer: A Psychological Profile* (New York: Basic Books, 1995), found that many of his clients suffered the same symptoms manifested in post-traumatic stress disorder (PTSD), a psychological response to extreme trauma. These symptoms include depression, anxiety, sleep disturbances, disassociation, flashbacks, and out-of-body experiences. Dutton's batterers had psychological profiles surprisingly similar to Vietnam War veterans who had been diagnosed with PTSD. Dutton argued that although abusers are rarely seen as victims, their psychological profiles reveal they have been victimized and suffered trauma. He wrote that the batterers' chronic anger and abusiveness pointed to a common source of early childhood trauma.

Researching his clients' childhood experiences, Dutton determined that the crucial factor in abusive behavior is the shame the men suffered as children. Dutton defined shame as an emotional response to an attack on the global sense of self. The men Dutton studied had experienced childhoods in which they had been continually humiliated, embarrassed, and shamed. He found that physical abuse alone did not predict later abusive behavior, but that the combination of shame and abuse was a dangerous mix.

According to Dutton, shame attacks a child's entire identity and teaches the child that he is worthless. Punishing a child at random also poses a serious attack on his identity. Because the punishment does not relate to a particular behavior, it teaches the child that his very being is wrong and unlovable. The child has no outlet for his rage and shame until he enters an intimate relationship. When

his bravado—the "tough guy" mask—is threatened, he responds with rage. The shame of his rage is too great to bear, so he blames the woman and the destructive pattern is established.

Dutton listed the early childhood experiences he believes make the strongest contributions to predicting wife assault in order of importance: feeling rejected by one's father, a lack of warmth from one's father, physical abuse from one's father, verbal abuse by one's father, and feeling rejected by one's mother.

Abuser Types

Research has increasingly focused on differing types of male batterers. Daniel G. Saunders, in "A Typology of Men Who Batter: Three Types Derived from Cluster Analysis" (*American Journal of Orthopsychiatry,* vol. 62, no. 2, 1992), surveyed 165 abusive men, using such psychological measures as childhood victimization, severity of violence, psychological abuse, domestic decision making, level of conflict, anger, jealousy, depression, the ability to make a good impression on others, and alcohol use. His pioneering work defined three types of batterers:

- Type I men are characterized as "family-only" aggressors. These men report low levels of anger, depression, and jealousy, and are the least likely to have been severely abused as children. They claim the most satisfaction in their relationships, the least marital conflict, and the least psychological abuse. Their violence is associated with alcohol about half the time. Members of this group suppress their anger until alcohol or stress triggers its release.

- Type II men are "generally violent" and are the most likely to be violent inside and outside the home. The majority have been severely abused as children, yet they report low levels of depression and anger. Their lower anger may reflect an attitude of "I don't get mad, I get even." Their violence is usually associated with alcohol, and they report the most frequent severe violence. Their attitudes about sex roles are more rigid than those of Type I men.

- Type III men report the highest levels of anger, depression, and jealousy. They are characterized as "emotionally volatile" aggressors. They are most likely to fear losing their partners and feel suicidal and angry. These men are not as physically aggressive as Type II men, but they are the most psychologically abusive and the least satisfied with their relationships. They also have the most rigid sex-role attitudes. About half of these men have previously received counseling and are thought to be the most likely to complete treatment.

Based on these three categories of batterers, Saunders proposed different types of counseling that would be most effective for each type. The family-only aggressor, Type I, might gain the most from an emphasis on the communication aspects of assertiveness training. He needs to learn how to express anger and understand his rights. He may be helped by couples counseling if his past violence level is low enough and if he remains nonviolent and committed to the relationship.

The Type II man may need help dealing with the psychic wounds of his childhood, stopping his abuse of alcohol, and learning how to express his feelings rather than by exploding. He also needs to recognize that his rigid sex-role notions are harmful. Saunders proposed that this type of abuser will probably require more than the standard three- to six-month treatment program.

The emotionally volatile man, Type III, must learn to express his feelings in nonaggressive ways and to accept his "weaker" feelings of jealousy and depression rather than express them through anger. He also needs to understand the damage caused by his psychological abuse and rigid sex-role beliefs.

In a follow-up study titled "Feminist-Cognitive-Behavioral and Process-Psychodynamic Treatments for Men Who Batter," Saunders went a step further than other researchers have done (*Violence and Victims,* vol. 4, 1996). While other researchers have hypothesized that identifying subtypes of batterers may help identify which treatments would be most effective for each type, Saunders actually evaluated different treatments for different types of batterers. He found that antisocial batterers did better in cognitive-behavioral group therapy, and "dependent" batterers did better in a new, psychodynamic treatment setting.

Survey of Typologies of Male Batterers

Amy Holtzworth-Munroe and Gregory L. Stuart reviewed fifteen studies of typologies of male batterers, including the Saunders study, and found that three dimensions of battering were generally used to distinguish among subtypes of batterers: severity of marital violence, whether the violence was directed at people other than the intimate partner, and the presence of personality disorders. They reported their findings in "Typologies of Male Batterers: Three Subtypes and the Differences Among Them" (*Psychological Bulletin,* vol. 116, no. 3, 1994). They synthesized the studies to propose a typology of three types of batterers: family only, dysphoric/borderline personality, and generally violent/antisocial.

In the researchers' conceptualization, family-only batterers are the least violent both in and outside the home. They do not suffer from personality disorders or other psychological disorders, they have low levels of abuse in their childhoods, and they have low levels of hostile attitudes toward women. Dysphoric/borderline batterers engage in moderate to severe abuse of their partners. They likely were abused themselves in childhood and are

psychologically distressed. They do not engage in violence outside the home. Violent/antisocial abusers engage in moderate to severe wife battering and exhibit violence outside the home, have hostile attitudes toward women, and are most likely to abuse substances and engage in other criminal behaviors.

Holtzworth-Munroe and other researchers later conducted a study titled "Testing the Holtzworth-Munroe and Stuart (1994) Batterer Typology" (*Journal of Consulting and Clinical Psychology,* vol. 68, 2000). It generally validated the initial hypotheses. The researchers conducted a follow-up study to determine whether batterer characteristics were stable over time; in other words, did batterers continue to differ on the individual characteristics related to intimate partner violence across time? Holtzworth-Munroe et al. went on in "Do Sub-Types of Maritally Violent Men Continue to Differ over Time?" to find that in fact, relationship violence is related to stable individual characteristics (the typologies) of the men (*Journal of Consulting and Clinical Psychology,* vol. 71, 2003).

Personality Differences and Treatment

Robert J. White and Edward W. Gondolf, in "Implications of Personality Profiles for Batterer Treatment," classified battering men by personality types with the intent to recommend treatment approaches for each type (*Journal of Interpersonal Violence,* vol. 15, May 2000). They found three levels of personality pathology that they characterized as low, moderate, and severe personality dysfunction. They also found that most batterers fell into one of two groups that cut across the personality types: narcissistic (overly focused on themselves) and avoidant/depressive.

The researchers argued that most batterers, whether avoidant or narcissistic, did not suffer from severe personality dysfunction and were therefore good candidates for cognitive-behavioral group therapy. This treatment could help the batterers with self-image problems as well as provide feedback to correct distorted thinking about relationships. The researchers stated that men with more severe personality problems (as many as 15% of batterers) would need additional attention within the group and possibly individualized psychological treatment. The researchers believed that the approach of different treatments for different batterers is overemphasized: "It appears that although one size does not fit all, one size appears to fit most," they wrote.

PROGRAM DROPOUT RATES

Dropout rates in battering programs are high, even though courts have ordered most clients to attend. Several studies indicate that 20% to 30% of the men who begin short-term treatment programs do not complete them. A 1990 survey of thirty programs of differing lengths found a wide range in completion rates. Half of the programs reported completion rates of 50% or less. If dropout rates are based on attendance at the intake session, rather than the first treatment session, noncompletion rates are even higher. A 1999 study that documented the dropout rate after the initial assessment found that 59% of those who completed the initial assessment never attended a single session and that 75% dropped out before the ten-week program was over.

High dropout rates in batterer intervention programs make it difficult to evaluate their success. Evaluations based on men who complete these programs focus on a very select group of highly motivated men who likely do not reflect the composition of the group when it began. Since a follow-up is not conducted with program dropouts, the men most likely to continue their violence, research generally fails to accurately indicate the success or failure of a given treatment program.

Certain characteristics are generally related to dropout rates. Bruce Dalton, in "Batterer Characteristics and Treatment Completion," found that the level of threat that the batterer perceived from the referral source (for example, the court) was, surprisingly, not related to program completion (*Journal of Interpersonal Violence,* vol. 16, December 2001). Unemployment is the one characteristic most consistently related to dropping out of treatment. Dalton theorized that these men both have trouble paying for the treatment and have a lower investment in the "official social order."

Other researchers have found that factors influencing completion rates of batterer intervention programs include youth, not being legally married, low income and little education, unstable work histories, criminal backgrounds, and excessive drinking or drug abuse. Voluntary clients, especially those with college educations, remain in treatment longer. Some researchers have found better attendance among college-educated men, regardless of whether their enrollment in a program is court ordered or voluntary. Such findings were reported by A. DeMaris in "Attrition in Batterers' Counseling: The Role of Social and Demographic Factors" (*Social Service Review,* Vol. 63, 1989); E. W. Gondolf in "A Comparison of Four Batterer Intervention Systems: Do Court Referral, Program Length, and Services Matter?" (*Journal of Interpersonal Violence,* Vol. 14, Issue 1, 1999); and J. Jacobs in *The Links between Substance Misuse and Domestic Violence: Current Knowledge and Debates* (London: Institute for the Study of Drug Dependence, 1999).

Nearly all professionals involved in domestic violence prevention and treatment programs concur that batterer intervention programs must address the issue of dropouts. Reducing or eliminating intake sessions and immediately engaging batterers in useful interventions may help to promote attendance and participation by immediately engaging participants in the treatment program. Counselors should provide more information about the purpose of the program in the preprogram orientation sessions. Other suggested retention measures include courtroom assistance, mentors, and stiffer and quicker punishment for dropouts. One study found that home visits after a batterer misses a meeting also help decrease dropout rates. Researchers on this subject include Bruce Dalton in "Batterer Characteristics and Treatment Completion" (*Journal of Interpersonal Violence,* Vol. 16, No. 12, December 2001) and A. DeMaris in "Attrition in Batterers' Counseling: The Role of Social and Demographic Factors" (*Social Service Review,* Vol. 63, 1989).

RECIDIVISM RATES

Recidivism, the tendency to relapse to old ingrained patterns of behavior, is a well-documented problem among persons in intimate partner violence treatment programs. In "Pattern of Reassault in Batterer Programs" (*Violence and Victims,* vol. 12, no. 4, 1997), Edward Gondolf reported his evaluation of four well-established batterer programs to assess the pattern of reassault or a return to battering. All the research sites had operated for five years or more and received at least forty to fifty referrals per month. Located in Pittsburgh, Pennsylvania; Denver, Colorado; and Dallas and Houston, Texas, the programs ranged from three to nine months in duration.

Of the 840 batterers recruited, 210 at each site, 82% were referred to the program by court order, and 18% entered the program voluntarily. Both batterers and their partners were interviewed by phone every three months for fifteen months after intake. The female partners of 79% of the batterers were interviewed at least once during the fifteen-month follow-up.

In follow-up reports on 662 batterers, 32% of the female partners reported at least one reassault during the fifteen months after treatment. Of the 210 reassault cases, 61% resulted in bruises or injuries, and 12% of victims required medical attention. The reassault rate was significantly higher for program dropouts than for participants who completed the program. Voluntary participants were also more likely to reassault their partners than court-ordered participants.

While the proportion of women who were reassaulted was relatively low, 70% of the women were subjected to verbal abuse, 45% were subjected to controlling behaviors, and 43% experienced threats. Nonetheless, 66% of the women said their "quality of life" had improved, and 73% reported feeling "very safe" during the follow-up periods.

Fourteen percent of first-time reassaults occurred in the first three months of the program, and 8% occurred within four to six months. Early reassault appeared to be a high-risk marker for continued abuse. Men who reassaulted their partners within the first three months were much more likely to repeat their attacks than were men who reassaulted for the first time after the first three months. The repeat offenders were also highly likely to use severe tactics and inflict injuries. Gondolf speculated that intervention may have been less effective for this group of men because of previous contact with the criminal justice system and/or severe psychological disorders.

Gondolf concluded that well-established programs seem to contribute to the cessation of assault, at least in the short term. For "resistant batterers," he recommended more extensive monitoring and intervention.

Other Studies

Saunders, in "Husbands Who Assault: Multiple Profiles Requiring Multiple Responses," reviewed the available information on male batterers and found that the recurrence of violence six months or more after treatment averages 35% across a number of studies (*Legal Response to Wife Assault*, [Newbury Park, CA: Sage, 1993]). For men who do not complete treatment, the average reassault rate is 52%. The men most likely to return to violence are on average younger, report alcohol problems, score higher for narcissism (excessive self-involvement) on psychological tests, and have longer histories of pretreatment violence.

Julia C. Babcock and Ramalina Steiner reported some cautiously optimistic findings in "The Relationship between Treatment, Incarceration, and Recidivism of Battering: A Program Evaluation of Seattle's Coordinated Community Response to Domestic Violence" (*Journal of Family Psychology*, vol. 13, no. 1, March 1999). Their research measured recidivism of domestic violence after arrest and completion or noncompletion of a mandatory, coordinated program of treatment involving the courts, probation officers, and treatment providers.

Babcock and Steiner followed 387 people arrested for misdemeanor domestic violence offences, thirty-one of whom were women. More than three-quarters of participants had no prior domestic violence convictions and 69% had no prior criminal history. The average age of participants was 32.7 years, 45% had graduated from high school, and 36% had attended college or were college graduates. About 41% of participants were white, 36% were African American, 6.6% were Hispanic, 8.6% were Asian American, and 7.8% identified themselves as "other." Half of the participants were employed and 31% were married.

Participants were referred to one of eleven certified domestic violence treatment programs. The majority attended programs that use the Duluth model, while the remainder participated in feminist, psychoeducational, and cognitive-behavioral men's groups. About 31% completed at least twenty-four sessions of treatment, and those batterers considered to have completed treatment attended an average of thirty-two sessions. In contrast, batterers who did not complete treatment attended an average of just 5.8 sessions. Treatment completers were generally first-time offenders, better educated, employed, and had less prior criminal involvement. Of the noncompleters, 58% did not attend any sessions, but the majority were not legally punished, despite their failure to attend court-ordered treatment.

Program completion was related to lower rates of recidivism—treatment completers had significantly fewer domestic violence arrests at follow-up than noncompleters, and this difference remained even when the researchers controlled for differences in prior criminal record and history. Batterers who had been court ordered to attend treatment and failed to complete it were more likely to commit further offenses than treatment completers. Babcock and Steiner concluded that their findings support the premise that completing treatment is directly related to reduced rates of domestic violence. They cautioned, however, that participants who completed treatment were probably not representative of the entire population of batterers—they likely had more to lose as a result of failure to complete treatment than the treatment dropouts.

Jill A. Gordon and Laura J. Moriarty in their study of the effect of batterer treatment on recidivism reported more pessimistic results ("The Effects of Domestic Violence Batterer Treatment on Domestic Violence Recidivism," *Criminal Justice and Behavior*, vol. 30, February 2003). They found that attending treatment had no impact on recidivism when comparing the treatment group as a whole with the experimental group. However, they also found that among the treatment group, the more sessions a batterer completed, the less likely he was to batter again. Batterers who completed all sessions were less likely to be rearrested for domestic violence than were batterers who had not completed all sessions.

CHAPTER 7
THE RESPONSE OF LAW ENFORCEMENT TO VIOLENCE AND ABUSE

THE POLICE RESPONSE

The police are often an abuse victim's initial contact with the judicial system, making the police response particularly important. The manner in which the police handle a domestic violence complaint will likely color the way the victim views the entire judicial system. Not surprisingly, when police project the blame for intimate partner violence on victims, the victims may be reluctant to report further abuse.

According to the 2002 National Crime Victimization Survey (NCVS), the police came to the aid of victims for about three-quarters (76%) of all violent crimes. In about two-thirds of incidents of rape and sexual assault, police came to victims (63.8%); 12.4% of victims went to police. Table 7.1 shows that police came to the aid of more victims of aggravated assault, simple assault, and robbery than victims of rape and sexual assault.

Family disturbance calls constitute the majority of calls received by police departments throughout the country, and historically such calls have not been taken seriously. In the mid-1960s, Detroit police dispatchers were instructed to screen out family disturbance calls unless they suspected "excessive" violence. A 1975 police guide, *The Function of the Police in Crisis Intervention and Conflict Management,* taught officers to avoid arrest at all costs and to discourage the victim from pressing charges by emphasizing the consequences of testifying in court, the potential loss of income, and other detrimental aspects of prosecution.

Arrest policies have changed significantly in the past twenty-five years. By 2002 all but one state (West Virginia) had moved to authorize probable cause arrests— arrest before the completion of the investigation of the alleged violation or crime—without a warrant in domestic violence cases. Police departments have adopted pro-arrest or mandatory arrest policies. Pro-arrest strategies include a range of sanctions from issuing a warning, to mandated treatment, to prison time.

WHO CALLS THE POLICE?

In the past, most women did not report incidents of abuse to the police. Several studies estimate that only about 10% of battering incidents are ever reported to authorities. The 1985 National Family Violence Survey found that only 6.7% of all husband-to-wife assaults were reported to police. When the assaults are categorized by severity as measured on a Conflict Tactics Scale, only 3.2% of minor violence cases and 14.4% of severe violence cases were reported.

There is some evidence that over time, slightly higher percentages of female victims have reported instances of intimate partner violence to the police. In "The 'Drunken Bum' Theory of Wife Beating" (*Physical Violence in American Families* [Piscataway, NJ: Transaction, 1990]), Glenda Kaufman Kantor and Murray Straus estimated that between 7% and 14% of intimate partner assaults are reported to police. A 1995 study using National Crime Victimization Survey data made the most optimistic projections, estimating that 56% of battering incidents were reported to the police. By 2002 the estimate drawn from the NCVS data was that slightly more than half of female victims filed police reports.

The women who chose not to report their abuse cited a variety of reasons, including fear of retaliation, loss of income, or loss of their children to child protection authorities. When abuse is reported to law enforcement agencies, it is often by health care professionals from whom the woman has sought treatment for her injuries. In many states, health professionals are mandated by law to report all instances of domestic violence to law enforcement authorities.

In an examination of the law enforcement response to mandated reporting by health professionals, Laura E. Lund surveyed domestic violence experts at thirty-nine police agencies in California. Her resulting report is titled "What Happens when Health Practitioners Report Domestic Vio-

TABLE 7.1

Percent distribution of police response to a reported incident, by type of crime, 2002

Type of crime	Number of incidents	Percent of incidents						
		Total	Police came to victim	Victim went to police	Contact with police—don't know how	Police did not come	Not known if police came	Police were at the scene
Crimes of violence	2,252,570	100%	76.0%	5.9%	0.0%[1]	12.5%	1.6%	3.9%
Rape/sexual assault[2]	133,130	100	63.8	11.4[1]	0.0[1]	20.7[1]	2.4[1]	1.8[1]
Robbery	315,980	100	80.7	8.5[1]	0.0[1]	8.0[1]	0.9[1]	1.9[1]
Aggravated assault	446,860	100	84.5	3.7[1]	0.0[1]	6.7[1]	0.4[1]	4.7[1]
Simple assault	1,356,600	100	73.4	5.4	0.0[1]	14.7	2.2[1]	4.3
Purse snatching/pocket picking	72,040	100	47.6	21.6[1]	0.0[1]	27.8[1]	3.0[1]	0.0[1]
Property crimes	6,909,730	100%	67.3%	5.1%	0.0%[1]	24.4%	1.9%	1.2%
Household burglary	1,726,780	100	85.4	2.4	0.0[1]	10.2	1.4[1]	0.6[1]
Motor vehicle theft	822,620	100	73.6	3.9	0.0[1]	17.6	2.0[1]	2.9[1]
Theft	4,360,330	100	58.9	6.5	0.0[1]	31.3	2.2	1.2

Note: Detail may not add to total shown because of rounding.
[1]Estimate is based on about 10 or fewer sample cases.
[2]Includes verbal threats of rape and threats of sexual assault.

SOURCE: "Table 106. Personal and Property Crimes, 2002: Percent Distribution of Police Response to a Reported Incident, by Type of Crime," in *Criminal Victimization in the United States, 2002 Statistical Tables,* U.S. Department of Justice, Bureau of Justice Statistics, National Crime Victimization Survey, 2002, http://www.ojp.usdoj.gov/bjs/abstract/cvusst.htm (accessed October 12, 2004)

lence Injuries to the Police? A Study of the Law Enforcement Response to Injury Reports" (*Violence and Victims,* vol. 14, no. 2, September 1999). She found that almost all had standard procedures for responding to domestic violence reports from health practitioners. But while the law mandates health practitioners to make these reports by telephone and in writing, she found that fewer than one-quarter of the police agencies consistently received both types of reports from health care providers.

Lund questioned whether California law enforcement agencies have adequate policies and procedures in place to respond to domestic violence complaints from health practitioners. Of the thirty-nine law enforcement agencies, thirty reported that when they receive a handwritten domestic violence report from a health care provider, they first search their own records to see whether the case is already under investigation. Many agencies also search for previous domestic violence cases or other crimes involving the alleged perpetrator.

Twenty-five law enforcement agencies said that if the health care professional does not report the abuse by telephone, it may be days or even weeks before police receive a handwritten abuse report. Often, the agencies noted, the reports lack essential information, such as a contact number for the victim, making it very difficult for investigators to match the incident with a crime report. In many cases the written reports from health practitioners cannot be matched to a previous report of an incident.

Most law enforcement agencies said they do attempt to conduct investigations when they receive these reports, known as "unmatched reports." The most common agency response to unmatched reports was to contact the victims. Fifteen agencies said this was their usual response or their

only response to unmatched reports. Only two of the fifteen agencies responded that they also attempt to contact the health practitioner who made the report and only one agency said it sends an officer to talk to the victim if the health practitioner provides an address but no phone number. It was unusual for agencies to have a policy of dispatching an officer based on an unmatched health practitioner report.

Lund argued that because law enforcement agencies receive relatively few health practitioner reports, with most of the reports received originating in hospital emergency rooms, problems exist in the implementation of mandatory reporting. The scarcity of the reports may be due, in part, to a lack of understanding of the law by health professionals, insufficient training in reporting techniques, or an unwillingness to report.

Lund also faulted police responses to reports from health practitioners, asserting that simply to report and respond is not adequate. Rather, health practitioners must report effectively and agencies must respond appropriately in order to help, rather than harm, domestic violence victims.

NATIONAL CRIME VICTIMIZATION SURVEYS

The National Crime Victimization Surveys (NCVS) are ongoing, nationwide surveys that gather data on criminal victimizations from a national sample of eighty thousand household respondents, ages twelve and older. The surveys provide a biannual estimate of crimes experienced by the public, whether or not a law enforcement agency was contacted about the crime.

It is well established that much intimate partner violence is unreported or underreported. Using seven years of data from the NCVS, statistician Callie Rennison

TABLE 7.2

Percent distribution of victimizations, by type of crime and whether or not reported to the police, 2002

		Percent of victimizations reported to the police			
Sector and type of crime	Number of victimizations	Total	Yes[2]	No	Not known and not available
All crimes	**23,036,030**	**100%**	**42.2%**	**56.5%**	**1.3%**
Personal crimes	**5,496,810**	**100%**	**48.4%**	**49.8%**	**1.7%**
Crimes of violence	5,341,410	100	48.5	49.7	1.8
Completed violence	1,753,090	100	60.4	39.0	0.6[1]
Attempted/threatened violence	3,588,320	100	42.7	55.0	2.3
Rape/sexual assault	247,730	100	53.7	46.3	0.0[1]
Rape/attempted rape	167,860	100	56.6	43.4	0.0[1]
Rape	90,390	100	57.3	42.7	0.0[1]
Attempted rape[3]	77,470	100	55.8	44.2	0.0[1]
Sexual assault[4]	79,870	100	47.8	52.2	0.0[1]
Robbery	512,490	100	71.2	28.3	0.5[1]
Completed/property taken	385,880	100	75.8	23.6	0.7[1]
With injury	169,980	100	79.8	20.2	0.0[1]
Without injury	215,890	100	72.6	26.2	1.2[1]
Attempted to take property	126,610	100	57.4	42.6	0.0[1]
With injury	42,600	100	92.6	7.4[1]	0.0[1]
Without injury	84,020	100	39.5	60.5	0.0[1]
Assault	4,581,190	100	45.7	52.3	2.0
Aggravated	990,110	100	56.6	40.5	2.8[1]
With injury	316,260	100	61.3	38.7	0.0[1]
Threatened with weapon	673,850	100	54.5	41.4	4.2[1]
Simple	3,591,090	100	42.7	55.6	1.8
With minor injury	906,580	100	54.8	44.2	1.0[1]
Without injury	2,684,510	100	38.6	59.4	2.1
Purse snatching/pocket picking	155,400	100	46.4	53.6	0.0[1]
Completed purse snatching	55,400	100	74.5	25.5[1]	0.0[1]
Attempted purse snatching	2,140[1]	100[1]	100.0[1]	0.0[1]	0.0[1]
Pocket picking	97,860	100	29.3[1]	70.7	0.0[1]
Property crimes	**17,539,220**	**100%**	**40.2%**	**58.6%**	**1.2%**
Household burglary	3,055,720	100	57.9	41.4	0.7[1]
Completed	2,597,310	100	58.8	40.4	0.8[1]
Forcible entry	1,017,660	100	77.2	21.7	1.1[1]
Unlawful entry without force	1,579,650	100	46.9	52.5	0.0[1]
Attempted forcible entry	458,410	100	52.9	47.1	0.0[1]
Motor vehicle theft	988,760	100	86.1	13.5	0.5[1]
Completed	780,630	100	95.8	3.9[1]	0.3[1]
Attempted	208,120	100	49.4	49.5	1.1[1]
Theft	13,494,750	100	32.8	65.8	1.4
Completed	13,039,920	100	32.7	65.9	1.4
Less than $50	4,186,570	100	17.1	81.8	1.1
$50–$249	4,455,080	100	28.3	70.6	1.1
$250 or more	3,270,530	100	56.4	42.8	0.8[1]
Amount not available	1,127,740	100	39.5	55.0	5.5
Attempted	454,830	100	36.5	62.5	1.0[1]

Note: Detail may not add to total shown because of rounding.
[1]Estimate is based on about 10 or fewer sample cases.
[2]Figures in this column represent the rates at which victimizations were reported to the police, or "police reporting rates."
[3]Includes verbal threats of rape.
[4]Includes threats.

SOURCE: "Table 91. Personal and Property Crimes, 2002: Percent Distribution of Victimizations, by Type of Crime and Whether or Not Reported to the Police," in *Criminal Victimization in the United States, 2002 Statistical Tables,* U.S. Department of Justice, Bureau of Justice Statistics, National Crime Victimization Survey, 2002, http://www.ojp.usdoj.gov/bjs/abstract/cvusst.htm (accessed October 12, 2004)

examined trends, including police notification, in *Intimate Partner Violence and Age of Victim, 1993–99* (Washington, DC: Bureau of Justice Statistics, 2001). She found that nearly three-quarters of intimate partner violence against females aged twelve to fifteen is not reported to police, and more than half of females aged sixteen to nineteen and over fifty do not make police reports.

According to the 2002 NCVS, about half of the victims of rape or sexual assault (53.7%) report the crime to the police. (See Table 7.2.) Women are more likely to report violent victimizations involving strangers (65.7%) than nonstrangers (51.2%). (See Table 7.3.) The survey also found that black females are more likely (61.7%) than white females (50.7%) to report violent victimizations to the authorities. (See Table 7.4.)

The reasons people give for their decision to report victimizations to the police are shown in Table 7.5. For all personal crimes, the highest proportion of victims (19.1%) said they reported the incident to prevent further crimes by the offender against them. Of other victims,

TABLE 7.3

Percent of victimizations reported to the police, by type of crime, victim-offender relationship and gender of victims, 2002

| | Percent of all victimizations reported to the police | | | | | | | | |
| Type of crime | All victimizations | | | Involving strangers | | | Involving nonstrangers | | |
	Both genders	Male	Female	Both genders	Male	Female	Both genders	Male	Female
Crimes of violence	48.5%	44.6%	53.0%	51.5%	47.9%	58.6%	45.5%	39.5%	49.7%
Completed violence	60.4	59.0	61.6	67.5	62.6	76.5	54.5	52.9	55.2
Attempted/threatened violence	42.7	38.9	47.8	44.8	41.7	50.7	40.4	34.5	45.7
Rape/sexual assault[2]	53.7	39.7[1]	55.8	57.9	22.8[1]	65.7	51.6	55.3[1]	51.2
Robbery	71.2	66.5	79.3	69.7	64.0	83.9	75.3	78.4	73.1
Completed/property taken	75.8	73.5	79.4	75.9	71.9	84.4	75.5	80.5	71.8
With injury	79.8	76.2	85.3	74.3	69.5	84.7[1]	88.7	91.9[1]	85.9[1]
Without injury	72.6	71.4	74.6	76.8	73.4	84.3	52.5[1]	51.0[1]	53.1[1]
Attempted to take property	57.4	47.4	78.7	50.1	42.4	81.3[1]	75.0[1]	72.2[1]	76.7[1]
With injury	92.6	90.0[1]	100.0[1]	87.9[1]	86.8[1]	100.0[1]	100.0[1]	100.0[1]	100.0[1]
Without injury	39.5	22.8[1]	70.6[1]	34.7[1]	20.5[1]	78.6[1]	54.5[1]	40.0[1]	61.5[1]
Assault	45.7	41.9	50.3	48.2	45.2	54.2	43.3	37.1	48.1
Aggravated	56.6	52.4	62.8	59.7	55.9	67.4	52.3	45.6	58.6
With injury	61.3	63.5	58.8	72.8	71.9	74.2	51.9	53.4	50.7
Threatened with weapon	54.5	48.1	65.2	55.5	51.1	64.9	52.6	40.7	65.5
Simple	42.7	38.6	47.3	44.1	41.3	49.6	41.5	35.1	46.2
With minor injury	54.8	49.6	59.0	58.4	52.4	72.6	52.9	46.3	55.8
Without injury	38.6	35.6	42.3	40.6	38.4	44.8	36.6	32.0	40.7

Note: Detail may not add to total shown because of rounding.
[1]Estimate is based on about 10 or fewer sample cases.
[2]Includes verbal threats of rape and threats of sexual assault.

SOURCE: "Table 93. Violent Crimes, 2002: Percent of Victimizations Reported to the Police, by Type of Crime, Victim-Offender Relationship and Gender of Victims," in *Criminal Victimization in the United States, 2002 Statistical Tables,* U.S. Department of Justice, Bureau of Justice Statistics, National Crime Victimization Survey, 2002, http://www.ojp.usdoj.gov/bjs/abstract/cvusst.htm (accessed October 12, 2004)

17.9% wanted to stop or prevent this crime, 14.6% said they reported to police because it was a crime, and 10.5% said they wanted to prevent the offender from assaulting anyone else. Other, less cited reasons included to punish the offender (7.2%), to catch the offender (6.9%), and a feeling of duty to notify the police (5.8%).

Other victims chose not to report personal crimes to the police. The reason offered most frequently for not reporting all types of personal crimes to the police was that the offense was a private or personal matter (21.2%). (See Table 7.6.) This reason was given more often by victims who chose not to report offenses committed by nonstrangers. (See Table 7.7.)

THE OUTCOME OF POLICE INTERVENTION

Eve Buzawa and Thomas Austin conducted a landmark study of four precincts of the Detroit Police Department and their responses to domestic violence in 1993. In "Determining Police Response to Domestic Violence Victims" (*American Behavioral Scientist,* vol. 36, no. 5, May 1993), they documented several factors that affected police decisions to arrest offenders:

- the presence of bystanders or children during the abuse
- the presence of guns and sharp objects as weapons
- an injury resulting from the assault
- the offender and victim sharing the same residence whether they were married or not

TABLE 7.4

Percent of victimizations reported to the police, by type of crime and gender and race or ethnicity of victims, 2002

| | Percent of all victimizations reported to the police | |
Characteristic	Crimes of violence*	Property crimes
Total	**48.5%**	**40.2%**
Male		
White	44.0	40.2
Black	48.0	46.8
Female		
White	50.7	38.1
Black	61.7	44.7
Male		
Hispanic	47.0	37.5
Non-Hispanic	44.0	41.5
Female		
Hispanic	55.5	39.9
Non-Hispanic	52.8	39.4

Note: Excludes data on persons of "Other" races. Excludes data on persons whose ethnicity was not ascertained.
*Includes data on rape and sexual assault, not shown separately.

SOURCE: "Table 91b. Violent Crimes, 2002: Percent of Victimizations Reported to the Police, by Type of Crime and Gender and Race or Ethnicity of Victims," in *Criminal Victimization in the United States, 2002 Statistical Tables,* U.S. Department of Justice, Bureau of Justice Statistics, National Crime Victimization Survey, 2002, http://www.ojp.usdoj.gov/bjs/abstract/cvusst.htm (accessed October 12, 2004)

- the victim's desire to have the offender arrested (of victims who expressed such a desire, arrests were made in 44% of the cases; when the victim did not

TABLE 7.5

Percent of reasons for reporting victimizations to the police, by type of crime, 2002

							Percent of reasons for reporting								
Type of crime	Number of reasons for reporting	Total	Stop or prevent this incident	Needed help due to injury	To recover property	To collect insurance	To prevent further crimes by offender against victim	To prevent crime by offender against anyone	To punish offender	To catch or find offender	To improve police surveillance	Duty to notify police	Because it was a crime	Some other reason	Not available
All personal crimes	2,388,410	100%	17.9%	1.7%	5.1%	0.4%	19.1%	10.5%	7.2%	6.9%	4.4%	5.8%	14.6%	4.6%	1.9%
Crimes of violence	2,294,390	100	18.5	1.8	4.1	0.3[1]	19.8	10.5	7.3	6.5	4.6	5.7	14.4	4.5	2.0
Completed violence	944,060	100	14.2	2.9[1]	8.6	0.5[1]	18.7	11.3	8.6	9.1	4.1	4.5	12.9	3.7	0.8[1]
Attempted/threatened violence	1,350,330	100	21.5	1.0[1]	1.0[1]	0.2[1]	20.5	10.0	6.3	4.6	4.9	6.5	15.5	5.1	2.8
Rape/sexual assault[2]	113,230	100	4.6[1]	0.0[1]	2.0[1]	0.0[1]	21.0[1]	20.7[1]	9.6[1]	17.9[1]	0.0[1]	0.0[1]	18.9[1]	5.3[1]	0.0[1]
Robbery	402,790	100	12.9	2.1[1]	20.5	0.6[1]	11.7	10.5	8.8	8.2	5.2[1]	2.8[1]	14.3	1.8[1]	0.6[1]
Completed/property taken	332,010	100	12.0	0.7[1]	23.7	0.7[1]	10.8	10.1	8.3[1]	9.0[1]	5.3[1]	3.4[1]	13.0	2.2[1]	0.8[1]
With injury	108,980	100	15.4[1]	2.3[1]	12.9[1]	0.0[1]	7.0[1]	10.1[1]	10.6[1]	7.9[1]	0.0[1]	1.9[1]	24.8[1]	4.8[1]	2.4[1]
Without injury	223,040	100	10.4[1]	0.0[1]	29.0	1.0[1]	12.6[1]	10.1[1]	7.1[1]	9.5[1]	7.9[1]	4.1[1]	7.2[1]	0.9[1]	0.0[1]
Attempted to take property	70,770	100	17.2[1]	8.4[1]	5.2[1]	0.0[1]	16.0[1]	12.2[1]	11.4[1]	4.6[1]	4.6[1]	0.0[1]	20.4[1]	0.0[1]	0.0[1]
With injury	47,230	100	5.6[1]	12.5[1]	0.0[1]	0.0[1]	24.0[1]	12.5[1]	11.1[1]	7.0[1]	7.0[1]	0.0[1]	20.4[1]	0.0[1]	0.0[1]
Without injury	23,540	100[1]	40.4[1]	0.0[1]	15.6[1]	0.0[1]	0.0[1]	11.7[1]	12.0[1]	0.0[1]	0.0[1]	0.0[1]	20.3[1]	0.0[1]	0.0[1]
Assault	1,778,370	100	20.6	1.8	0.6[1]	0.3[1]	21.5	9.9	6.8	5.3	4.7	6.7	14.2	5.1	2.4
Aggravated	525,190	100	13.8	2.1[1]	0.7[1]	0.5[1]	20.8	15.0	9.0	9.7	4.4[1]	6.2	11.9	4.2[1]	1.6[1]
Simple	1,253,180	100	23.5	1.7[1]	0.5[1]	0.2[1]	21.8	7.8	5.9	3.5	4.9	6.9	15.1	5.5	2.8
Purse snatching/pocket picking	94,020	100	2.7[1]	0.0[1]	29.6[1]	2.3[1]	2.7[1]	10.5[1]	4.6[1]	16.1[1]	0.0[1]	7.8[1]	17.8[1]	5.4[1]	1.4[1]
All property crimes	9,064,910	100%	7.6%	0.1%*	24.7%	5.3%	9.9%	6.8%	4.1%	7.3%	6.3%	6.0%	17.7%	3.0%	1.4%
Household burglary	2,468,020	100	10.4	0.2[1]	19.9	4.0	12.2	6.4	4.8	7.5	7.2	5.5	18.4	2.2	1.2
Completed	2,191,050	100	9.3	0.2[1]	22.4	4.4	11.2	6.9	5.2	7.1	6.5	5.7	17.5	2.3	1.2[1]
Forcible entry	1,233,030	100	9.3	0.4[1]	19.3	4.9	11.3	7.7	6.4	7.5	7.7	6.7	15.3	2.0[1]	1.4[1]
Unlawful entry without force	958,020	100	9.3	0.0[1]	26.4	3.9	11.1	5.9	3.8	6.6	5.0	4.4	20.2	2.7	0.9[1]
Attempted forcible entry	276,970	100	19.7	0.0[1]	0.0[1]	0.9[1]	20.0	2.3[1]	1.6[1]	10.3[1]	12.9	3.5[1]	25.7	1.6[1]	1.5[1]
Motor vehicle theft	1,050,840	100	4.8	0.0[1]	35.5	10.3	6.1	5.6	4.9	7.2	6.8	5.5	11.7	1.3[1]	0.3[1]
Completed	904,690	100	4.6	0.0[1]	41.0	10.3	4.1	4.7	5.0	7.6	4.3	5.2	11.5	1.6[1]	0.0[1]
Attempted	146,150	100	6.0[1]	0.0[1]	1.4[1]	10.2[1]	18.5[1]	10.9[1]	4.3[1]	4.5[1]	21.9	7.2[1]	13.3[1]	0.0[1]	1.8[1]
Theft	5,546,050	100	6.8	0.1[1]	24.7	4.9	9.5	7.2	3.7	7.2	5.8	6.3	18.6	3.6	1.7
Completed	5,355,180	100	6.6	0.1[1]	25.6	4.7	9.6	7.1	3.7	7.1	5.6	6.3	18.5	3.5	1.6
Attempted	190,870	100	11.0[1]	0.0[1]	0.0[1]	8.8[1]	8.0[1]	11.0[1]	2.5[1]	8.6[1]	10.8[1]	7.5[1]	21.3	5.8[1]	4.8[1]

Note: Detail may not add to total shown because of rounding. Some respondents may have cited more than one reason for victimizations to the police.

[1]Estimate is based about 10 or fewer sample cases.

[2]Includes verbal threats of rape and threats of sexual assault.

SOURCE: "Table 101. Personal and Property Crimes, 2002: Percent of Reasons for Reporting Victimizations to the Police, by Type of Crime," in *Criminal Victimization in the United States, 2002 Statistical Tables*, U.S. Department of Justice, Bureau of Justice Statistics, National Crime Victimization Survey, 2002, http://www.ojp.usdoj.gov/bjs/abstract/cvusst.htm (accessed October 12, 2004)

TABLE 7.6

Percent of reasons for not reporting victimizations to the police, by type of crime, 2002

		Percent of reasons for not reporting					
Type of crime	Number of reasons for not reporting	Total	Reported to another official	Private or personal matter	Object recovered; offender unsuccessful	Not important enough	Insurance would not cover
All personal crimes	**3,200,150**	**100%**	**17.0%**	**21.2%**	**15.7%**	**4.9%**	**0.1%[1]**
Crimes of violence	3,105,890	100	17.1	21.7	15.8	5.1	0.1[1]
Completed violence	830,960	100	14.2	17.4	9.5	1.7[1]	0.3[1]
Attempted/threatened violence	2,274,930	100	18.2	23.3	18.1	6.3	0.0[1]
Rape/sexual assault[2]	133,690	100	2.7[1]	8.6[1]	9.2[1]	3.8[1]	0.0[1]
Robbery	196,020	100	9.0[1]	6.9[1]	10.7[1]	5.5[1]	1.4[1]
Completed/property taken	138,080	100	8.1[1]	4.3[1]	10.7[1]	1.8[1]	2.0[1]
With injury	59,820	100	0.0[1]	4.2[1]	9.1[1]	4.1[1]	4.6[1]
Without injury	78,260	100	14.4[1]	4.3[1]	11.9[1]	0.0[1]	0.0[1]
Attempted to take property	57,940	100	10.9[1]	13.4[1]	10.9[1]	14.3[1]	0.0[1]
With injury	3,130[1]	100[1]	0.0[1]	0.0[1]	0.0[1]	0.0[1]	0.0[1]
Without injury	54,810	100	11.5[1]	14.1[1]	11.5[1]	15.1[1]	0.0[1]
Assault	2,776,190	100	18.4	23.4	16.5	5.1	0.0[1]
Aggravated	478,910	100	10.5	22.2	8.3	4.7[1]	0.0[1]
Simple	2,297,280	100	20.0	23.7	18.2	5.2	0.0[1]
Purse snatching/pocket picking	94,260	100	11.9[1]	2.8[1]	10.1[1]	0.0[1]	0.0[1]
All property crimes	**12,958,170**	**100%**	**9.7%**	**5.2%**	**25.7%**	**3.4%**	**2.4%**
Household burglary	1,685,780	100	3.9	4.9	21.0	3.2	3.0
Completed	1,397,180	100	2.8	4.2	20.3	3.7	3.6
Forcible entry	303,380	100	2.8[1]	5.0[1]	12.1	0.9[1]	2.3[1]
Unlawful entry without force	1,093,800	100	2.9	4.0	22.5	4.5	3.9
Attempted forcible entry	288,600	100	8.9[1]	8.2[1]	24.4	0.7[1]	0.0[1]
Motor vehicle theft	152,140	100	9.9[1]	6.2[1]	32.0	1.4[1]	1.5[1]
Completed	30,210[1]	100[1]	7.6[1]	23.7[1]	12.6[1]	0.0[1]	0.0[1]
Attempted	121,930	100	10.5[1]	1.9[1]	36.8	1.8[1]	1.9[1]
Theft	11,120,240	100	10.6	5.2	26.3	3.4	2.4
Completed	10,754,160	100	10.7	5.1	25.9	3.4	2.4
Attempted	366,080	100	7.6[1]	7.9[1]	38.4	4.6[1]	1.9[1]

Note: Detail may not add to total shown because of rounding.
Some respondents may have cited more than one reason for not reporting victimizations to the police.
[1]Estimate is based on about 10 or fewer sample cases.
[2]Included verbal threats of rape and threats of sexual assault.

SOURCE: "Table 102. Personal and Property Crimes, 2002: Percent of Reasons for Not Reporting Victimizations to the Police, by Type of Crime," in *Criminal Victimization in the United States, 2002 Statistical Tables,* U.S. Department of Justice, Bureau of Justice Statistics, National Crime Victimization Survey, 2002, http://www.ojp.usdoj.gov/bjs/abstract/cvusst.htm (accessed October 12, 2004)

want the offender arrested, arrests were made in only 21% of the cases)

Interviewing 110 victims, Buzawa and Austin found that 85% of victims were satisfied with the police response. Not surprisingly, they were particularly satisfied when the police responded to their preferences for arresting or not arresting the offenders.

Lynette Feder, in "Police Handling of Domestic and Nondomestic Assault Calls: Is There a Case for Discrimination?" (*Crime and Delinquency,* vol. 44, no. 2, April 1998), found that domestic assault calls are nearly twice as likely to result in arrests than are nondomestic assault calls. However, overall rates of arrest are fairly low—arrests are made in 23% of domestic assault calls and 13% of nondomestic assault calls. Feder identified four variables that determine the probability of arrest: the presence of the offender when the police arrive, the victim's desire for the arrest of the offender, the extent of the victim's injuries, and the offender's disrespectful demeanor toward police.

Victims' Attitudes toward Police Response

Raquel Kennedy Bergen interviewed forty women who had been physically abused and raped by their husbands. In *Wife Rape: Understanding the Response of Survivors and Service Providers* (Thousand Oaks, CA: Sage, 1996), she reported that only 37% of the women, or fifteen out of forty, contacted the police for help on at least one occasion. Three women in the study felt it was impossible to call the police because their spouses were members of the police department. One participant reported that during several interviews with the police, the officers made a point of asking embarrassing questions and repeatedly asked for intimate details. Another woman who found the police unresponsive lied to get them to come to her aid. About 80% of victims who did call the police were not satisfied with the officers' responses. Ultimately, only eight of the spouses were charged with rape.

The results of a 2003 study, however, conflicted with Bergen's results. In "Perceptions of the Police by Female Victims of Domestic Partner Violence," researchers

TABLE 7.7

Percent of reasons for not reporting victimizations to the police, by victim-offender relationship and type of crime, 2002

Relationship and type of crime	Number of reasons for not reporting	Percent of reasons for not reporting													
		Total	Reported to another official	Private or personal matter	Object recovered; offender unsuccessful	Not important enough	Insurance would not cover	Not aware crime occurred until later	Unable to recover property; no ID no.	Lack of proof	Police would not want to be bothered	Police inefficient, ineffective, or biased	Fear of reprisal	Too inconvenient or time consuming	Other reasons
Involving strangers															
Crime of violence	1,457,920	100%	13.3%	18.6%	19.2%	6.5%	0.2%[1]	0.3%[1]	0.0%[1]	5.3%	6.9%	4.6%	3.1%	3.5%	18.7%
Rape/sexual assault[2]	45,960	100%	0.0[1]	5.0[1]	26.9[1]	0.0[1]	0.0[1]	8.9[1]	0.0[1]	0.0[1]	7.1[1]	7.1[1]	4.6[1]	0.0[1]	40.3[1]
Robbery	120,830	100%	8.7[1]	2.3[1]	10.2[1]	1.8[1]	2.3[1]	0.0[1]	0.0[1]	17.8[1]	6.4[1]	26.6	5.7[1]	4.4[1]	14.0[1]
Assault	1,291,130	100%	14.2	20.6	19.7	7.1	0.0[1]	0.0[1]	0.0[1]	4.4	6.9	2.4	2.8	3.5	18.4
Involving nonstrangers															
Crime of violence	1,647,970	100%	20.5	24.5	12.9	3.8	0.0[1]	0.6[1]	0.6[1]	1.1[1]	3.1	1.7[1]	6.0	1.7[1]	23.6
Rape/sexual assault[2]	87,720	100%	4.1[1]	10.5[1]	0.0[1]	5.8[1]	0.0[1]	0.0[1]	0.0[1]	3.7[1]	0.0[1]	0.0[1]	41.1	0.0[1]	34.7
Robbery	75,190	100%	9.4[1]	14.3[1]	11.6[1]	11.5[1]	0.0[1]	0.0[1]	3.9[1]	10.2[1]	13.7[1]	3.9[1]	3.0[1]	3.4[1]	15.2[1]
Assault	1,485,050	100%	22.0	25.9	13.7	3.3	0.0[1]	0.6[1]	0.5[1]	0.4[1]	2.7	1.7[1]	4.1	1.7[1]	23.4

Note: Detail may not add to total shown because of rounding.
Some respondents may have cited more than one reason for not reporting victimizations to the police.
[1]Estimate is based on about 10 or fewer sample cases.
[2]Includes verbal threats of rape and threats of sexual assault.

SOURCE: "Table 104. Personal Crimes of Violence, 2002: Percent of Reasons for Not Reporting Victimizations to the Police, by Victim-Offender Relationship and Type of Crime," in *Criminal Victimization in the United States, 2002 Statistical Tables*, U.S. Department of Justice, Bureau of Justice Statistics, National Crime Victimization Survey, 2002, http://www.ojp.usdoj.gov/bjs/abstract/cvusst.htm (accessed October 12, 2004)

Robert Apsler, Michele R. Cummins, and Steven Carl investigated "what female victims of domestic violence wanted from the police, the extent to which they perceived they obtained what they wanted, and how helpful they found the actions of the police."

The authors found that women in the study were very satisfied with the police response to their call. They believed the police had been very helpful, and more than 80% of the women said they would definitely call the police for help in the future. The authors emphasized that this police department had recently instituted policies specifically designed to help battered women.

A Source of Frustration

There can be little doubt that "domestic quarrels" cause great frustration to the police. According to the *FBI Law Enforcement Bulletin* (October 1997), domestic violence calls repeatedly involve the same homes, diverting resources from other areas while often resulting in no legal action against offenders. Police claim 90% of domestic violence calls are repeat calls and that police typically know the callers by the location. Both victims and police officers find these situations frustrating. Battered women think the police are sometimes insensitive and the officers become exasperated after responding to multiple calls from the same person.

Research has found that few women will file complaints against their batterers. In spite of significant legislative changes, police officers still meet victim resistance to arresting an abusive partner. Furthermore, researchers have documented a fact that many battered women have long suspected: that arrests do not decrease repeat offenses.

Kathleen Ferraro and Lucille Pope, in "Battered Women, Police and the Law" (*Legal Responses to Wife Assault* [Thousand Oaks, CA: Sage, 1993]), examined the cultural context of law enforcement's attitude to arrest. Based on 440 hours of field observation of the Phoenix, Arizona, police, Ferraro and Pope concluded that among the most influential factors in police attitudes are the officers' background beliefs about race and class. Women from low-income, minority communities are more likely to be seen as "enmeshed in a culture of violence." A specific violent event is likely to be viewed as part of a larger pattern of culture and therefore beyond the scope of police intervention.

Ferraro and Pope found in past research that while the police express frustration that women refuse to press charges, the proportion of cases dropped because of the victim's reluctance—13%—is not much higher than the 10% dropped because of the inadequacy of police reports documenting the evidence. Police blame not only the women for refusing to file charges, but also the courts for

undermining the seriousness of the crime by failing to impose jail sentences or probation. A review of court cases cited by Ferraro and Pope found that only one out of 250 cases of wife assault actually ended up with a report to police, a court conviction, and a serious sentence.

Ferraro and Pope observed that some officers resent the time it takes to process an arrest. They view domestic violence calls as a time-consuming effort that could be better devoted to other police work. One officer complained that she was unable to respond to an armed robbery call because she was transporting a woman to a shelter. Police officers are not often rewarded or promoted for their efforts to prevent intimate partner violence but are recognized for their work on high-profile crimes, such as illegal drug trafficking or armed robberies.

Traditional Attitudes Prevail

George Rigakos, in "Constructing the Symbolic Complainant: Police Subculture and the Nonenforcement of Protective Orders from Battered Women" (*Violence and Victims,* vol. 10, no. 3, 1995), studied how police officers' attitudes influenced the treatment women received in a suburb of Vancouver, British Columbia. He found that a traditional masculine culture contributed to negative stereotypes of women as liars, manipulators, and unreliable witnesses.

According to Rigakos, interviews with police officers and justice officials revealed four major themes. First, justice officials and police felt they were doing all they could for women but contended that other institutions impeded their work. Police officers blamed the legal system, charging the courts with liberally issuing unenforceable restraining and protective orders. In addition, judges issued these orders incorrectly, according to the police. For their part, the justices blamed the police for lack of enforcement. They believed the police misunderstand the law and fail to respond adequately.

Second, the police in this study held conservative attitudes about marriage that resulted in their excusing men's abusive behavior. Officers expressed preferences for women who adhered to traditional behaviors, such as mothering and housekeeping.

Third, because traditional beliefs influenced police attitudes toward the victims, many male officers seemed determined to make the women's behavior appear "unreliable." Some felt that the women were using restraining orders to manipulate their husbands to give themselves advantages in custody battles and divorces. Even some female officers blamed the women.

Fourth, the officers made generalizations that were supported by their beliefs about the women but were not substantiated by official court records. The officers believed that after they had spent tremendous amounts of

...me and effort to prepare a case, the women frequently did not pursue the charges. These negative perceptions of the women produced "selective memory" that magnified every instance of a battered woman failing to appear to testify against a partner and diminished the number of times when the women followed through with legal action.

Rigakos's survey of court records for 1993 found that out of forty-nine cases, five women were "uncooperative," three were no-shows, one refused to testify, and one stated she had lied. Rigakos concluded that the feelings of betrayal engendered by the small number of women who became reluctant witnesses tended to overshadow the hundreds of successful prosecutions. These few cases stood out because of their strong personal effect on the witnessing officers and their consistency with the officers' prevailing patriarchal views.

Robert J. Kane examined patterns of arrest of batterers who violate restraining orders in "Police Responses to Restraining Orders in Domestic Violence Incidents" (*Criminal Justice and Behavior,* vol. 27, no. 5, October 2000). Although all violators in his study were required by Massachusetts state law to be immediately arrested, in reality only between 20% and 40% of violators of restraining orders are taken into custody. Kane found that restraining orders had no significant effect on arrest rate; instead, police perception of imminent danger to the victim was the strongest predictor of arrest. He also found that as the number of domestic violence calls from one victim to police increased, the rate of arrest decreased, regardless of whether a restraining order was in place. Kane suggested that further studies should be done into variations in arrest rates that include personal characteristics of police officers and the social contexts of the couples involved in domestic violence incidents.

NOT ALL VICTIMS WHO SEEK POLICE ATTENTION ARE THE SAME

Investigators Robert Apsler, Michelle Cummins, and Steven Carl speculate that the female victims who seek police aid are very likely the most frightened women, and that they are seeking assistance to prevent future instances of abuse. In "Fear and Expectations: Differences among Female Victims of Domestic Violence Who Come to the Attention of Police" (*Violence and Victims,* vol. 17, no. 4, August 2002), they reviewed police officers' interviews of ninety-five consecutive victims who came to the attention of a police department in a suburb of Boston.

The study participants had either contacted the police department via telephone or by personal appearance at the police station to request intervention in a violent intimate partner dispute. Police officers administered a standardized questionnaire that included questions about the severity of the abuse victims had experienced, their level of fear, and their expectations about the future. About half the victims were living with their abusers at the time the incident occurred.

Apsler, Cummins, and Carl found that just one-quarter of respondents said they were very afraid of their abusers. Another 6% were fairly afraid, 12% said they were slightly afraid, and 36% claimed they were not at all afraid of their abusers. Taken together, these latter two groups accounted for nearly half of participants reporting little or no fear of their abusers.

The results were similar in terms of participants' expectations of future abuse. Apsler, Cummins, and Carl found that just 21% of victims thought future abuse was very likely, and well over half of women surveyed said future abuse was not at all likely or only slightly likely. These findings challenge long-standing beliefs that the victims who tend to come to the attention of the police are those who most fear future abuse.

Interestingly, there were no statistically significant relationships found between victims' expectations of future violence and whether they lived with their abusers, had children under eighteen years old, or were able to support themselves financially. A less surprising result was that victims' expectations of future abuse strongly influenced their desired future relationships with their offenders. A strong majority of the participants (90%) who thought future abuse was fairly or very likely wanted to permanently separate from the offenders. In contrast, only about half of the women who thought further abuse was not at all likely wanted permanent separations.

The researchers concluded that the differences between victims of domestic violence and their varied expectations when seeking police attention point to a need for law enforcement agencies to offer a variety of police responses tailored to individual victim's needs. For example, they suggested that mandatory arrest of victims' aggressors might not be helpful as a universally applicable strategy for all victims, especially women who do not fear further abuse. On the other hand, very fearful victims might be reassured and experience greater security if police maintained regular, ongoing contact with them following the incident. Apsler, Cummins, and Carl added that police follow-up might also send a powerful message to perpetrators—that they are under surveillance and that future violations will not be tolerated.

DOES ARREST HELP?

The Bureau of Justice Statistics, in the fact sheet *Preventing Domestic Violence against Women,* stated that about one in four of all violent offenders incarcerated in local jails in 1996 had committed their offense against an intimate. These same violent offenders were also about twice as likely to be convicted of assault than if the same act was committed against a stranger. (See Figure 7.1.)

FIGURE 7.1

Profile of convicted violent offenders in local jails, 1996

Convicted violent offenders in local jails

Intimate violence 23.6%	Other relatives violence 8.6%	Friend/ acquaintance violence 25.9%	Stranger violence 41.9%
Homicide 4.7%	Homicide 2.0%	Homicide 8.6%	Homicide 7.5%
Rape/ sexual assault 12.3%	Rape/ sexual assault 52.4%	Rape/ sexual assault 23.5%	Rape/ sexual assault 3.6%
Robbery 2.4%	Robbery 3.7%	Robbery 14.1%	Robbery 46.8%
Assault 72.3%	Assault 34.4%	Assault 46.4%	Assault 36.6%

Note: Intimate violence includes violent offenses committed against current and former spouses, boyfriends, and girlfriends.

SOURCE: "Profile of Convicted Violent Offenders in Local Jails," in *Violence by Intimates: Analysis of Data on Crimes by Current or Former Spouses, Boyfriends, and Girlfriends,* U.S. Department of Justice, Bureau of Justice Statistics, 1998, http://www.ojp.usdoj.gov/bjs/pub/pdf/vi.pdf (accessed October 21, 2004)

Of the violent offenders convicted of a crime against an intimate, the majority, 72.3%, were serving time for assault, 12.3% were incarcerated for rape or sexual assault, and 4.7% were convicted of homicide. The remaining 2.4% were convicted of robbing an intimate.

The fact sheet also noted that half of all inmates serving time in local jails had been previously placed under a restraining or protective order. Four out of ten of these inmates had criminal justice status or a protective order in effect against them at the time of the offense.

The Bureau of Justice Statistics report supported arrest in domestic violence cases, stating that it could:

• prevent future criminal behavior

• prevent further injury to the victim

• demonstrate to the offender that he will face legal consequences

• demonstrate to the victim, the offender, and the community that domestic violence is criminal behavior

• increase the number of offenders subject to prosecution, court supervision, treatment, and other community intervention

Arrest gained popularity as a tactic after the publication of a series of six studies funded by the National Institute of Justice known as the Spouse Assault Replication Program. All of the studies were designed to explain how arrest in domestic violence cases could serve as a deterrent to future violence. L. W. Sherman and R. A. Berk, the authors of the influential first study in the series, "The Spe-

cific Deterrent Effects of Arrest for Domestic Assau.." found that "the arrest intervention certainly did not make things worse and may well have made things better" (*American Sociological Review,* vol. 49, no. 2, April 1984).

Although Sherman and Berk cautioned about generalizing from the results of a small study dealing with a single police department in which few police officers properly followed the test procedure, they concluded that in instances of domestic violence, an arrest is advisable except in cases where it would be clearly counterproductive. At the same time, Sherman and Berk recommended allowing police a certain amount of flexibility when making decisions about individual situations, on the premise that police officers must be permitted to rely on professional judgment based on experience.

Arrest Is Not More Effective

Sherman and Berk's study had a tremendous impact on police practices, despite the fact that five other Spouse Assault Replication Program studies found arrest had little or no effect on domestic violence recurrence—for example, J. David Hirschel et al. in "The Failure to Deter Spouse Abuse" (*Journal of Research in Crime and Delinquency,* vol. 29, no. 1, 1992). A survey conducted two years after the Sherman and Berk report found more than a fourfold increase in the number of police departments reporting arrest as their preferred policy in domestic violence disputes.

Arrest Does Deter Some Men

Sherman et al. were among the first investigators to examine and report rates of recidivism in their Milwaukee police study, "Crime, Punishment and Stake in Conformity: Legal and Extralegal Control of Domestic Violence" (*American Sociological Review,* vol. 57, 1992). The study found that arrest deters men with strong attachments to their local communities, perhaps through employment, friends, or family. Batterers who have little "stake in conformity," such as the unemployed and unmarried, have a tendency to become more violent in response to arrest. However, this landmark study did not consider other variables that might have influenced the results. For example, employed offenders might have less violent histories, less stressful home life, or may be older—all factors that might affect their rates of recidivism.

Peter G. Jaffe et al. in "The Impact of Police Laying Charges" (*Legal Responses to Wife Assault—Current Trends and Evaluations* [Newbury Park, CA: Sage, 1993]), studied the effect of police intervention in London, Ontario. The participants were ninety female victims of assault. Fifty-two of the women had called for police intervention and filed criminal charges, fourteen had received police intervention but no charges were filed, and twenty-four had neither received police help nor filed charges. Although arrest alone did not decrease the violence in this study, it was a significant deterrent when charges were filed. Jaffe et al. urged that police support be integrated into a community response that includes all aspects of support for battered women.

Warrantless Probable Cause Arrests

In the early 1970s, it was legal for the police to make probable cause arrests without a warrant for felonies, but only fourteen states permitted it for misdemeanors. Because the crime of simple assault and battery is a misdemeanor in most states, family violence victims were forced to initiate their own criminal charges against a batterer. By 2002, West Virginia was the only state that did not authorize warrantless probable cause misdemeanor arrests in domestic violence cases. However, more than half of the states have added qualifiers, such as visible signs of injury or report of the violence within eight hours of the incident. Most state codes authorizing warrantless arrests require police to inform victims of their rights, which include the acquisition of protection orders, as well as referral to emergency and shelter facilities and transportation.

Mandatory Arrests

By 1992, fifteen states, the District of Columbia, and dozens of municipalities had instituted a mandatory arrest policy whenever police were called to a domestic violence situation. Some battered women's advocates do not support mandatory arrest. They fear that poor and minority families are treated more harshly than middle-class families and that if the police arrive and both spouses are bloodied by the fight, both will be arrested, forcing the children into foster care. In Connecticut, where a strict arrest policy is mandatory, the dual arrest rate is 14%.

Recent data suggest that mandatory arrests may actually increase violence, especially if the batterer is unemployed or has a criminal record. Some observers suggest that mandatory arrest should be replaced with mandatory action, such as providing transportation to a shelter or granting the victim the option to have the offender arrested. Mandatory action would allow police officers to make decisions appropriate to each individual case.

Some police departments have adopted a presumptive arrest policy. This policy means that an arrest should be made unless clear and compelling reasons exist not to arrest. Presumptive arrest provisions forbid officers from basing the decision to arrest on the victim's preference or on a perception of the victim's willingness to testify or participate in the proceedings. Proponents point out that arresting an offender gives the victim a respite from fear and an opportunity to look for help. Furthermore, they claim it prevents bias in arrests.

Evan Stark, in "Mandatory Arrest of Batterers: A Reply to Its Critics" (*Do Arrests and Restraining Orders Work?* [Newbury Park, CA: Sage, 1996]), offered reasons for a mandatory arrest policy other than deterrence. Stark asserted that mandatory arrest policies provide:

- a standard against which to judge variation in police responses

- immediate protection from current violence and time for victims to consider their options

- measurable reductions in the overall incidence of domestic violence directly (because arrest might deter recidivism) and indirectly, by sending a clear message that battering is unacceptable

- access for victims to services and protection that would not be available outside the criminal justice system

However, David Hirschel and Ira W. Hutchinson found support for a police policy of taking victim preferences into account in the decision to arrest in their study "The Voices of Domestic Violence Victims: Predictors of Victim Preference for Arrest and the Relationship between Preference for Arrest and Revictimization" (*Crime & Delinquency,* vol. 49, no. 2, April 2003). Victims based their preferences for arrest on the seriousness of the violence and the perpetrators' prior abusive behavior; victims in fact proved to be good judges of the seriousness of the violence and the likelihood of it recurring. The researchers found that victims who wanted their abusers arrested were more likely to suffer subsequent abuse than were victims who did not want their batterers arrested. "Based on these data," the authors wrote, "victim desire for arrest of the offender would appear to be a factor that police should take into account in determining subsequent action."

Police Response Can Empower Victims

Researchers Carolyn Hoyle and Andrew Sanders contended that police intervention in cases of domestic violence can do one of two things—either further intimidate women or actually help them to improve their own circumstances. In "Police Response to Domestic Violence: From Victim Choice to Victim Empowerment?"(*British Journal of Criminology,* vol. 40, 2000), they examined the views of victims about the value of criminal justice interventions in light of pro-arrest policies and the establishment of specially trained domestic violence units and officers.

Hoyle and Sanders interviewed sixty-five women in three communities in Thames, England, to find out what the victims wanted when they called the police to intervene in domestic disputes. In earlier studies, Hoyle and Sanders characterized the police policy as "victim's choice"—the police approached each instance of domestic violence according to the woman's preferences about pursuing legal action. This policy was widely criticized because it allowed victims to decide on actions without consideration of the consequences of nonprosecution on perpetrators and victims. Critics also felt that many women were not actually expressing their true wishes and that their choices were coerced or influenced by fear of retribution from their abusers.

Since 1993, Thames police policy has shifted from victim's choice to pro-arrest, on the premise that arrest and prosecution better serve the interests of victims and the community at large. The policy changed in response to U.S. research findings that arrest correlates with short-term reductions in domestic violence. The new British policy based on these findings favored immediate intervention—arresting the abusers—and longer-term intervention—pressing charges that presumably might result in sentences of rehabilitation or incarceration. The authors argued that this policy is the opposite of the previous one because it assumes that policy makers are more capable of deciding on correct courses of action than the victims themselves.

More than half (thirty-one) of the survey participants called the police with the intent of having the offender arrested, but the majority of these women did not wish to pursue prosecution. The balance either wanted the offender removed from the scene—simply to get a break from the abuse—or wanted the police to calm the agitated man. The women cited a wide range of reasons for their choices, from fear of retaliation, to a desire to remain married, to genuine sympathy for a substance-abusing or otherwise impaired spouse.

Hoyle and Sanders found that arrest, with or without prosecution, might in some instances act as a deterrent, but it does not reduce violence. They asserted that arrest is most effective when combined with other strategies, such as treatment programs, incentives to reduce recidivism, and social supports for women. They termed this the "victim empowerment model" and proposed that it might prove more effective than the exclusively legal remedies provided by either the victim's choice or pro-arrest policies.

Hoyle and Sanders concluded that battered women are a diverse group in need of different kinds of support. They also observe that victims' preferences are shaped by a variety of factors and that an ideal approach would be to support each victim to change her circumstances in order to reduce coercion and to help her to make different choices, including the decision to end the violent relationship.

JoAnn Miller, in "An Arresting Experiment: Domestic Violence Victim Experiences and Perceptions," focused on the Spouse Assault Replication Program victims' perceptions of police interventions and arrest (*Journal of Interpersonal Violence*, vol. 18, no. 7, July 2003). She examined two concepts of power: personal power (control of economic and social resources) and legal power (perceived empowerment in response to police intervention).

Miller found that women did not use their sense of personal power (derived from an independent income) to end domestic violence. But, she found, victims' perception of legal power (derived from their satisfaction with the police action taken) could be used to feel safer and to control interactions with violent partners in the future. She concluded that "the most reasonable criminal justice and social service responses to domestic violence are those that consider the victim's needs by taking into account her subjective experiences, her cultural and social resources, and her personal and legal resources." In other words, mandatory arrest policies tend to undermine victims' personal power because they do not take into account individual victims' needs.

STALKING

Many abused women who leave their partners feel threatened and remain in physical danger of further attacks. One form of threatening behavior, stalking, is generally defined as harassment that involves repeated visual or physical proximity; nonconsensual communication; verbal, written, or implied threats; or a combination of these acts that would cause a reasonable person fear. Stalking is a series of actions, usually escalating from legal but annoying acts, such as following or repeatedly phoning the victim, to violent or even fatal actions.

Not all stalking incidents involve abusive couples or intimate relationships. A stalker may fixate on an acquaintance or a stranger as the object of obsession. Celebrity stalking cases have been highly publicized but they account for a very small percentage of stalking incidents. Stalking most often involves intimates or former intimates and starts or continues after a victim leaves the relationship. And it is a widespread problem. In *Stalking and Domestic Violence: The Third Annual Report to Congress under the Violence against Women Act* (Washington, DC: Violence against Women Grants Office, U.S. Department of Justice, 1998), researchers estimated that 8.1 million women and more than two million men have been stalked in their lifetimes.

Researchers using National Violence against Women Survey data estimate that one out of twelve American women and one out of forty-five American men have been stalked at some point in their lives. An estimated 1% of all women respondents and 0.4% of all male respondents were stalked in the twelve months prior to the NVAWS. These percentages represent more than one million women and 370,000 men who are stalked annually in the United States.

Stalkers: Who Are They?

Although stalking is considered a "gender-neutral" crime, the majority of victims are women and the main perpetrators are men. Young adults are the primary targets—52% of victims were between the ages of eighteen

FIGURE 7.2

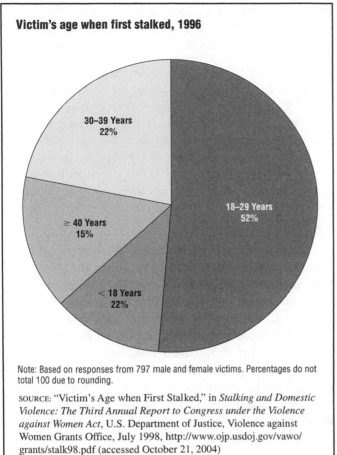

Victim's age when first stalked, 1996

30–39 Years 22%

≥ 40 Years 15%

< 18 Years 22%

18–29 Years 52%

Note: Based on responses from 797 male and female victims. Percentages do not total 100 due to rounding.

SOURCE: "Victim's Age when First Stalked," in *Stalking and Domestic Violence: The Third Annual Report to Congress under the Violence against Women Act*, U.S. Department of Justice, Violence against Women Grants Office, July 1998, http://www.ojp.usdoj.gov/vawo/grants/stalk98.pdf (accessed October 21, 2004)

FIGURE 7.3

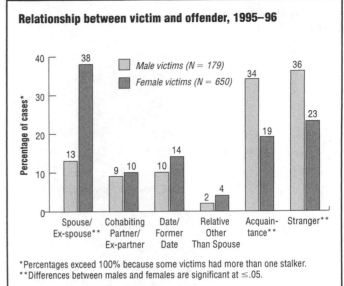

Relationship between victim and offender, 1995–96

Male victims (N = 179)
Female victims (N = 650)

Spouse/Ex-spouse** — 13, 38
Cohabiting Partner/Ex-partner — 9, 10
Date/Former Date — 10, 14
Relative Other Than Spouse — 2, 4
Acquaintance** — 34, 19
Stranger** — 36, 23

*Percentages exceed 100% because some victims had more than one stalker.
**Differences between males and females are significant at ≤.05.

SOURCE: "Exhibit 7. Relationship between Victim and Offender," in *Stalking and Domestic Violence: The Third Annual Report to Congress under the Violence against Women Act*, U.S. Department of Justice, Violence against Women Grants Office, July 1998, http://www.ojp.usdoj.gov/vawo/grants/stalk98.pdf, accessed October 21, 2004

and twenty-nine. Another 22% were between thirty and thirty-nine years old when the stalking began, and 15% were forty years old or older. (See Figure 7.2.)

As suspected, the survey found that most victims knew their stalker. Only 23% of the female victims and 36% of male victims were stalked by strangers. Most women were stalked by intimate partners. Overall, 62% of the female and 32% of male victims were stalked by current or former intimates. Figure 7.3 shows the relationship between stalkers and victims—female victims were stalked by spouses and former spouses nearly three times as often as male victims.

Most stalkers follow or spy on their victims, place unwanted phone calls, and send unwanted letters or other items. The pattern of harassment is similar whether the victim is male or female. Eighty-two percent of all female stalking victims and 72% of all male stalking victims reported being followed or spied on, or found the stalker standing outside their home or workplace. Sixty-one percent of the females and 42% of the males reported receiving phone calls from the stalker. Twenty-nine percent of the women and 30% of the men reported property damage by the stalker, while 9% of the women and 6% of the male victims said the stalker either killed or threatened to kill their family pet.

When the Violence Occurs

Victims' advocates and counselors have long held that women are at the greatest risk of violence when they end a relationship with a batterer. This assumption is based on findings that divorced or separated women report more intimate partner violence than married women. In addition, interviews conducted with men who killed their wives reveal that the violence escalated or was precipitated by separation or threats of separation from their partners.

Many female stalking victims (43%) reported that they were stalked after ending their relationship with intimate partners, although 36% said they were stalked both before and after the breakup. Twenty-one percent of the victims said the stalking began before they terminated their relationships. (See Figure 7.4.)

According to findings released in *Extent, Nature, and Consequences of Intimate Partner Violence: Findings from the National Violence against Women Survey* (Washington, DC: National Institute of Justice and Centers for Disease Control and Prevention, July 2000), separated women are nearly four times more likely to report rape, physical assault, or being stalked by their spouses than women who live with their husbands. In comparison, men who live apart from their spouses are nearly three times as likely to report being victimized by their wives than men who live with their spouses. These findings support the widely held belief that there is an increased risk of partner violence for both men and women once an abusive relationship ends.

While 43% of all stalking victims said the stalking began after they ended their relationship, only 6.3% of

FIGURE 7.4

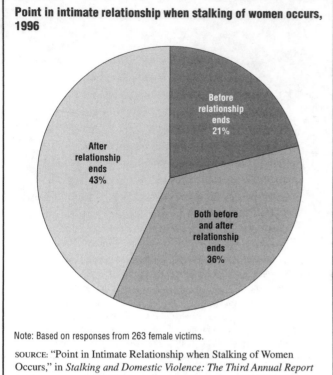

Point in intimate relationship when stalking of women occurs, 1996

Before relationship ends 21%

Both before and after relationship ends 36%

After relationship ends 43%

Note: Based on responses from 263 female victims.

SOURCE: "Point in Intimate Relationship when Stalking of Women Occurs," in *Stalking and Domestic Violence: The Third Annual Report to Congress under the Violence against Women Act*, U.S. Department of Justice, Violence against Women Grants Office, July 1998, http://www.ojp.usdoj.gov/vawo/grants/stalk98.pdf (accessed October 21, 2004)

rape victims and 4.2% of physical assault victims reported victimization after they terminated their relationship. (See Figure 7.5.) These findings suggest that most rapes and violent assaults against women by their partners occur during the relationship, but stalking is more likely to occur after the relationship is terminated.

Legal Response to Stalking

About half of the stalking victims in the National Violence against Women Survey (53.1%) reported stalking to the police. In most cases, the victim made the report. Police were significantly more likely to arrest or detain a suspect stalking a female victim (25.1%) than one stalking a male victim (16.7%). Other police responses included referrals to the prosecutor or court (23.3%), referral to victim services (13.8%), and advice on self-protective measures (33.2%). In 18.9% of the cases, police did nothing.

Of those victims who reported their stalking to the police, about half were satisfied with the actions taken by the police, and about the same proportion indicated they felt police interventions had improved their situations or that the police had done all they could. Victims who thought police actions were inadequate had hoped that their assailants would be jailed (42%) and that their complaints would be treated more seriously (20%). Another 16% had wanted police to do more to protect them from their assailants.

Victims who chose not to report their stalking to the police said they felt their stalking was not a police matter (20%), they believed police would be unable to help them (17%), or they feared reprisal from their stalkers (16%).

Not unexpectedly, because women were more likely to be stalked by intimate partners with a history of violence, female victims were significantly more likely than male victims to obtain protective or restraining orders. According to *Stalking and Domestic Violence: The Third Annual Report to Congress under the Violence against Women Act* (Washington, DC: U.S. Department of Justice, July 1998), of those who obtained protective orders, 68.7% of the women and 81.3% of the men said their stalker violated the order.

Carol E. Jordan, T. K. Logan, Robert Walker, and Amy Nigoff studied the disposition of stalking cases and published the results in "Stalking: An Examination of the Criminal Justice Response" (*Journal of Interpersonal Violence,* vol. 18, no. 2, February 2003). They examined the cases of 390 males charged with stalking from fiscal year 1999, and found that most misdemeanor and felony charges of stalking were dismissed. Only 28.5% of the charged stalkers were convicted. The authors concluded that although the majority of stalking cases are dismissed, those cases that are not dismissed have a fair chance of resulting in conviction.

Antistalking Legislation

All states and the District of Columbia have laws making stalking a crime, but whether it is a felony or a misdemeanor varies by state. In 1996 the Interstate Stalking Punishment and Prevention Act, part of the National Defense Authorization Act for 1997, made interstate stalking a felony. This federal statute addresses cases that cross state lines. In the past, interstate offenses were difficult for state law enforcement agencies to take action against.

Several state legislatures have amended their antistalking laws after constitutional challenges or judicial interpretations of the law made it difficult to prosecute alleged stalkers. For example, in 1996 the Texas Court of Criminal Appeals, in *Long v. Texas,* ruled that the 1993 Texas antistalking law was unconstitutional because it addressed conduct protected by the First Amendment. Legislators amended the statute in January 1997 to stipulate that to violate the statute, an alleged offender must knowingly engage in conduct that he or she "reasonably believes the other person will regard as threatening."

According to the U.S. Department of Justice Office for Victims of Crime, the variation in state stalking laws has to do with the type of repeated behavior that is prohibited, and whether by definition stalking must include a threat. Laws also are based on the victim's reaction to the stalking, and the stalker's intent. The U.S. Department of Jus-

FIGURE 7.5

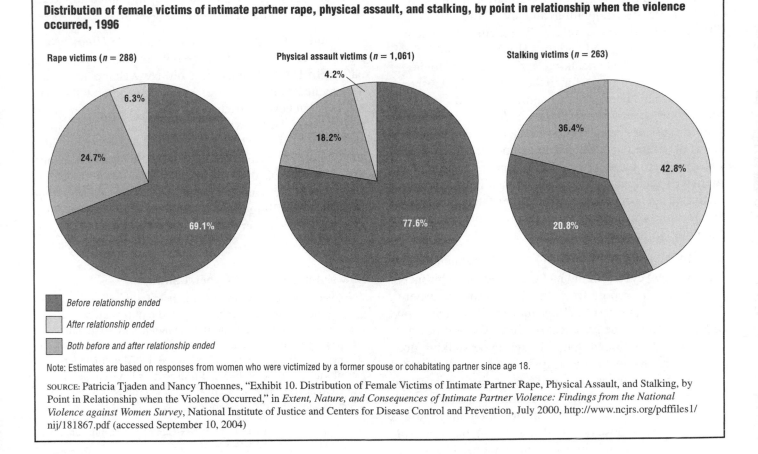

Distribution of female victims of intimate partner rape, physical assault, and stalking, by point in relationship when the violence occurred, 1996

Rape victims (*n* = 288)   Physical assault victims (*n* = 1,061)   Stalking victims (*n* = 263)

6.3%   24.7%   69.1%

4.2%   18.2%   77.6%

36.4%   42.8%   20.8%

Before relationship ended

After relationship ended

Both before and after relationship ended

Note: Estimates are based on responses from women who were victimized by a former spouse or cohabitating partner since age 18.

SOURCE: Patricia Tjaden and Nancy Thoennes, "Exhibit 10. Distribution of Female Victims of Intimate Partner Rape, Physical Assault, and Stalking, by Point in Relationship when the Violence Occurred," in *Extent, Nature, and Consequences of Intimate Partner Violence: Findings from the National Violence against Women Survey*, National Institute of Justice and Centers for Disease Control and Prevention, July 2000, http://www.ncjrs.org/pdffiles1/ nij/181867.pdf (accessed September 10, 2004)

tice legal series bulletin *Strengthening Antistalking Statutes* (January 2002) detailed state legislative changes to better define prohibited conduct so that supreme courts would not find the statutes "unconstitutionally vague." For example, the Oregon legislature removed the term "legitimate purpose" from its statute when its Supreme Court determined it did not adequately describe the prohibited behavior. Similarly, the Supreme Court of Kansas sought increased precision when it requested that the state's stalking statute provide measures of behaviors such as "alarm, annoy and harassment," arguing that actions that alarm or annoy one person may not alarm or annoy another.

Stalking Interventions

Criminal justice officials and victim service providers continue to develop and refine programs, strategies, and protocols to address stalking with an emphasis on enhancing victim safety. According to *Domestic Violence and Stalking: The Second Annual Report to Congress under the Violence against Women Act* (Washington, DC: U.S. Department of Justice, 1997), intervention strategies must strike a balance between stopping the stalking and protecting the victim.

"Suspect intervention" and "victim intervention" are important aspects of the Los Angeles Police Department

Stalking and Threat Assessment Team response to stalking cases. Suspect intervention is the process of gathering, documenting, and analyzing information to assess the potential danger of the stalker. It also includes arrests, protection orders, confiscation of weapons, and face-to-face meetings with stalking suspects.

Victim intervention includes educating the victims about stalking, instructing victims about self-protective measures and how they can assist police to establish and pursue cases, and recommending therapeutic interventions, such as support groups or self-defense training, to help the victims regain control over their lives. The Los Angeles Police Department Stalking and Threat Assessment Team and a comparable program in New York City have been lauded for their effective training for personnel and for dedicating resources to pursue and combat stalking crimes.

As police departments and victim service agencies implement new and modified strategies, those that prove to be effective deterrents to stalking will serve as models. The U.S. Department of Justice is committed to supporting basic research to better understand intimate partner violence and stalking. Evaluation of these efforts will better inform public policy decision makers and guide officials to develop effective prevention and intervention programs.

Cyberstalking

Cyberstalking—online harassment and threats that can escalate to frightening and even life-threatening offline violence—is a relatively recent phenomenon. Brian H. Spitzberg and Gregory Hoobler's study of college students, "Cyberstalking and the Technologies of Interpersonal Terrorism," found that almost a third responded that they had experienced some degree of computer-based harassment and pursuit (*New Media & Society,* vol. 4, no. 1, 2002). The authors wrote that "it stands to reason that if there are classes of people who elect, or are driven obsessively, to pursue intimacy with others that these pursuers will seek whatever means are available that might increase their access to the objects of their pursuit, and that people's increasing exposure on and through the computer will make them more accessible as victims."

Although the extent of the problem is difficult to measure, by 1999 cyberstalking had generated enough concern to warrant the report from the U.S. attorney general, *Cyberstalking: A New Challenge for Law Enforcement and Industry,* to then vice president Al Gore. The attorney general's report cautioned that although cyberstalking does not involve physical contact, it should not be considered less dangerous than physical stalking. In fact, the ease and anonymous nature of online communication coupled with increased access to personal information may pose a greater threat because potential stalkers unable or unwilling to confront victims in person may not hesitate to send menacing electronic mail messages. Finally, although there is no research to support or refute the contention that cyberstalking leads to more serious violent relationships, recent incidents investigated by representatives of the media and reports from law enforcement agencies underscore the potential for dire consequences.

CASES MAKE HEADLINE NEWS. The attorney general's report recounted three of many serious instances of cyberstalking that attracted attention in the media and among policymakers. The first successful prosecution under California's cyberstalking law was in Los Angeles, where a fifty-year-old man stalked a twenty-eight-year-old woman who had refused his advances. He posted her name and telephone number online along with messages saying she wanted to be raped. The Internet posts prompted men to knock on the woman's door, often during the night, in the hopes of fulfilling the fantasy her stalker had posted. In April 1999, the accused pleaded guilty to stalking and solicitation of sexual assault and was sentenced to a six-year prison term.

Another California case involved an honors graduate student at the University of San Diego who entered a guilty plea after sending, over the course of a year, hundreds of violent and menacing e-mail messages to five female university students he had never met. He also faces up to six years in prison. The third case cited in the report

was prosecuted in Massachusetts, where a man repeatedly harassed coworkers via e-mail and attempted to extort sexual favors from one of them.

In July 2002, the CBS News program *48 Hours* investigated a lethal case of cyberstalking that shocked the nation. In 1999 a twenty-year-old New Hampshire resident named Amy Boyer was killed by a cyberstalker she had met, but never befriended or dated, years earlier in the eighth grade. Unknown to Boyer, her stalker had apparently obsessed over her for years and had constructed a Web site that described his stalking of Boyer and his plans to kill her. He used an investigation service to discover where she worked and ambushed her as she left, shooting her and then killing himself. Boyer's death inspired her parents to speak out and champion anti-cyberstalking laws, which as of July 2002 were in place in twenty states.

Law Enforcement and Cyberstalking

Cyberspace has become a fertile field for illegal activity. By the use of new technology and equipment, which cannot be policed by traditional methods, cyberstalking has replaced traditional methods of stalking and harassment. Because cyberstalking has led to offline incidents of violent crime, police and prosecutors have cooperated to devise strategies to resolve these problems through the criminal justice system."

—Linda Fairstein, chief of the Sex Crimes Prosecution Unit, Manhattan District Attorney's Office

Cyberstalking presents some unique law enforcement challenges. Offenders are often able to use the anonymity of online communication to avoid detection and accountability for their actions. Appropriate interventions and recourse are unclear because often the stalker and his victim have never been in physical proximity to one another. Complicating the situation, the identity of the stalker may be difficult to determine. In Dallas a judge issued a temporary restraining order to stop an alleged offender from stalking his victim over the Internet. According to an October 1996 article that appeared in the *Dallas Morning News,* because the alleged stalker's address was unknown, the restraining order was served through e-mail and posted on the Internet.

Furthermore, in many jurisdictions law enforcement agencies are unprepared to investigate cyberstalking cases because they lack the expertise and training. The attorney general's study found that some victims had been advised by law enforcement agents to simply "turn off their computers" or to "come back should the offender confront or threaten them offline."

Finally, some state and local law enforcement agencies are frustrated in their efforts to track down cyberstalkers by the limits of their statutory authority. For example, the Cable Communications Policy Act of 1984 bars the release of cable subscriber information to law enforcement agencies without advance notice to the subscriber and a court order. Because a growing number of Internet users receive services via cable, the act inadvertently grants those wishing to remain anonymous for purposes of cyberstalking some legal protection from investigation. The attorney general's report called for modifications to the act to include provisions to help law enforcement agents gain access to the identifying information they need while maintaining privacy safeguards for cable customers. "It may be ironic," wrote Spitzberg and Hoobler, "that to combat the risks of cyberstalking, law enforcement may need the very tools of electronic surveillance and intrusion that are currently the source of many citizens' fundamental fears of privacy invasion."

CHAPTER 8

DOMESTIC VIOLENCE—THE LAWS AND THE COURTS

Before the 1962 landmark case *Self v. Self*, when the California Supreme Court ruled that "one spouse may maintain an action against the other for battering," women had no legal recourse against abusive partners. The judicial system had tended to view wife abuse as a matter to be resolved within the family. Maintaining that "a man's home is his castle," the U.S. government traditionally had been reluctant to violate the sanctity of the home. Furthermore, many legal authorities persisted in "blaming the victim," maintaining that the wife was, to some degree, responsible for her own beating by somehow inciting her husband to lose his temper. Yet even after the landmark California case, turning to the judicial system for help was still unlikely to bring assistance to or result in justice for victims of spousal abuse. Jurisdictions throughout the United States continued to ignore the complaints of battered women until the late 1970s.

LANDMARK LEGAL DECISIONS

Many victims of domestic violence have sought legal protection from their abusive partners. This section summarizes the outcomes of several landmark cases that not only helped to define judicial responsibility, but also shaped the policies and practices aimed at protecting victimized women.

Baker v. The City of New York

Sandra Baker was estranged from her husband. In 1955 the local Domestic Relations Court issued a protective order directing her husband, who had a history of serious mental illness, "not to strike, molest, threaten, or annoy" his wife. Baker called the police when her husband created a disturbance at the family home. When a police officer arrived, she showed him the court order. The officer told her it was "no good" and "only a piece of paper" and refused to take any action.

Baker went to the Domestic Relations Court and told her story to a probation officer. While making a phone call, she saw her husband in the corridor. She went to the probation officer and told him her husband was in the corridor. She asked if she could wait in his office because she was "afraid to stand in the room with him." The probation officer told her to leave and go to the waiting room. Minutes later, her husband shot and wounded her.

Baker sued the City of New York, claiming that the city owed her more protection than she was given. The New York State Supreme Court Appellate Division, in *Baker v. The City of New York* (1966), agreed that the city of New York failed to fulfill its obligation. The court found that she was "a person recognized by order of protection as one to whom a special duty was owed . . . and peace officers had a duty to supply protection to her." Neither the police officer nor the probation officer had fulfilled this duty and both were found guilty of negligence. Since the officers were representatives of the city of New York, Baker had the right to sue the city.

Equal Protection

Another option desperate women have used in response to unchecked violence and abuse is to sue the police for failing to offer protection, alleging that the police violated their constitutional rights to liberty and equal protection under the law.

The Equal Protection Clause of the Fourteenth Amendment provides that no state shall "deny to any person within its jurisdiction the equal protection of the laws." This clause prohibits states from arbitrarily classifying individuals by group membership. If a woman can prove that a police department has a gender-based policy of refusing to arrest men who abuse their wives, she can claim that the policy is based on gender stereotypes and therefore violates the equal protection laws.

THURMAN V. CITY OF TORRINGTON. Between October 1982 and June 1983 Tracey Thurman repeatedly called the Torrington, Connecticut, police to report that her estranged husband was threatening her life and that of her child. The police ignored her requests for help no matter how often she called or how serious the situation became. She tried to file complaints against her husband but city officials ignored her.

Even when her husband was finally arrested after attacking her in full view of a policeman and after a judge issued an order prohibiting him to go to his wife's home, the police continued to ignore Thurman's pleas for help. Her husband violated the order and came to her house and threatened her. When she asked the police to arrest her husband for violating his probation and threatening her life, they ignored her. She obtained a restraining order against her husband, which he violated, but again the police failed to take any action.

On June 10, 1983, Thurman's husband came to her home. She called the police. He then stabbed her repeatedly around the chest, neck, and throat. A police officer arrived twenty-five minutes later but did not arrest her husband, despite the attack. Three more policemen arrived. The husband went into the house and brought out their child and threw him down on his bleeding mother. The officers still did not arrest him. While his wife was on the stretcher waiting to be placed in the ambulance, he came at her again. Only at that point did police take him into custody. Thurman later sued the city of Torrington, claiming she was denied equal protection under the law.

In *Thurman v. City of Torrington* (1984), the U.S. District Court for Downstate Connecticut agreed, stating:

> City officials and police officers are under an affirmative duty to preserve law and order, and to protect the personal safety of persons in the community. This duty applies equally to women whose personal safety is threatened by individuals with whom they have or have had a domestic relationship as well as to all other persons whose personal safety is threatened, including women not involved in domestic relationships. If officials have notice of the possibility of attacks on women in domestic relationships or other persons, they are under an affirmative duty to take reasonable measures to protect the personal safety of such persons in the community.

> [A] police officer may not knowingly refrain from interference in such violence, and may not automatically decline to make an arrest simply because the assailant and his victim are married to each other. Such inaction on the part of the officer is a denial of the equal protection of the laws.

For the federal district court, there could be little question that "such inaction on the part of the officers was a denial of the equal protection of the laws." The police could not claim that they were promoting domestic harmony by refraining from interference in a marital dispute because research had conclusively demonstrated that police inaction supports the continuance of violence. There could be no question, the court concluded, that the city of Torrington, through its police department, had "condoned a pattern or practice of affording inadequate protection or no protection at all, to women who complained of having been abused by their husbands or others with whom they have had close relations." The police had, therefore, failed in their duty to protect Tracey Thurman and deserved to be sued.

The federal court jury awarded Thurman $2.3 million in compensatory damages. Almost immediately, the state of Connecticut changed the law, calling for the arrest of assaultive spouses. In the twelve months following the new law, arrests for domestic assault almost doubled from 12,400 to 23,830.

Due Process

The Due Process Clause of the Fourteenth Amendment provides that "no State shall deprive any person of life, liberty, or property without due process of law," protecting against state actions that are unfair or arbitrary. It does not, however, obligate the state to protect the public from harm or provide services that would protect them. Rather, a state may create special conditions in which that state has constitutional obligations to particular citizens because of a "special relationship between the state and the individual." Abused women have used this argument to claim that being under a protection order puts them in a "special relationship."

DESHANEY V. WINNEBAGO COUNTY DEPARTMENT OF SOCIAL SERVICES. The "special relationship" and the gains women achieved in *Thurman* lost their power with the Supreme Court case of *DeShaney v. Winnebago County Department of Social Services* (1989). A young boy, Joshua DeShaney, was repeatedly abused by his father. Despite repeated hospitalizations, the Department of Social Services insisted that there was insufficient evidence to remove the child from the home. Eventually, the father beat the boy into a coma, causing permanent brain damage. The boy's mother, who did not have custody, sued the Department of Social Services for not intervening. The Supreme Court ruled that the due process clause does not grant citizens any general right to government aid and that a "special relationship" is a custodial relationship. The court's decision noted, "The facts of this case are undeniably tragic" but "the affirmative duty to protect arises not from the state's knowledge of the individual's predicament or from its expressions of intent to help him, but from the limitations that it has imposed on his freedom to act on his own behalf, through imprisonment, institutionalization, and other similar restraint of personality."

The court concluded,

> It is well to remember once again that the harm was inflicted not by the State of Wisconsin, but by Joshua's

father. The most that can be said of the state functionaries in this case is that they stood by and did nothing when suspicious circumstances dictated a more active role for them. The people of Wisconsin may well prefer a system of liability that would place upon the State and its officials the responsibility for failure to act in situations such as the present one. . . . But they should not have it thrust upon them by this Court's expansion of the Due Process Clause of the Fourteenth Amendment.

Although this case concerned a child, it also applied to abused women. Following *DeShaney*, women have been unable to win a case on the basis of due process or equal protection. Jena Balistreri's case against the police department of Pacifica, California, began before *DeShaney*, but unfortunately for her, it was not finally decided until after the *DeShaney* precedent had been established.

BALISTRERI V. PACIFICA POLICE DEPARTMENT. Jena Balistreri first called police in February 1982 when her husband beat her. The police refused to arrest him, and one of the officers stated that Balistreri deserved the beating. In November 1982 Balistreri obtained a restraining order forbidding her husband from "harassing, annoying, or having contact with her." Despite repeated vandalism that included crashing his car into her garage and firebombing her home, the police refused to take Balistreri seriously. She turned to the courts in an effort to force police to restrain her husband.

Two out of the three judges of the U.S. Court of Appeals for the Ninth Circuit, both women, found that Balistreri's case might convince a jury that the police were guilty either of "intentional harassment" or "reckless indifference to her safety." The police's conduct, the judges wrote, "strongly suggest[s] an intention to treat domestic abuse cases less seriously than other assaults, as well as an animus against abused women," and their behavior may "violate equal protection."

Regarding the due process claim, Balistreri argued that she had a special relationship with the state because the police knew she was being terrorized and she had a protection order. Two judges ruled she might have a claim to a "special relationship" and the state might, after all, have "a duty to take reasonable measures to protect Balistreri from her estranged husband."

The third judge dissented, stating that the restraining order "heightens the state's awareness" of her risk of harm, "but the mere existence of the order" created no "special relationship" to the state and imposed no constitutional duty to protect her. The case was initially returned to the lower courts for further proceedings. After *DeShaney*, however, the court reversed its decision and threw out Balistreri's due process claim.

MACIAS V. IHDE. During the eighteen months before her estranged husband Avelino Macias murdered her at her place of work, Maria Teresa Macias had filed twenty-two police complaints. In the months before her death, Avelino Macias sexually abused his wife, broke into her home, terrorized, and stalked her. The victim's family filed a wrongful death lawsuit against the Sonoma County, California, Sheriff's Department, accusing the department of failing to provide Macias equal protection under the law and of discriminating against her as a Hispanic and a woman.

The U.S. District Court for the Northern District of California dismissed the case because Judge D. Lowell Jensen said there was no connection between Macias's murder and how the sheriff's department had responded to her complaints. Although the lower court had dismissed the family's claim, on July 20, 2000, the U.S. Court of Appeals for the Ninth Circuit reversed the earlier decision and ruled that the lawsuit could proceed with the discovery phase and pretrial motions. Judge Arthur L. Alarcon of the U.S. Court of Appeals for the Ninth Circuit conveyed the unanimous opinion of the court when he wrote, "It is well established that there is no constitutional right to be protected by the state against being murdered by criminals or madmen. There is a constitutional right, however, to have police services administered in a nondiscriminatory manner—a right that is violated when a state actor denies such protection to disfavored persons."

After this decision, the case proceeded to trial. On June 18, 2002, Sonoma County agreed to pay $1 million to the Macias family in order to settle the case. The settlement agreement did not include an admission of any wrongdoing by the county. Nevertheless, domestic violence activists lauded the result. Kim Gandy, president of the National Organization for Women, stated, "This settlement shows that law enforcement cannot get away with denying equal protection under the law to victims of domestic violence."

KEY DOMESTIC VIOLENCE LEGISLATION

While appealing to the judicial system for help will not solve all the problems an abused woman faces, the reception a battered woman can expect from the system—police, prosecutors, and courts—has improved markedly over the past several years. The Violence against Women Act, signed into law by President Bill Clinton in September 1994, did much to help. The act simultaneously strengthened prevention and prosecution of violent crimes against women and provided law enforcement officials with the tools they needed to prosecute batterers. Although the system is far from perfect, legal authorities are far more likely to view abuse complaints as legitimate and serious than they had in the past.

The Violence against Women Act

A key provision in the Violence against Women Act, the civil rights provisions of Title III, declared that violent crimes against women motivated by gender violate victims' federal civil rights—giving victims access to federal courts for redress for the first time. In testifying in favor of the passage of the act, Sally Goldfarb, an attorney for the National Organization for Women (NOW), told Senate members, "The enactment of civil rights legislation would convey a powerful message: that violence motivated by gender is not merely an individual crime or a personal injury, but is a form of discrimination, an assault on a publicly shared ideal of equality. When half of our citizens are not safe at home or on the streets because of their sex, our entire society is diminished" (Prepared Statement of Sally Goldfarb, Senior Staff Attorney, NOW Legal Defense and Education Fund. Senate Hearing 103-51, November 16, 1993. Hearing before the Subcommittee on Civil and Constitutional Rights of the Committee on the Judiciary House of Representatives. Serial No. 51). When the Violence against Women Act was passed into law, the text of the civil rights provision was:

> Federal civil rights action as specified in this section is necessary to guarantee equal protection of the laws and to reduce the substantial adverse effects on interstate commerce caused by crimes of violence motivated by gender; and the victims of crimes of violence motivated by gender have a right to equal protection of the laws, including a system of justice that is unaffected by bias or discrimination and that, at every relevant stage, treats such crimes as seriously as other violent crimes.

In 1999, the civil rights section of the act was tested in the U.S. Supreme Court. Christy Brzonkala, an eighteen-year-old freshman at Virginia Polytechnic Institute, was violently attacked and raped by two men, Antonio Morrison and James Crawford, on September 21, 1994. Brzonkala did not immediately report the rape, and no physical evidence of the rapes was preserved. Two months later, she filed a complaint with the school; after learning that the college took limited action against the two men, she withdrew from the school and sued her assailants for damages in federal court.

Brzonkala's case reached the Supreme Court in 1999. Briefs in favor of giving victims of gender-based violence access to federal courts were filed by dozens of groups—the American Medical Women's Association, the National Association of Human Rights Workers, the National Coalition against Domestic Violence, and the National Women's Health Network among them—as well as the briefs filed by law scholars and human rights experts. But the majority of the Supreme Court (five to four) decided that Congress could not enact a law giving victims of gender-motivated violence access to federal civil rights remedies. The majority opinion emphasized that "the Constitution requires a distinction between what is truly national and what is truly local"—and they ruled that the violent assault of Christy Brzonkala was local (United States, Petitioner v. Antonio J. Morrison et al. [no. 99-5],

Christy Brzonkala, Petitioner v. Antontio J. Morrison et al. [no. 99-29]. Argued January 11, 2000. Decided May 15, 2000. *United States Supreme Court Reports, Lawyer's Edition*. Volume 146 L Ed. 2d, No. 6).

In October 2000, Congress responded to the Supreme Court decision by passing new legislation, the Victims of Trafficking and Violence Protection Act of 2000. The new statute included these titles: Strengthening Law Enforcement to Reduce Violence against Women, Strengthening Services to Victims of Violence, Limiting the Effects of Violence on Children, and Strengthening Education and Training to Combat Violence against Women. The act allocated $3.3 billion over five years to fund traditional support services along with prevention and education about dating violence, rape, and stalking via the Internet, as well as new programs for transitional housing and expanded protection for immigrant women. The new act did not mention women's civil rights.

Other Federal Laws and Public Policies

The following are among other federal laws and public policies aimed at addressing violent crimes against women:

• The Family Violence Prevention and Services Act of 1992 supported the development and expansion of shelters and other services for victims of domestic violence as well as programs to prevent family violence.

• The Hillory J. Farias and Samantha Reid Date Rape Drug Prohibition Act of 2000 made it illegal to manufacture, distribute, or dispense gamma hydroxybutyric acid (GHB, also known as "Liquid Ecstasy") and created a special unit to evaluate abuse and trafficking of GHB and other drugs associated with instances of sexual assault.

• The Social Security Administration in 1998 changed its rules governing new social security numbers. Previously, women needed to provide evidence that an abuser was using a social security number to locate her or evidence that the violence was life-threatening. With the new law, women need only to provide written corroboration of domestic violence from a third party, such as a doctor, lawyer, clergy member, or even a family member or friend, in order to obtain a new number.

• A Postal Service Release of Information Final Rule was published January 25, 2000, and became effective February 24, 2000. If an individual postal customer presents the U.S. Postal Service with a court order of protection, then the postal service may not disclose identifying information such as address, location, or post office box, unless ordered by the court.

• A Final Rule on Documentation of Immigrants and Nonimmigrants—Visa Classification Symbols was published on June 18, 2001. This rule amended PL

TABLE 8.1

Reasons for rejections of firearm transfer applications, 1999–2003

Reason for rejection	FBI		State and local agencies					
	2003	1999–2003	2003	2002	2001	2000	1999	1999–2003
Total	100%	100%	100%	100%	100%	100%	100%	100%
Felony indictment/conviction	38.6	54.5	44.8	51.8	57.7	57.6	72.5	58.1
Other criminal history[1]	24.3	15.0	—	—	—	—	—	—
Domestic violence								
Misdemeanor conviction	12.2	13.3	11.7	10.4	10.6	8.9	9.0	10.0
Restraining order	5.0	4.4	3.8	3.5	3.7	3.3	2.1	3.2
State law prohibition[2]	—	—	10.4	9.9	7.0	4.7	3.5	6.7
Fugitive	4.7	3.3	7.8	8.0	5.8	4.3	5.0	5.9
Illegal alien	2.4	1.1	1.1	0.8	0.4	0.2	0.2	0.5
Mental illness or disability	0.5	0.4	2.4	1.4	1.2	1.0	0.5	1.2
Drug addiction	8.0	5.8	1.8	1.3	1.0	0.7	1.0	1.1
Local law prohibition	—	—	1.2	0.9	0.5	0.2	0.2	0.6
Other[3]	4.3	2.1	14.9	12.0	12.1	19.2	6.0	12.8

— Not available or not applicable.

[1]Includes multiple DUI's, non-NCIC warrants, and other unspecified criminal history disqualifiers.

[2]FBI denies on State prohibitors but does not separate them out under this category.

[3]Includes persons dishonorably discharged from the Armed Services, persons who have renounced their U.S. citizenship, and other unspecified persons.

SOURCE: "Table 5. Reasons for Rejection of Firearm Transfer Applications, 1999–2003," in *Background Checks for Firearm Transfers, 2003*, U.S. Department of Justice, Bureau of Justice Statistics, NCJ 204428, September 2004, http://www.ojp.usdoj.gov/bjs/pub/pdf/bcft03.pdf (accessed October 22, 2004)

106-386 to create new nonimmigrant categories for victims of trafficking for illicit sexual purposes and slavery and those who have suffered abuse, such as battering, and other forms of violence.

In addition, on January 26, 2001, the U.S. Sentencing Commission published the Sentencing Guidelines for United States Courts, which increased the base sentencing levels for offenses and required stricter sentences for stalking, domestic violence, and cases involving the use of GHB.

Domestic Violence Gun Ban

The Omnibus Consolidated Appropriations Act of 1997 included a domestic violence gun ban. The law prohibits batterers convicted of domestic violence crimes or those with domestic violence protection orders filed against them from owning or carrying guns. During 1997, background checks of potential handgun buyers prevented an estimated sixty-nine thousand purchases. Most of those rejected (62 %) had been convicted of a felony or were under felony indictment. Domestic violence misdemeanor convictions represented nearly 10% of the rejections, while domestic violence restraining orders accounted for 2%.

On November 30, 1998, the permanent provisions of an even tighter handgun ban, the Brady Handgun Prevention Act, went into effect. These provisions require background checks for anyone seeking to transfer ownership of a gun, which includes pawnshop transactions as well as purchases from retail gun shops.

From the inception of the Brady Act on March 1, 1994, through December 31, 2003, more than 53 million applications for firearm permits or transfers were subjected to background investigations. Of these applications, about

1,102,000 were rejected, according to *Background Checks for Firearm Transfers, 2003* (Washington, DC: Bureau of Justice Statistics, NCJ 204428, September 2004). In 2003, about 17% of those rejected were rejected because the Federal Bureau of Investigation or state or local police agencies found that applicants had been either convicted of a domestic violence misdemeanor or had a protective order issued against them. (See Table 8.1.) After prior felony convictions, domestic violence was the second leading reason for rejecting applicants' gun permit requests.

RESPONSES TO THE BAN. The passage of the domestic violence gun ban was a victory for the battered women's movement but generated an outcry in the law enforcement community. Because the ban applied retroactively, anyone, including police officers, convicted of domestic violence before passage of the law on September 30, 1996, lost the right to possess and carry firearms.

The law has been hotly debated. Some people feel that law enforcement officers and military personnel who use firearms in their professional duties should be exempt from the prohibition. Others want to apply the ban only to those convicted of domestic violence after the date when the gun ban was enacted. Still others maintain that all persons convicted of such offenses should be prohibited from carrying firearms. Legislation has been introduced that would apply the ban only to those convicted after September 30, 1996, and that would exempt government employees, such as military and police.

After the domestic violence gun ban passed, John W. Magaw of the federal Bureau of Alcohol, Tobacco, Firearms and Explosives advised police officers to turn over their firearms to a third party if they had ever been convicted of a domestic violence misdemeanor. Most police groups claimed that the law unfairly punished officers who committed domestic violence offenses in the past, and requested that exceptions be made for police officers who would be unable to conduct their law enforcement duties without firearms. However, in 1999 the Supreme Court rejected a policeman's argument that he had the right to carry a gun even though he had pleaded guilty to domestic violence (*Gillespie v. City of Indianapolis*, 1999 U.S. App. Lexis 15117).

In 1998, at the request of the U.S. Department of Justice, the International Association of Chiefs of Police drafted the *Model Policy on Police Officer Domestic Violence*. In an attempt to address the domestic violence problem before it cost an officer his or her job, the policy took a "continuum" approach, including these increasing levels of intervention:

• prevention, education, and training

• early warning and intervention

• incident response protocols

• victim safety and protection

• administrative and prosecutorial actions after an incident

Although the policy focuses on early prevention and intervention strategies, it also states that officers convicted of domestic abuse will be removed from their enforcement positions and either terminated or reassigned. It calls on police departments to screen recruits for any indications of violent or abusive tendencies and to conduct background checks for histories of domestic violence or abuse.

Despite the increased restrictions mandated by the Brady Act, convicted batterers and those subject to an order of protection can still buy guns. Loopholes in state and federal laws allow batterers to purchase guns. In many states, private gun owners can sell their firearms without background checks. In addition, many states keep incomplete records of domestic violence offenders and orders of protection. The Bureau of Justice Statistics has made recommendations to address these holes in domestic violence record keeping in its report *Background Checks for Firearm Transfers, 2003* (Washington, DC: Bureau of Justice Statistics, NCJ 204428, September 2004). Still other evidence suggests that some gun dealers knowingly allow people who are not legally eligible to purchase firearms to buy them through a third party.

FILING CHARGES

In the past, the victims shouldered the burden of filing charges in domestic violence cases. Prosecutors and the courts offered victims little support or protection. Currently, the decision to charge offenders in cases of domestic violence is notable for having less to do with legal

criteria than with evaluation of the victims' and offenders' personal attributes. Prosecutors are more likely to charge in cases where victims suffer serious injuries and defendants have a record of previous arrests. Negative characteristics in the offender, such as alcohol or drug use and the failure to comply with the police and courts, increase the likelihood that charges will be pressed. Yet, the same attributes in the abused woman call into question her status as an innocent victim. Eve Buzawa and Carl Buzawa explored these issues in *Current Controversies on Family Violence* (Newbury Park, CA: Sage, 1993). In the book they stated that more than a third of misdemeanor domestic violence cases would have been felony offenses of rape, robbery, or aggravated assault had they been committed by strangers rather than intimates.

Who should file the charges: the state through the prosecutor or the victim? In *Confronting Domestic Violence: A Guide for Criminal Justice Agencies* (Washington, DC: National Institute of Justice, 1986), advocates for the state filing the charges argued that this policy would:

• clearly establish spouse abuse as a crime

• force prosecutors to take domestic violence cases seriously and eliminate their reluctance to handle these cases because of their view that victims tend to seek dismissals or refuse to testify

• protect the community as a whole, since presumably innocent bystanders might be injured during future violence

• strengthen the criminal justice system's control over prosecution and increase the number of batterers convicted and held accountable for their actions (either through incarceration or court-ordered intervention)

• reduce the likelihood that batterers will intimidate and harass victims because they hold the victims responsible for their prosecution

Those recommending that victims file the charge argue:

• Battered women, when given full information, have the right and the ability to decide whether they want criminal justice intervention. For example, a battered woman might choose not to prosecute because she prefers civil remedies, faces life-threatening danger, fears race-biased sentencing, or would lose critical financial support.

• Civil remedies may be appropriate in some cases. If batterer counseling is viewed as a critical intervention, then it can be mandated through properly monitored and enforced civil protection orders, as well as through criminal action.

• There are other ways to address the potential for victim intimidation and harassment, including statutes that make intimidation of a witness a substantive crime and the use of protection orders a condition of release.

- Policies that eliminate victim discretion may serve to alienate battered women and discourage them from calling police or seeking other legal intervention in the future, thereby placing them in jeopardy of extreme injury or death.

Cheryl Hanna, in "No Right to Choose: Mandated Victim Participation in Domestic Violence Prosecutions," argued that many jurisdictions now have pro-prosecution policies that "treat domestic violence as a serious crime and recognize the ambivalence that abused women bring to the process" (*Harvard Law Review*, June 1996). However, not all pro-prosecution policies are the same—they might be "hard" or "soft." Under hard policies, batterers are prosecuted regardless of victims' wishes; government attorneys are required to file criminal charges against domestic violence offenders, and abused women are given no option to drop the case. However, under the soft policies of most jurisdictions, prosecutors do not force victims to take part in criminal proceedings, but instead provide support services and encouragement to continue the process of prosecuting abusers.

Should a Woman Be Forced to File?

Advocates who favor the victim filing charges agree that when the lives of others are clearly endangered, battered women must be expected to cooperate with the prosecution. To pressure women to testify, some prosecutors have charged them with filing false police reports and perjury or lying to the court. In rare instances, they have been jailed. Some prosecutors see this as a further abuse of an already demoralized woman, while others claim that allowing the woman to drop charges sends the message that the court does not take her problems seriously.

Victims' advocates claim that when the courts help women file charges and support them throughout the process, many more women follow through—an endorsement for "soft" pro-prosecution policies. For example, in Brockton, Massachusetts, a court found that 71% of women who obtained restraining orders did not appear at their hearings ten days later. In comparison, in a Quincy, Massachusetts, court with a separate office for restraining orders and support groups for the women, only 2.8% of the women failed to show at their hearings.

Some research reports an unintended result of hard, no-drop policies: Battered women who were given the option to drop charges were at lower risk for subsequent violence than women who were not allowed to drop charges. Simply being able to participate in decision making with authorities served to empower the women. This finding is consistent with the observations of Carolyn Hoyle and Andrew Sanders in "Police Response to Domestic Violence: From Victim Choice to Victim Empowerment?" (*British Journal of Criminology*, vol. 40, 2000), who advocated for policies to empower, rather than to further disable victims of domestic violence.

THE COURTS

An appeal to the American judicial system should be an effective method of obtaining justice. For battered women, however, this has not always been the case. In the past, ignorance, social prejudices, and uneven attention from the criminal justice system all tended to underestimate the severity and importance of battering crimes against women. Although society has become significantly less tolerant of domestic violence, and laws in many states criminalize behavior previously considered acceptable, old attitudes and biases continue to plague intimate partner violence and spouse abuse cases in the courts.

Intimate partner abuse cases are often complicated by evidence problems because domestic violence usually takes place behind closed doors. The volatile and unpredictable emotions and motivations influencing the behavior of both the abuser and victim may not always fit neatly into the organized and systematic framework of legal case presentation. Finally, training mandates to ensure that prosecutors and judges are better informed about the social and personal costs of domestic violence, along with society's changing attitudes toward abuse, influence the responses of the judicial system.

Keeping the Family Together

Traditionally, the family has been the basis of American society. While the value of an intact family cannot be underestimated, the traditional family is one of the fastest changing aspects of our culture. Preserving an unhappy marriage "for the children's sake" is much less common than it was just two generations ago. Nonetheless, there are still many women, police officers, lawyers, judges, and other community opinion leaders, such as members of the clergy, politicians, and social scientists, who feel that only the most extreme instances of abuse justify breaking up a family.

In the past, many judges backed away from the responsibility to punish batterers under the pretense of protecting and preserving the family. *Confronting Domestic Violence*, cited above, quoted a judge who claimed, "Even if the woman shows up in my court with visible injuries, I don't really have any way of knowing who is responsible or who I should kick out of the house. Yes, he may have beaten her but nagging and a sharp tongue can be just as bad. Maybe she used her sharp tongue so often . . . she provoked him to hit her."

Confronting Domestic Violence offered evidence that attitudes are changing and cited several judges' statements from the bench. "I don't care if she's your wife or not," one judge declared. "A marriage license is not a hitting license. If you think that the courts can't pin you for assaulting your wife, you are sadly mistaken." When another defendant claimed his girlfriend had provoked a beating, the judge warned, "This is your problem, not your girlfriend's. You will damage your next relationship in the same way if you don't get help." Another judge took the pressure off a wife testifying against her abusive husband by saying, "It's not your wife's fault that she's here to testify. She has no choice. I could have arrested her to make her come. She's not prosecuting you. The city is. She's required to tell the truth. It's perjury if she doesn't."

Alcohol and Drug Abuse and Domestic Violence Cases

Alcohol, and later illegal drug abuse, has sometimes been considered the cause of domestic violence. Authorities base this conclusion on studies like that of William Fals-Stewart in "The Occurrence of Partner Physical Aggression on Days of Alcohol Consumption: A Longitudinal Diary Study." He found that the likelihood of physical aggression toward intimate partners among battering males entering outpatient alcoholism or domestic violence treatment programs was eight to eleven times higher on days when the male partner consumed alcohol (*Journal of Consulting and Clinical Psychology*, vol. 71, no. 1, 2003). Even though a causal link has not been established, courts and other authorities encourage and mandate that substance abusers seek treatment on the assumption that curing a drinking or drug problem would bring an end to abuse.

Some researchers, however, refute the hypothesis that completing substance abuse treatment programs effectively serves to reduce rates of intimate partner violence or prevent recurrences of battering. These researchers include Julia C. Babcock and Ramalina Steiner, writing in "The Relationship between Treatment, Incarceration, and Recidivism of Battering: A Program Evaluation of Seattle's Coordinated Community Response to Domestic Violence" (*Journal of Family Psychology*, vol. 13, no. 1, March 1999).

Obstacles to Prosecuting Abusers

One of the most formidable problems in prosecuting abusers is the victim's reluctance to cooperate. Although many abused women have the courage to initiate legal proceedings against their batterers, some are later reluctant to cooperate with the prosecution because of their emotional attachment to their abusers. Other sources of their reluctance are fear of retaliation, mistrust or lack of information about the criminal justice system, or fear of the demands of court appearances. These are among findings by Lisa Goodman, Lauren Bennett, and Mary Ann Dutton (cited below) and JoAnn Miller in "An Arresting Experiment: Domestic Violence Victim Experiences and Perceptions" (*Journal of Interpersonal Violence*, vol. 18, no. 7, July 2003). A victim's fear and ambivalence about testifying, and the importance of her behavior as a witness, can undoubtedly discourage some prosecutors from taking action.

On the other hand, a victim might choose not to move forward with the prosecution because the violence ceases temporarily following the arrest while the batterer is in custody. Most women do not want their husbands to go to jail with the attendant loss of income and community standing. They simply want their husbands to stop beating them.

Religious convictions, economic dependency, and family influence to drop the charges place great pressure on victimized women. Consequently, many prosecutors, some of whom believe abuse is a purely personal problem and others who believe winning the case is unlikely, test the victim's resolve to make sure she will not back out. This additional pressure drives many women to drop the charges because after being controlled by their husbands, they feel that the judicial system is repeating the pattern by abusing its power. Hence, the prosecutors' fears contribute to the problem, creating a self-perpetuating cycle.

A STUDY OF VICTIMS' WILLINGNESS TO COOPERATE. In "Obstacles to Victims' Cooperation with the Criminal Prosecution of Their Abusers: The Role of Social Support" (*Violence and Victims*, vol. 14, no. 4, Winter 1999), Goodman, Bennett, and Dutton explored the reasons many domestic violence victims refuse to cooperate in the prosecution of their abusers.

Goodman, Bennett, and Dutton studied ninety-two abused women in Washington, D.C., whose partners had been arrested on misdemeanor domestic abuse charges, such as simple assault, threats, or destruction of personal property. Almost 90% of the women were African-Americans aged eighteen to forty-six; they had lived with their abusive partners for, on average, a little more than three years.

The participants generally reported high levels of physical violence during the previous year with 90% reporting at least one instance of severe physical violence. More than half reported an instance of "minor" sexual assault and a comparable proportion reported severe injury from sexual abuse or physical assault.

The victims all struggled with a number of health and socioeconomic problems. More than half were unemployed, about three-quarters reported symptoms consistent with a diagnosis of clinical depression, and about one-fifth met the criteria for substance abuse. Despite these difficulties, Goodman, Bennett, and Dutton found that more than half of the women cooperated with the prosecution at the time of the defendant's first scheduled trial date, about twelve weeks into the case. Women who received tangible support, such as help with taking care of their children or an emergency loan, were about twice as likely to cooperate with the prosecution of their abuser as women who received little support. Researchers cited several possible reasons for this finding. Although 82.7% of the participants were not financially dependent on the abuser, some indicated that the abuser provided other forms of support, such as child care or transportation. When families or friends provided these types of support, the victims were more likely to seek help from the criminal justice system and cooperate with prosecutors.

Surprisingly, the researchers found that the relationship between emotional support and cooperation with prosecutors was not significant. Similarly, institutional support, whether from police or victim advocates, was also unrelated to cooperation. Psychological factors also were unrelated to cooperation—neither level of depression nor degree of emotional attachment to the abuser had an effect. This finding refuted the common perception that the battered woman is too depressed, helpless, or attached to the abuser to cooperate in his prosecution. Instead, Goodman, Bennett, and Dutton's findings showed that many domestic violence victims persevere in the face of depression and the sometimes complex emotional attachment to their partner.

Consistent with findings from earlier studies, Goodman, Bennett, and Dutton found that the more severe the violence, the more likely the abuse women were to cooperate with prosecutors. Participants rearing children with the abuser were also more likely to cooperate, perhaps because these women hoped that the criminal justice system would force the abuser into treatment.

In contrast, women with substance abuse problems were less than half as likely as other women to cooperate with the prosecution. Goodman, Bennett, and Dutton concluded that the women who used alcohol or drugs believed that the abuse was partly their fault or that a judge would not take them seriously. Some also feared that their substance abuse might negatively affect the court proceedings and possibly even lead to criminal charges or the loss of their children.

DIFFERING RESPONSES TO STRANGER AND NONSTRANGER CRIME

The victim-offender relationship is an important factor in determining how the offender is treated by the criminal justice system. In general, strangers are treated more harshly because stranger offenses are considered more heinous and the true targets of the justice system. As a result, the criminal law is strictly enforced against them. On the other hand, the justice system has traditionally perceived nonstranger offenses as a victim's misuse of the legal system to deal with strained interpersonal relationships.

Several studies confirm that while intimate partners are frequently charged with and convicted of more serious offenses, stranger offenders generally receive longer sentences. In addition, most intimate partner crimes never go to sentencing, because victims drop charges or settle out of court. Those cases that do proceed through the judicial system are likely to be the more serious crimes.

PROTECTION ORDERS

A victim in any state may go to court to obtain a protection order prohibiting an abuser from harming her. Also referred to as "restraining orders" or "injunctions," civil orders of protection are legally binding court orders that prohibit an individual who has committed an act of domestic violence from further abusing the victim. Although the terms are often used interchangeably, restraining orders usually refer to short-term or temporary sanctions, while protection orders have longer duration and may be permanent. These orders generally prohibit harassment, contact, communication, and physical proximity to the victim. Although protection orders are common and readily obtained, they are not always effective.

All states and the District of Columbia have laws that allow an abused adult to petition the court for an order of protection. States also have laws to permit persons in other relationships with the abuser to file for protection orders. Relatives of the victim, children of either partner, couples in dating relationships, same-sex couples, and former spouses are among those who can file for a protection order in a majority of the states, the District of Columbia, and Puerto Rico. In Hawaii and Illinois, those who shelter an abused person can also obtain a protective order against the abuser.

In addition to violent physical abuse, petitioners may file for protection orders in other circumstances, including sexual assault, marital rape, harassment, emotional abuse, and stalking. Protection orders are valid for varying lengths of time depending on the state. In thirty states, the orders are in force for six months to a year. In Illinois and Wisconsin the orders last two years, and in California and Hawaii they are in effect for three years. Furthermore, some states have extended the time during which a general or incident-specific protective order is effective. For example, a no-contact order issued against a stalker convicted in California remains in effect for ten years. In Iowa, five-year protection orders are issued and additional five-year extensions may be obtained. New Jersey offers permanent protective orders, and a conviction for stalking serves as an application for a permanent restraining order. Judges in Connecticut may issue standing criminal restraining orders that remain in effect until they are altered or revoked by the court.

Protection orders give victims an option other than filing a criminal complaint. Issued quickly, usually within twenty-four hours, they provide safety for the victim by barring or evicting the abuser from the household. However, this judicial protection has little meaning if the police do not maintain records and follow through with arrest should the abuser violate the order. Statutes in most states make violating a protection order a matter of criminal contempt, a misdemeanor, or even a felony.

The "full faith and credit" provision of the Violence against Women Act was passed to establish nationwide enforcement of protection orders in courts throughout the country. States, territories, and tribal lands were ordered to honor protection orders issued in other jurisdictions—although the act did not mandate how these orders were to be enforced. Most states have amended their state domestic violence codes or statutes to reflect the new requirement, although the states vary widely on how easy it is for battered women to get their protection orders enforced. Courts and law enforcement agencies in most states have access to electronic registries of protection orders, both to verify the existence of an order and to assess whether violations have occurred.

Effects of Protection Orders

In the National Center for State Court study *Civil Protection Orders: The Benefits and Limitations for Victims of Domestic Violence* (Washington, DC: National Institute of Justice, 1997), Susan Keilitz et al. reported that most women who petitioned for a civil protection order had suffered physical abuse for some time. One-quarter of the women interviewed endured abuse for more than five years before obtaining a protection order.

The researchers found that temporary protection orders may be useful even when the victim does not follow through to obtain a permanent order. When victims were asked why they did not return for permanent protection orders, most said that their abusers had stopped bothering them.

Although abusers often violate the protection orders in some way, the orders generally deter repeated incidents of physical and psychological abuse. Keilitz et al. found that the majority of abuse victims felt that civil protection orders protected them against repeated incidents of abuse and helped them regain a sense of well-being. In the initial interviews, 72.3% of the women who had received protection orders reported that their lives had improved. At the six-month follow-up interviews, the proportion had increased to 85.3%. More than 90% reported feeling better about themselves and 80.5% felt safer.

About 72% of participants in the initial interviews reported no continuing problems following the petition for protection orders, compared to 65.3% six months later. The follow-up interviews showed that reports of stalking increased from 4.1% to 7.2%. Reports of repeated physical and psychological abuse also increased. Abusers with a criminal history of violent offenses were more likely to violate protection orders, prompting the researchers to

observe that criminal prosecution may be required to stop abusive behavior in this group of perpetrators.

The Strength of a Protective Order

A federal report titled *Enforcement of Protective Orders* (Washington, DC: U.S. Department of Justice, January 2002) observed that while all states have passed some form of legislation to benefit victims of domestic violence, and thirty-two states have integrated these rights at the constitutional level, the scope and enforcement of these rights varies. The report called for law enforcement agencies, prosecutors, and judges to be completely informed about the existence and specific terms and requirements of orders and to act to enforce them. John W. Gilles, the director of the U.S. Department of Justice, Office for Victims of Crime, asserted that "[u]nequivocal, standardized enforcement of court orders is imperative if protective orders are to be taken seriously by the offenders they attempt to restrain."

Permanent Civil Protection Orders Reduce Risk

The results of research on civil protection orders were presented by Victoria Holt et al. in "Civil Protection Orders and Risk of Subsequent Police-Reported Violence" (*Journal of the American Medical Association*, vol. 288, no. 5, August 7, 2002). The study was supported by the Centers for Disease Control and Prevention, the National Institutes of Health, and the National Institute of Justice as part of the Interagency Consortium on Violence against Women and Family Violence Research. The researchers investigated whether obtaining a protection order acts to reduce the risk of subsequent police-reported intimate partner violence.

Holt et al. reviewed the cases of 2,691 female victims of intimate partner violence reported to the Seattle Police Department between August 1, 1998, and December 31, 1999. They looked at rates of police-reported physical and psychological abuse in the twelve months following the incident according to the victim's protection order status. Temporary protection orders were generally in effect for two weeks and permanent protection orders were usually in effect for one year. The researchers also followed those victims who chose not to obtain protection orders.

The researchers found that having a permanent protection order in effect was associated with an 80% reduction in police-reported physical violence in the twelve months following an incident of intimate partner violence. They also reported that women who had obtained temporary protection orders were more likely than victims with no protection orders to be psychologically abused in the six months after the reported incident of intimate partner violence.

Holt et al. speculated that temporary protection orders may have restrained abusers from inflicting physical violence, producing a commensurate increase in psychological abuse. They observed that while temporary orders were linked to increased psychological abuse, the orders did not generate the increased physical violence that many victims and service providers fear will ensue. The researchers concluded that concern about increased physical violence after obtaining temporary protection orders may be unfounded, and permanent protection orders may be more powerful deterrents to prevent violence recurrence than previously believed.

CHAPTER 9
WHEN WOMEN KILL THEIR PARTNERS

Women do not kill their intimate partners nearly as often as men do. The National Crime Victimization Surveys estimate that intimate partner homicide accounts for just 4% of murders of men but about one-third of the murders of women.

However, when women do kill, they are most likely to kill an intimate partner or other family member. In *Women Offenders,* a special report from the Bureau of Justice Statistics (Washington, DC: Office of Justice Programs, NCJ 175688, 1999), researchers stated that of the sixty thousand slayings committed by women between 1976 and 1997, just over 60% were committed against a nonstranger.

According to the Federal Bureau of Investigation's *Supplementary Homicide Report,* in 2002, 7% of all known murder offenders were female. Their victims were often their spouses or intimate partners. A 1994 Department of Justice study on "murder in families" analyzed ten thousand cases and determined that women made up more 41% of those charged in familial murders, but only 10.5% of those charged with murder overall.

In 2002, 388 male homicide victims (3.1%) and 1,202 female homicide victims (31.9%) were killed by an intimate partner. There are regional variations in the rates of intimate partner homicide. When the National Center for Injury Prevention and Control (part of the Centers for Disease Control and Prevention) analyzed Federal Bureau of Investigation data, southern and western states were found to have the highest rates of intimate partner homicide. Figure 9.1 shows the geographic variation of intimate partner homicide among white females by state, and Figure 9.2 displays the rates of intimate partner homicide by state for black females. Centers for Disease Control researchers also reported in *Morbidity and Mortality Weekly Report Surveillance Summaries* (vol. 50, no. SS03, October 12, 2001) that the risk of intimate partner homicide increases with population size—rates in metro-politan areas with more than 250,000 persons are two to three times higher than rates in cities with fewer than ten thousand residents.

Figure 9.3 shows that the number of males killed by intimate partners dropped by 71.4% between 1976 and 2002. Researchers and advocates for battered women attribute this dramatic decline to the widespread availability of support services for women, including shelters, crisis counseling, hotlines, and legal measures such as protection and restraining orders. These services offer abused women options for escaping violence and abuse other than taking their partners' lives. Other factors that may have contributed to the decline are the increased ease of obtaining divorce and the generally improved economic conditions for women.

SPOUSAL MURDER DEFENDANTS

In the report *Spouse Murder Defendants in Large Urban Counties* (Washington, DC: Bureau of Justice Statistics, 1995), researchers Patrick A. Langan and John W. Dawson reported on their examination and analysis of 540 spouse homicide cases in the nation's seventy-five largest counties—59% of the killers were husbands and 41% were wives. Even though Langan and Dawson analyzed data from crimes and court decisions that took place more than a decade ago, they explained that "[The Bureau of Justice Statistics] knows from long experience with surveying courts that changes in case processing are quite gradual. The report's results are, therefore, likely to be applicable today."

Nearly all the wives used weapons—95% of female suspects used a gun or knife. Men used those weapons only 69% of the time. Not surprisingly, in view of their generally larger size, strength, and body weight, husbands are far more likely than wives to strangle or beat their spouses to death.

FIGURE 9.1

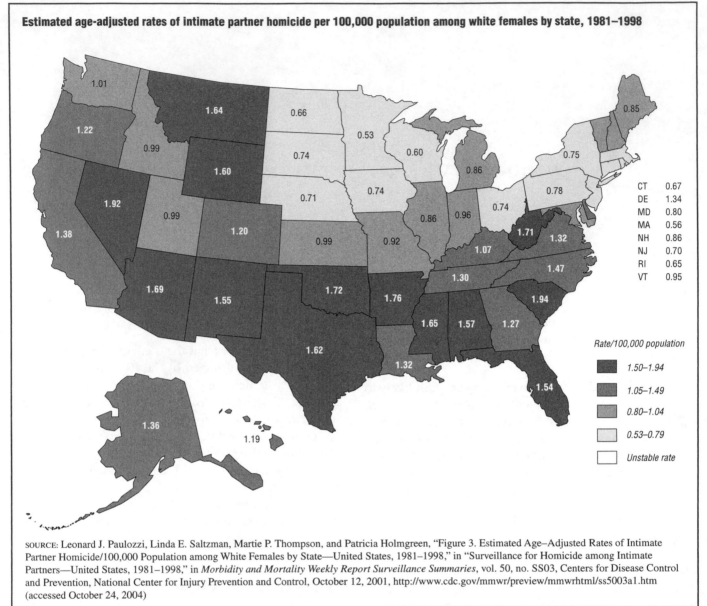

Estimated age-adjusted rates of intimate partner homicide per 100,000 population among white females by state, 1981–1998

CT	0.67
DE	1.34
MD	0.80
MA	0.56
NH	0.86
NJ	0.70
RI	0.65
VT	0.95

Rate/100,000 population

- 1.50–1.94
- 1.05–1.49
- 0.80–1.04
- 0.53–0.79
- Unstable rate

SOURCE: Leonard J. Paulozzi, Linda E. Saltzman, Martie P. Thompson, and Patricia Holmgreen, "Figure 3. Estimated Age–Adjusted Rates of Intimate Partner Homicide/100,000 Population among White Females by State—United States, 1981–1998," in "Surveillance for Homicide among Intimate Partners—United States, 1981–1998," in *Morbidity and Mortality Weekly Report Surveillance Summaries*, vol. 50, no. SS03, Centers for Disease Control and Prevention, National Center for Injury Prevention and Control, October 12, 2001, http://www.cdc.gov/mmwr/preview/mmwrhtml/ss5003a1.htm (accessed October 24, 2004)

Langan and Dawson also found that, proportionally, twice as many husbands (20%) killed in fits of jealousy. In addition, husbands who killed their wives were more likely to be substance abusers than wives who killed their husbands. Nearly one-third (31%) of the husbands had a history of drug abuse, compared to 9% of the wives. Almost one-quarter (22%) of the husbands were using drugs at the time of the crime, and two-thirds, or 66%, were drinking alcohol, compared to 3% and 37%, respectively, for the women. Another later study funded by the National Institute of Justice confirmed the high likelihood that when husbands murder or attempt to murder their wives, they are also abusing alcohol and drugs. Phyllis Sharps, Jacquelyn C. Campbell, Doris Campbell, Faye Gary, and Daniel Webster reported their findings in "Risky Mix: Drinking, Drug Use, and Homicide" (*National Institute of Justice Journal*, no. 250, November 2003).

Wives on Trial

Although women in Langan and Dawson's study were about as likely as men to be prosecuted, stand trial, or plead guilty to killing their spouses, female defendants were less likely to serve jail time. In part, this finding resulted from a larger percentage of husbands being convicted (41%) than wives (31%). Researchers found women were seven times more likely than men to be acquitted at trial.

Female defendants were also less likely to serve life sentences for killing their spouses than were male defendants. Convicted men were sentenced to prison terms more than twice as long as those received by convicted women. About half as many wives as husbands received life sentences (8% compared to 15%). Among wives sentenced to prison, only 15% received a sentence of twenty

FIGURE 9.2

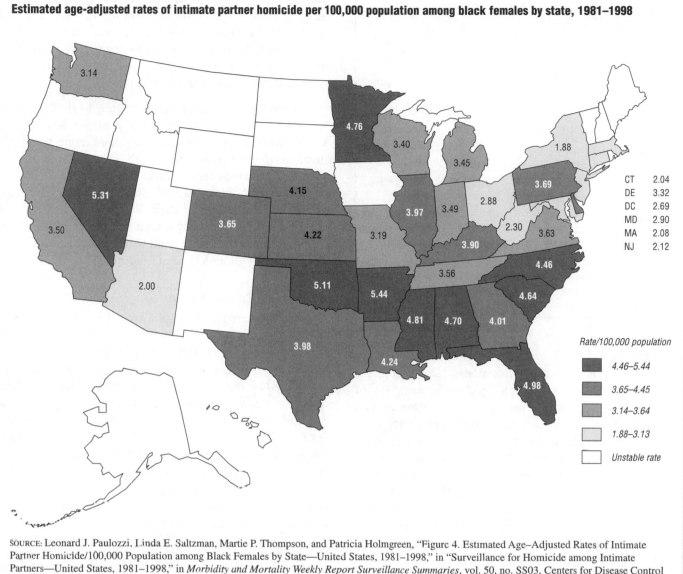

Estimated age-adjusted rates of intimate partner homicide per 100,000 population among black females by state, 1981–1998

CT	2.04
DE	3.32
DC	2.69
MD	2.90
MA	2.08
NJ	2.12

Rate/100,000 population

- 4.46–5.44
- 3.65–4.45
- 3.14–3.64
- 1.88–3.13
- Unstable rate

SOURCE: Leonard J. Paulozzi, Linda E. Saltzman, Martie P. Thompson, and Patricia Holmgreen, "Figure 4. Estimated Age–Adjusted Rates of Intimate Partner Homicide/100,000 Population among Black Females by State—United States, 1981–1998," in "Surveillance for Homicide among Intimate Partners—United States, 1981–1998," in *Morbidity and Mortality Weekly Report Surveillance Summaries*, vol. 50, no. SS03, Centers for Disease Control and Prevention, National Center for Injury Prevention and Control, October 12, 2001, http://www.cdc.gov/mmwr/preview/mmwrhtml/ss5003a1.htm (accessed October 24, 2004)

years or more, compared to 43% of the husbands. Wives in general received considerably shorter prison sentences than husbands, six years versus 16.5 years.

In 44% of wife defendant cases, there was evidence that the wife had acted in response to a violent attack from her husband at the time of the killing. In contrast, just 10% of the husbands claimed that their victims had assaulted them at the time of the murder. The researchers observed that "[i]n many instances in which wives were charged with killing their husbands, the husbands had assaulted the wife, and the wife then killed in self-defense. That might explain why wives had a lower conviction rate than did husbands." With strong legal defense and detailed documentation of abuse, many women are able to successfully argue that after suffering years of mental and/or physical abuse at the hands of their abusers, they suffer from what is known as battered woman syndrome

and killed in self-defense. In fact, battered woman syndrome has become a recognized defense in courtrooms throughout the country. At least some scholars, however, advocate relying on evidence of "battering and its effects" rather than testimony of a "syndrome" that reduces the issues facing battered women to a psychological problem and does not fit every victim's circumstances. Kathleen J. Ferraro explores the issue in her study, "The Words Change, But the Melody Lingers: The Persistence of the Battered Woman Syndrome in Criminal Cases Involving Battered Women" (*Violence against Women*, vol. 9, no. 1, January 2003).

FACTORS THAT INFLUENCE THE MURDER OF HUSBANDS BY WIVES

In one of the first studies of wives who murdered their abusive partners, *When Battered Women Kill* (New York:

FIGURE 9.3

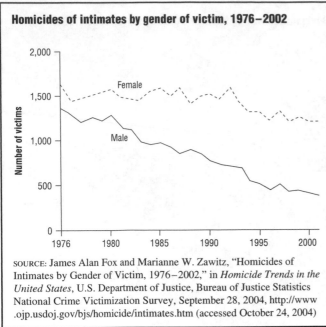

Homicides of intimates by gender of victim, 1976–2002

SOURCE: James Alan Fox and Marianne W. Zawitz, "Homicides of Intimates by Gender of Victim, 1976–2002," in *Homicide Trends in the United States*, U.S. Department of Justice, Bureau of Justice Statistics National Crime Victimization Survey, September 28, 2004, http://www .ojp.usdoj.gov/bjs/homicide/intimates.htm (accessed October 24, 2004)

The Free Press, 1987), Angela Browne of the Family Research Laboratory at the University of New Hampshire compared forty-two women charged with murdering or seriously injuring their spouses with 205 abused women who had not killed their husbands. Wondering why some women were unable to see that their partners were dangerously violent, she found that some of the personal characteristics of men inclined to violent, abusive behavior were the same qualities that initially attracted the women to them. For example, a woman might initially perceive a man who always wanted to know where she had been as intensely romantic. Only later, when she was unable to act or move without her partner's supervision, might she realize that she had become a virtual prisoner of her controlling mate.

Browne asserted that the intensity of these early relationships further serves to isolate the women. Women may be denied contact with family and friends to the extent that a casual conversation with a neighbor may provoke abuse. A woman may come to see her partner's behavior as extremely jealous and possessive. This pathological protectiveness is communicated by an abuser's belief that his partner belongs exclusively to him and is a possession to be used as he pleases. Browne found that many abusive husbands feared or believed their wives were sexually promiscuous. These mistaken beliefs frequently prompted extreme sexual assault.

Rape

Browne's findings suggest a link between the frequency of marital rape and homicide potential. More than 75% of women who had committed homicide claimed they were forced to have sexual intercourse with their

husbands, compared to 59% in the group of women who had not killed their husbands. Some 39% of the former group had been raped more than twenty times, compared to 13% of the latter group. One woman Browne interviewed said, "It was as though he wanted to annihilate me. . . ; as though he wanted to tear me apart from the inside out and simply leave nothing there."

According to Raquel Kennedy Bergin in *Wife Rape* (Thousand Oaks, CA: Sage, 1996), about 60% of the women who are raped in their marriages report that their husbands have threatened to kill them. Three of the women in her study reported that they were finally able to break free of their abusive relationships when they realized that they would kill their husbands if they did not leave. About half the sample confessed to thinking about killing their partners but did not believe they could actually follow through with their murderous plans.

Murder and Suicide Threats

Men murdered by their spouses had often threatened to kill their partners. In Browne's study, 83% of the men killed by their wives had threatened to kill someone, compared to 59% of the men whose wives did not kill them. Men killed by their wives had used guns to frighten their spouses and were sometimes killed with their own weapons. Nearly two-thirds (61%) of this group also threatened to kill themselves. Many of the threats were made when women tried to leave the relationship or when the men were depressed. Browne questioned whether the suicide threats were genuine expressions of wishes to die or whether they were used to manipulate the women in efforts to make them feel guilty and prevent them from leaving.

Studies have found that battered women often contemplate suicide because they see no other escape from the cycle of abuse, and that as many as a third of women who do commit suicide each year have been abused by a male partner. Neil Websdale explored the subject in "Reviewing Domestic Violence Deaths" (*National Institute of Justice Journal,* no. 250, November 2003). One woman in Browne's study expressed her wish to escape abuse when she decided not to seek help after a severe beating because she thought "[death] might not be so bad; like passing out only you never get beaten again."

Drug Use and Physical Abuse

When Browne compared abused women who had murdered their spouses and women who had not, she found that in the homicide group, 29% of the men had used drugs daily or almost daily versus only 7.5% of the men in the other group. There were even sharper differences in reported alcohol use. Twice as many (80%) of the men killed by their wives were reportedly drunk every day, compared with 40% of the abusive men not killed by their spouses.

Lenore Walker, a renowned expert in domestic violence who is often hired as an expert witness in homicide cases, researches and testifies in cases where women have killed their husbands after they pass out from drinking. She argued that women, convinced the beatings will resume when the men awake, take the opportunity to murder their abusers. Autopsies show that these victims had blood alcohol levels of up to three times greater than the measure normally defined as intoxicated.

In addition, 92% of the men killed by their wives had been arrested for crimes ranging from drunk driving to murder, compared with 77% of the abusive men not killed by their wives. A common feature of the marriages where the wife killed her spouse was that the wife did not know anything about her husband's criminal past, including his arrest records.

LEGAL ISSUES SURROUNDING BATTERED WOMEN WHO KILL

In legal cases involving battered women who kill their abusers, the defendants often admit to the murder and reveal a history of physical abuse. The charge is usually first- or second-degree murder, which is murder with malicious intent either with or without premeditation. The outcome of these trials depends on three main issues: self-defense, equal force, and imminent versus immediate danger. Expert witnesses are crucial in an abused woman's trial to explain how these issues are different for cases involving battered women than for other homicide cases.

Self-Defense

Women often plead that they killed in self-defense, a plea that requires proof that the woman used such force as was necessary to avoid imminent bodily harm. Self-defense was originally intended to cover unexpected attacks by strangers and did not take into account a past history of abuse or a woman's fear of renewed violence. Traditionally applied, a self-defense plea does not exonerate a woman who kills during a lull in the violence, for example, when the drunken abuser passes out.

Many observers feel that self-defense law is problematic, inadequate, and/or not appropriate for use in self-defense cases of battered women, according to Diane Follingstad et al. in "The Impact of Elements of Self-Defense and Objective versus Subjective Instructions on Jurors' Verdicts for Battered Women Defendants" (*Journal of Interpersonal Violence,* vol. 12, no. 5, 1997). Traditionally, self-defense permits an individual to use physical force when he or she reasonably believes it is necessary to counteract imminent or immediate danger of serious bodily harm. Furthermore, a person must use only a reasonable amount of force to stop the attack and cannot be the one who provoked the encounter or initiated the violence. To justify the use of reciprocal deadly force, most juris-

dictions require that the defendant reasonably believes the attacker is using or is about to use deadly force. Some jurisdictions further require that before resorting to deadly force, the defendant must make an effort to retreat, although this is not required in most courts if the attack took place in the defendant's own home.

Advocates of battered women have succeeded in convincing many courts to accept a subjective standard of determining whether a battered woman who killed her husband was protecting her own life. This concession allows the court to judge the circumstances of the crime in relation to the special needs of battered women and not according to the strict definition of "self-defense." This looser definition is especially important for women who killed during a lull in the violence, because a strict interpretation of "imminent danger" does not provide legal justification for their actions.

A subjective standard asks a jury to understand what is reasonable for a battered woman. Susannah Marie Bennett, in "Ending the Continuous Reign of Terror: Sleeping Husbands, Battered Wives, and the Right of Self-Defense" (*Wake Forest Law Review,* 1989), explained the critical difference as viewing the appearance of danger subjectively, from the perspective of one who saw and knew what the defendant saw and knew. An objective standard still governs whether a reasonable person, in similar circumstances and with the same perceptions, would also have acted in self-defense. This is the "hybrid" definition of self-defense that supporters of battered women encourage the courts to adopt.

According to Gena Rachel Hatcher in "The Gendered Nature of Battered Woman Syndrome: Why Gender Neutrality Does not Mean Equality," in order for this hybrid definition to work, the court must first be subjective in understanding the woman's circumstances. Next, it must be objective in deciding that, given the situation, she truly did act in a reasonable manner (*New York University Annual Survey of American Law,* 2003). Courts have already accepted the notion that self-defense does not require perfect judgment in a violent situation, only reasonableness. Justice Oliver Wendell Holmes, in *Brown v. United States* (1921), said "[d]etached reflection cannot be demanded in the presence of an uplifted knife." Battered women and their advocates have asked the courts to revise their definitions of imminent danger and proportionate force in cases involving domestic violence.

Equal Force

Self-defense permits the use of equal force, which is defined as the least amount of force necessary to prevent imminent bodily harm or death. Women, however, who are generally physically weaker than men and who know the kind of physical damage their batterers can inflict, may justifiably feel that they are protecting their lives when shooting unarmed men. In *State v. Wanrow* (1977), the Washington Supreme Court ruled that it was permissible to instruct the jury that the objective standard of self-defense does not always apply.

Yvonne Wanrow was sitting up at night fearful that a male neighbor, who she thought had molested the child in her care, was going to make good on his threats to break into the house where she was staying. When the large, intoxicated man did enter, Wanrow, who was incapacitated with a broken leg, shot him. The court ruled, "The respondent was entitled to have the jury consider her actions in the light of her own perception of the situation, including those perceptions that were the product of our nation's long and unfortunate history of sex-discrimination. . . . Until such time as the effects of that history are eradicated, care must be taken to assure that our self-defense instructions afford women the right to have their conduct judged in light of the individual physical handicaps that are the product of sex discrimination. To fail to do so is to deny the right of the individual woman involved to trial by the same rules that are applicable to male defendants."

Imminent versus Immediate Danger

Traditionally, self-defense required that the danger be immediate, meaning that the danger was present at the very moment the decision to respond was made, in order to justify the use of force, as noted by Kimberly Kessler Ferzan in "Defending Imminence: From Battered Women to Iraq" (*Arizona Law Review,* 46, Summer 2004). Accepting imminent danger, or danger that is about to occur, as justification for action permits the jury to understand the motivations and dynamics of a battered woman's behavior. A history of abuse may explain why a defendant might react to the threat of violence more quickly than a stranger would in the same circumstances. In *Wanrow,* the Washington Supreme Court found that when the jury considered a woman's actions based on immediate danger, it was required to focus only on the time immediately before the defendant's actions. "It is clear that the jury is entitled to consider all of the circumstances surrounding the incident in determining whether [the] defendant had reasonable grounds to believe grievous bodily harm was about to be inflicted," the court wrote.

Lenore Walker observed in *Terrifying Love: Why Battered Women Kill and How Society Responds* (New York: Harper and Row, 1989) that it is often hard for a jury to understand how a woman can be continuously afraid of a man with whom she lives. Walker insisted, however, that her own research and that of others had repeatedly demonstrated that battered women know their abusers' potential for violence and live in constant fear, even when they have developed coping skills that enable them to continue living with their violent partners. Fully 85% of the four hundred battered women Walker interviewed felt they could or would be killed at some time by their abusers.

Juries and Expert Testimony

Whether a woman will be convicted depends largely on the jury's attitude, or the judge's disposition when it is not a jury trial, and the amount of background and personal history of abuse that the judge or jury is permitted to hear. Juries that have not heard expert witnesses present the battered woman defense are often unsympathetic to women who kill their abusive partners.

Regina Schuller et al. in "Jurors' Decisions in Trials of Battered Women Who Kill: The Role of Prior Beliefs and Expert Testimony" (*Journal of Applied Psychology,* vol. 24, no. 4, 1994) found that jurors who learned about battered woman syndrome from expert testimony were more likely to believe the defendant feared for her life, that she was in danger, and that she was trapped in the abusive relationship. Equipped with knowledge and understanding of battering and its effects, jurors handed down fewer murder convictions than were issued by a control group of jurors who were not given this specialized information.

Using mock jury trials, Schuller et al. examined whether a potential juror's belief in a "just world" would influence how he or she receives and responds to expert testimony. A strong belief in a just world would lead a juror to reason that a person deserves his or her fate. Persons holding strong "just world" beliefs would decide that when a woman is abused, she must be responsible for the beating in some way or she must deserve and share responsibility for the outcome. The study found that women who did not accept the concept of a just world were especially receptive to, and influenced by, expert testimony. Men, however, independent of their beliefs, were generally more resistant to the influence of expert witnesses.

When judges opt not to permit expert testimony, it is frequently because they do not wish the expert to influence jurors about the specific circumstances and details of the case. In some states, an expert witness is only permitted to speak generally about battering and its effects and may not comment about the individual woman on trial. On the other hand, some states permit the expert to express an opinion on the ultimate question of whether the battered defendant's behavior was reasonable in view of her circumstances.

A CASE STUDY: *STATE V. NORMAN.* In *State v. Norman* (1989), the North Carolina Court of Appeals overturned a lower court's verdict of voluntary manslaughter for a woman who fatally shot her husband while he was sleeping, because the original court had failed to instruct the jury on self-defense. In the final appeal, however, the North Carolina Supreme Court reversed that opinion and reaffirmed the validity of the first court's traditional objective standard of self-defense, resulting in a conviction of voluntary manslaughter. Kimberly Kessler Ferzan discusses the case in "Defending Imminence: From Battered Women to Iraq," cited above.

The defendant, Judy Norman, had been continually abused during her twenty-five-year marriage to her husband, J. T. He had beaten her with every available weapon, forced her into prostitution, and required her to eat dog food from a bowl on the floor. He had thrown her down stairs when she was pregnant with their youngest child, causing her to give birth prematurely, and often threatened to "cut her heart out" or "cut her breast off." Dr. William Tyson, an expert witness at the trial, characterized her situation as "torture, degradation, and reduction to an animal level of existence where all behavior was marked purely by survival."

On this final occasion, J. T. was arrested for drunk driving. After his release from jail, he came home to vent his anger on his wife, beating her repeatedly over thirty-six hours. In the past, Judy had gone to Mental Health Services and the Department of Social Services for help, but her husband had always come to get her, reaffirming her belief that her husband was invulnerable to the law. In her mind, the only choices left were to kill him or to die.

The defense relied heavily on expert testimony about battered woman syndrome and the theory of learned helplessness. The court ruled that reasonable, deadly fear is not only theoretically possible, but also real, and may have been present in Judy's mind. Susannah Marie Bennett, in "Ending the Continuous Reign of Terror" (cited above), applauded the court of appeals decision to accept the special circumstances of battered women, asserting that, by recognizing self-defense as a concern, the court validated the view that a defendant may reasonably fear imminent harm from a sleeping person.

But Bennett argued that the court of appeals was wrong to claim that "therefore, a battered spouse who kills a passive abuser can satisfy the traditional elements of self-defense under an objective analysis." Bennett pointed out that the imminency requirement may stop the woman from employing the right of self-defense at the one time it would work: when the abuser is passive. Instead, the rule directs the woman to wait until she could be completely defenseless—during or just prior to a battering incident—before she can justifiably save her life. Thus, the court essentially recognized that the requirement of imminent danger may be met by events outside of an actual attack or a threat of attack, but only in the special circumstances of battered spouses. This recognition, Bennett contended, is a monumental exception to the general principle of self-defense.

By accepting this definition of self-defense, the court cannot claim to have used an objective standard. Bennett suggested that the reason the North Carolina Supreme Court overturned the court of appeals decision was because the latter court may have tried to mask its move to subjectivity and that it would have been better off to admit that it was relaxing its standard in order to accommodate killings that do not objectively meet traditional self-defense criteria.

Bennett concluded that instead of adhering to outdated concepts and a rigid interpretation of self-defense, the court of appeals made an honest effort to take up the legal aspects of spousal abuse. The court demonstrated significant insight by recognizing the plight of victims of battering—a predicament created by the deadly combination of battering and its effects and strict judicial adherence to standards that were never intended to address such situations. Accordingly, the court ruled with a compassionate and insightful opinion that is part of a growing trend in self-defense law.

On July 7, 1989, North Carolina Governor James G. Martin commuted Judy Norman's six-year manslaughter sentence to time she had already served.

SHOULD THE LAW BE CHANGED?

Some observers believe that by acknowledging the differences between men and women and accepting different conduct from each, the courts are moving perilously closer to providing two standards of justice. A woman can be permitted to use a gun in self-defense in cases where a man cannot, and she may need the extra help of an expert witness to explain her motivation to a jury. Is this a step in the right direction for the courts? Are the courts only now incorporating changes needed to resolve and adjudicate previously unconsidered situations? Have women been discriminated against and is society only now righting the wrongs?

Those opposed to changing the law claim that many domestic disputes are more complicated than battered women's advocates portray. For example, Sonny Burmeister, the president of the Georgia Council for Children's Rights, an organization that lobbies for equal treatment for men in child custody cases, believes that women are trying to write a customized set of laws, depicting men as violent and women as victims, thereby absolving women from the social and legal consequences of their actions.

Incorrect Assumptions

Some observers object to revising the law, claiming that these modifications will permit women to kill their husbands indiscriminately. By allowing such change, they argue, the law is sending a message to society that revenge is acceptable, even permitted, under the law.

Holly Maguigan, a defense attorney and law professor, argued in "Battered Women and Self-Defense: Myths and Misconceptions in Current Reform Proposals" (*University of Pennsylvania Law Review*, vol. 140, no. 2, 1991) that the law does not need to be changed, but rather, needs to be properly applied. According to Maguigan, the effort to change the law is based on two incorrect assumptions. The first is that juries convict battered women for killing in nonconfrontational circumstances, such as during a lull in the violence or when a man is sleeping. The second assumption is that the current definitions of self-defense apply only to men of roughly equal size and power. Some insist that the law ignores the social context of the battered woman's actions. Maguigan countered that reformers have not carefully examined the law as it stands and that when the reformers explain what they mean by "a fair trial" they are referring to a not-guilty verdict.

Studies show that a large majority of women kill their abusers during a confrontation and not during a break in the attack. Angela Browne in her *When Battered Women Kill* (cited above) estimated that at least 70% of women who have killed their abusers did so during a confrontation. Other researchers have estimated that as many as 90% of such women kill under confrontational circumstances. Maguigan examined 223 cases and found that 75% involved confrontations, 8% involved "sleeping-man" situations, and 4% were contract killings. In 8% of the cases, the defendant was the aggressor in a lull in the violence, and in the remaining 5% there was not enough background in the court opinions to establish the accurate details of the events.

Maguigan asserted that nearly every jurisdiction decides questions of equal force on a case-by-case basis and does not ban a woman from using a weapon against an unarmed man. Courts have recognized for years that use of a weapon by a battered woman against an unarmed man does not necessarily constitute disproportionate force. In *Kress v. State* (1940), the Tennessee Supreme Court reversed the conviction of a woman who shot her husband in the midst of an attack. "Where a great bodily violence is being inflicted or threatened upon a person by one much stronger and heavier, with such determined energy that the person assaulted may reasonably apprehend death or great bodily injury, he is justifiable in using a deadly weapon," the court wrote.

Furthermore, the law in every state permits a history of past abuse to be presented in court. Cases of abused women who have killed their partners and who claimed self-defense are not new. They date back at least to 1902, long before Walker conceived of the battered woman syndrome. Maguigan showed that jurisdictions that accept imminent danger as opposed to immediate danger are more likely to present the history of abuse to the jury to explain the reasonableness of the woman's conduct.

A Misapplication of the Law

Maguigan's analysis revealed that convictions of battered women usually result from a misapplication of the law, not from the unjust structure of the law. She found that 40% of the guilty verdicts were later reversed in higher courts, a rate significantly higher than the national average rate of reversal of 8.5% in homicide cases in general. Problems arose when trial court judges interpreted the women's acts as vigilantism and did not permit instruction to the jury on self-defense or presentation of history-of-abuse evidence. In *State v. Branchal* (1984), the trial judge commented that the court "did not want to condone spousal retaliation for past violence."

Maguigan concluded that in most jurisdictions it is the failure of the trial judges to apply general standards of self-defense, not the legal definition of self-defense, that prevents battered women from obtaining fair trials. Neither current proposals for legal redefinition nor creation of separate standards will remedy problems resulting from a refusal to apply the law. If legal exceptions are made, there is a danger that trial judges will apply the law too strictly, possibly excluding some women. A trial judge in Missouri, for example, made a decision (subsequently reversed on appeal) that testimony on battered woman syndrome did not apply to a defendant because she was not legally married to the abuser.

Maguigan cautioned that when the law defines a special group of people, it eliminates others, and in this situation it could deny expert witnesses or special instructions on self-defense because an individual defendant's case did not meet the strict definition of a battered woman. She suggested that flexibility and general terms are more beneficial, citing the proposed rule of evidence for the New York State courts as an example: "If scientific, technical or other specialized knowledge will assist the trier of fact to understand the evidence or to determine a fact in issue, a witness qualified as an expert by knowledge, skill, experience, training or education, may testify."

According to Maguigan, the laws to provide women with fair trials are already in place. What is needed is for jurisdictions to understand and accept the legal precedents of imminent rather than immediate danger and to allow evidence of a history of battering and expert testimony to explain the reasonableness of a battered woman's reaction.

CALIFORNIA LAW FREES BATTERED WIFE WHO KILLED HER HUSBAND. On October 25, 2002, Marva Wallace, a forty-four-year-old high school graduate and mother of two, was freed after serving seventeen years in state prison for the murder of her abusive husband. Wallace was the first person released under a California law enacted in January 2002 aimed at inmates convicted prior to 1992, for whom expert testimony on battered woman syndrome was not presented at trial. The law allows these inmates to file writs of habeas corpus (protection against illegal imprisonment) asking that convictions be overturned or sentences reduced and enabling them to petition for new trials.

In Wallace's case, her husband began to abuse her just two months into her marriage. According to court documents, her husband's beatings often left her bloodied and bruised. He refused to allow Wallace to work, isolated her from her family, and would not give her money to support her children. A substance abuser, Wallace's husband had previously abused his first wife.

On the day she killed him, Wallace asked her husband if she could take her two-year-old daughter to visit the girl's grandmother. Her husband became angry, slapped her, and forced her to perform oral sex in front of her daughter. Shortly after these events, she shot him with a gun that was in their home.

Although friends and family testified at the trial that Wallace had been abused, there was no expert witness to present the effects of abuse on Wallace's mental state. She was convicted of first-degree murder and sentenced to twenty-seven years to life in state prison.

In an article that appeared in the October 26, 2002, *Los Angeles Times,* David S. Wesley, the judge who overturned the murder conviction, acknowledged that Wallace had been a battered wife and that she was convicted in 1985 when much less was known and understood about intimate partner violence. Judge Wesley ordered a new trial in the case and released Wallace on her own recognizance. During the new trial, testimony of her battering and its effects was presented, and she was allowed to plead guilty to a lesser charge, voluntary manslaughter. She was sentenced to eight years of time already served.

CHAPTER 10

INTIMATE PARTNER VIOLENCE ISSUES AND ATTITUDES

Recent adoption and use of the term "intimate partner violence," instead of "wife battering," "spouse abuse," or "domestic violence," is one sign of changing views about violent relationships. Intimate partner violence describes a broader range of abusive relationships, including psychological abuse and social isolation, and acknowledges that violence occurs among unmarried and same-sex partners as well as among persons who do not live together. Also, the term is generally used to describe "a continuing pattern of behavior rather than a single violent act," according to a report of the American Medical Association's Council on Scientific Affairs titled *AMA Data on Violence between Intimates* (http://www.ama-assn.org/ ama/pub/category/13577.html, December 2000 [accessed January 31, 2005]).

The Centers for Disease Control and Prevention (CDC) recognizes that use of consistent terminology is vital for researchers collecting data about the scope of the problem. The centers made a move to establish tracking systems, identify high-risk populations, and assess the results of prevention programs with the publication of *Intimate Partner Violence Surveillance: Uniform Definitions and Recommended Data Elements* by Linda E. Saltzman, Janet L. Fanslow, Pamela M. McMahon, and Gene A. Shelley (Atlanta, GA: The Centers for Disease Control and Prevention, 2002). The report attempted to standardize terminology in order to enable researchers, health care professionals, and policy makers to use the same terms to describe comparable violent acts.

VIOLENCE ON OUR MINDS

Americans are worried about violence and violent crimes. Surveys find that violent crime, violence in schools and among young people, and the depiction of violence in the media are all causes for concern.

A 2003 poll by the Center for the Advancement of Women found that 92% of women polled listed "reducing domestic violence and sexual assault" as a top priority for the women's movement ("Progress and Perils: New Agenda for Women," June 2003). An October 1998 Harris Poll found that 6% of respondents said they thought it was very likely they would be hit by a spouse or partner, an additional 8% felt it was somewhat likely, and 1% admitted that it had already happened to them. In view of the stigma associated with intimate partner violence and the reluctance to admit or disclose it, the finding that 15% of survey respondents thought it likely to occur or had occurred in their personal relationships was significant.

A poll by Harris Interactive published in the *Sourcebook of Criminal Justice Statistics 2002* (Washington, DC: Bureau of Justice Statistics, 2003) compared survey responses given in 1994, 1999, and 2001 to questions about the factors Americans believe contribute to violence in U.S. society. Although the most frequently named causes remained constant through each survey year—in 2001, 86% cited "lack of adult supervision" and 60% said "easy availability of handguns"—the percentage of respondents attributing violence to these factors declined from 1994 to 2001. The biggest drop was in the proportion of persons blaming television news media for encouraging violence—from 39% in 1999 to 30% in 2001.

Men and Women View Domestic Violence Differently

A 1997 survey commissioned by Women's Work, a program of Liz Claiborne, Inc., and conducted by the public opinion research firm Roper Starch Worldwide, found that men and women define domestic violence and abusive behavior differently. Interviews with a random sample of 1,011 adults nationwide revealed that while men and women basically agree that acts and threats of physical violence are abusive, they disagree about the behaviors that constitute psychological abuse.

Controlling behaviors, such as dictating the clothes a woman must wear, was considered abusive by more than

FIGURE 10.1

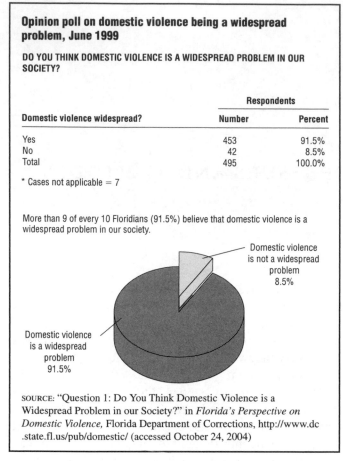

Opinion poll on domestic violence being a widespread problem, June 1999

DO YOU THINK DOMESTIC VIOLENCE IS A WIDESPREAD PROBLEM IN OUR SOCIETY?

	Respondents	
Domestic violence widespread?	Number	Percent
Yes	453	91.5%
No	42	8.5%
Total	495	100.0%

* Cases not applicable = 7

More than 9 of every 10 Floridians (91.5%) believe that domestic violence is a widespread problem in our society.

Domestic violence is not a widespread problem 8.5%

Domestic violence is a widespread problem 91.5%

SOURCE: "Question 1: Do You Think Domestic Violence is a Widespread Problem in our Society?" in *Florida's Perspective on Domestic Violence,* Florida Department of Corrections, http://www.dc.state.fl.us/pub/domestic/ (accessed October 24, 2004)

FIGURE 10.2

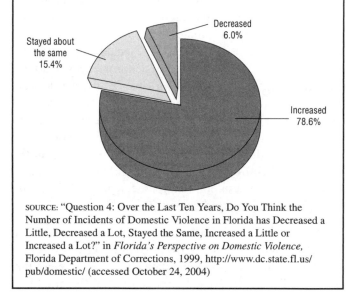

Opinion poll on the increase or decrease of domestic violence in Florida, June 1999

OVER THE LAST TEN YEARS, DO YOU THINK THE NUMBER OF INCIDENTS OF DOMESTIC VIOLENCE IN FLORIDA HAS DECREASED A LITTLE, DECREASED A LOT, STAYED THE SAME, INCREASED A LITTLE OR INCREASED A LOT?

	Respondents	
10 year change in domestic violence	Number	Percent
Increased a lot	219	48.9%
Increased a little	133	29.7%
Stayed about the same	69	15.4%
Decreased a little	23	5.1%
Decreased a lot	4	0.9%
Total	448	100.0%

*Cases not applicable = 54

The majority of respondents (78.6%) believe that over the past 10 years, the number of incidents of domestic violence in Florida has increased. Only 6.0% believe domestic violence has decreased over the past 10 years. Women felt that it has increased more (84.3%) than men (70.2%).

Stayed about the same 15.4%

Decreased 6.0%

Increased 78.6%

SOURCE: "Question 4: Over the Last Ten Years, Do You Think the Number of Incidents of Domestic Violence in Florida has Decreased a Little, Decreased a Lot, Stayed the Same, Increased a Little or Increased a Lot?" in *Florida's Perspective on Domestic Violence,* Florida Department of Corrections, 1999, http://www.dc.state.fl.us/pub/domestic/ (accessed October 24, 2004)

half the female respondents, but only 33% of men said it was definitely abusive behavior. Less than one-quarter of males thought that withholding money from a wife or girlfriend was abusive, while 37% of women felt it was definitely abusive and 74% thought it probably was.

A greater proportion of women (78%) than men (67%) viewed enforced social isolation—preventing a woman from contact with family and friends—as abusive. Fully 85% of women and 75% of men thought that a man's cursing or insulting his partner in front of others constituted abuse.

About three-quarters of all survey respondents considered violence directed at women by their partners as among the major problems facing the country, and 21% thought it was a minor problem. Two percent said it was not a problem at all. More women (85%) felt domestic violence was a major problem than men (69%).

More than half of all respondents reported that they knew someone directly involved in intimate partner violence, as either a victim or perpetrator. Slightly more women (59%) than men (54%) said they knew someone involved in an abusive relationship. Nearly one-third of respondents knew that about one out of four women is affected by domestic violence, but 37% admitted that they did not know enough about the problem to estimate how frequently it occurs.

The State of Florida Weighs in on Domestic Violence

In June 1999 the Florida Department of Corrections surveyed state residents about how they felt about domestic violence. Survey respondents were representative of the Florida population and ranged in age from eighteen to eighty-nine years—the average age of respondents was 45.5 years. The survey was composed of approximately 40% men and 60% women.

More than nine out of ten Floridians thought domestic violence is a widespread problem in society, and a large majority (78.6%) felt that their state had seen an increase in the number of incidents of domestic violence during the past decade. Only 6% felt the number of incidents of domestic violence had dropped. (See Figure 10.1 and Figure 10.2.) Official statistics from the Florida Department of Law Enforcement supported public perceptions—reported domestic violence crime had increased by 9%—

TABLE 10.1

Opinion poll on percentage of physically abusive men, June 1999

WHAT PERCENTAGE OF MEN DO YOU THINK HAVE EVER PHYSICALLY ABUSED THEIR WIVES OR GIRLFRIENDS?

Percentage of men who have abused wives or girlfriends	Respondents	
	Number	Percent
0–10%	47	11.7%
11–20%	54	13.4%
21–30%	90	22.2%
31–40%	58	14.4%
41–50%	64	15.9%
51–60%	27	6.7%
61–70%	24	6.0%
71–80%	23	5.7%
81–90%	10	2.5%
91–100%	6	1.5%
Total	403	100.0%

*Cases not applicable = 99

SOURCE: "Question 2: What Percentage of Men Do You Think Have Ever Physically Abused Their Wives or Girlfriends?" in *Florida's Perspective on Domestic Violence,* Florida Department of Corrections, 1999, http://www.dc .state.fl.us/pub/domestic/ (accessed October 24, 2004)

FIGURE 10.3

Opinion poll on the witnessing of physical abuse by a man toward his wife or girlfriend, June 1999

HAVE YOU EVER WITNESSED A MAN PHYSICALLY ABUSING HIS WIFE OR GIRLFRIEND?

Witnessed abuse?	Respondents	
	Number	Percent
Yes	219	43.7%
No	282	56.3%
Total	501	100.0%

*Cases not applicable = 1

Over 1 in 3 (43.7%) Floridians have actually witnessed a man physically abusing his wife or girlfriend.

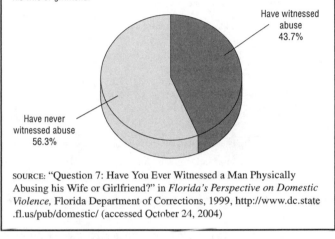

SOURCE: "Question 7: Have You Ever Witnessed a Man Physically Abusing his Wife or Girlfriend?" in *Florida's Perspective on Domestic Violence,* Florida Department of Corrections, 1999, http://www.dc.state .fl.us/pub/domestic/ (accessed October 24, 2004)

and the Florida Task Force on Domestic and Sexual Violence confirmed that only about one-seventh of all domestic assaults are reported to police.

On average, survey respondents said they believed that nearly 40% of men have physically abused an intimate partner at some point in their lives. (See Table 10.1.) Female respondents (42.5%) were more likely than male respondents (32.9%) to believe that men abused their intimate partners.

More than half the respondents (55.5%) knew at least one victim of domestic violence. Nearly 43% of those respondents said the victim was a friend and more than one-quarter said an immediate family member had been a victim of domestic violence. More than one in three respondents (43.7%) reported that they had actually witnessed a man physically abusing his wife or girlfriend. (See Figure 10.3.)

The survey respondents were asked what they believed caused domestic violence. The most frequently cited causes were women's reluctance to leave their abusers (89.8%), partners' inability to communicate and resolve differences (79.4%), drug and alcohol problems (78.4%), and the economic reality that many women are forced to choose between poverty and remaining with their abusers (76.7%). Respondents also thought that many men learned violent behavior in their homes during childhood and adolescence (73.1%), and they believed that the breakdown of the traditional family unit contributed to violence (67.6%).

Almost 65% of those surveyed said the courts did little to protect battered women, and 21.9% said they felt domestic violence exists because police didn't do enough

to stop it. (See Table 10.2.) More than eight out of ten respondents wanted police to arrest persons suspected of partner violence, and more than 85% want to see offenders who caused serious bodily harm to their victims imprisoned. (See Table 10.3.) More than three-quarters believed that abusers should be both punished and forced to receive treatment; less than 8% felt that punishment without treatment was sufficient.

To compare how survey participants viewed domestic violence in comparison to violence in the community, researchers asked respondents how a man who had beaten up his wife at home should be punished and how a man who had beaten up another man in a bar should be punished. Overall, the respondents did not believe these violent acts should be punished differently. Almost 70% favored imprisoning a man who assaulted a woman at home, and 74% would jail a man who assaulted another man in a bar.

Most respondents said that not enough taxpayer money was being spent on preventing and treating intimate partner violence and enforcing laws against it. Eight out of ten of the respondents would support a tax increase to pay for more counseling for victims. Nearly three-quarters would agree to a tax increase to fund more shelters for victims, and more than two-thirds of respondents were willing to spend more tax dollars to treat offenders.

TABLE 10.2

Opinion poll on the causes of domestic violence, June 1999

Causes	Percent	
	Agree	Disagree
Domestic violence continues because most women will not leave the men who abuse them.	89.8%	10.2%
Domestic violence is the result of a couple's inability to communicate and resolve conflicts.	79.4%	20.6%
Drug and alcohol problems are the primary cause of domestic violence.	78.4%	21.6%
Many women have to choose between living on their own and being poor or staying in the home where they are being battered.	76.7%	23.2%
Most men learn to be violent because they were beaten or witnessed violence in their home when they were growing up.	73.1%	26.9%
Domestic violence is caused by the breakdown of the traditional family.	67.6%	32.4%
The court system does very little to protect abused women.	64.9%	35.1%
Domestic violence is a result of unequal relationships between men and women.	54.3%	45.7%
Domestic violence exists because police won't stop it.	21.9%	77.1%
It's none of my business if a husband physically abuses his wife during an argument inside their own home.	14.8%	85.2%

*Those who neither agreed nor disagreed were not used to calculate valid percentages.

SOURCE: "Question 8: Causes of Domestic Violence," in *Florida's Perspective on Domestic Violence,* Florida Department of Corrections, 1999, http://www.dc.state.fl.us/pub/domestic/ (accessed October 24, 2004)

TABLE 10.3

Opinion polls on police intervention in domestic violence cases/imprisonment of serious offenders, June 1999

WHEN THE POLICE HAVE BEEN CALLED TO A HOME, DO YOU THINK AN ARREST SHOULD BE MADE WHEN THE POLICE SUSPECT THAT DOMESTIC VIOLENCE HAS OCCURRED?

Arrest if police suspect domestic violence?	Respondents	
	Number	Percent
Yes	397	86.3%
No	63	13.7%
Total	460	100.0%

*Cases not applicable = 42

More than 8 in 10 Floridians (86.3%) believe that an arrest should be made when the police suspect domestic violence has occurred. More women (90.3%) believed that an arrest should be made when the police suspect domestic violence has occurred, compared to men (80.1%).

DO YOU THINK IMPRISONMENT IS THE APPROPRIATE PUNISHMENT FOR DOMESTIC VIOLENCE INCIDENTS INVOLVING SERIOUS BODILY INJURIES?

Is imprisonment the appropriate punishment?	Respondents	
	Number	Percent
Yes	412	85.3%
No	71	14.7%
Total	483	100.0%

*Cases not applicable = 19

SOURCE: "Question 10: When the Police Have Been Called to a Home, Do You Think an Arrest Should Be Made when the Police Suspect that Domestic Violence has Occurred?" and "Question 11: Do You Think Imprisonment is the Appropriate Punishment for Domestic Violence Incidents Involving Serious Bodily Injury?" in *Florida's Perspective on Domestic Violence,* Florida Department of Corrections, 1999, http://www.dc.state.fl.us/pub/domestic/ (accessed October 24, 2004)

The respondents believed the most effective strategies for reducing domestic violence were counseling for victims, public education, treatment for abusers, and placing restraining orders on convicted offenders. More female respondents (73.9%) than males (51.8%) thought treatment of abusers would be very effective. Similarly, 80.8% of women favored counseling for victims, compared to 58.8% of men.

When they were questioned about their willingness to help victims of intimate partner violence, nine out of ten respondents said they would call the police if they heard an assault occurring next door. Nearly all the woman surveyed (94.5%) said they would telephone police and 87.9% of men indicated they would contact police. Furthermore, the overwhelming majority (93%) said they would testify in court about an assault they had seen.

Survey respondents were asked whether they agreed or disagreed with the 1997 legislation that made it illegal for a person convicted of domestic violence to own a firearm. Most respondents (89%) agreed with the law, with women expressing more support than men (92.9% and 79.4%, respectively). Furthermore, nine out of ten respondents said neither law enforcement officers nor military personnel should be exempt from the legislation prohibiting convicts or subjects of an injunction from possessing a firearm.

Only 40% of respondents were aware of batterer intervention programs and less than 8% said they knew of a man involved in one of the programs. Nonetheless, a full 91.8% of those surveyed felt that it should be mandatory for all men charged with domestic violence to attend batterer intervention programs.

The majority of survey respondents thought more public attention would help victims of domestic violence. Figure 10.4 shows that 56.7% of the respondents believed the media had not directed enough attention to domestic violence issues.

How Do Women Feel about Mandatory Reporting of Domestic Violence?

There is considerable controversy about mandatory reporting requirements among health care professionals, patients, and advocates for domestic violence prevention. From 1991 to 1994 California, Colorado, Rhode Island, and Kentucky passed laws requiring health professionals to report cases of intimate partner violence to the police. Proponents of mandatory reporting claim it increases identification and prosecution of abusers and improves data collection. Critics feel it compromises victims' autonomy, may increase the risk of further violence by perpetrators, and endangers patient-practitioner trust and confidentiality.

FIGURE 10.4

Opinion poll on domestic violence in the media, June 1999

ON THE ISSUE OF DOMESTIC VIOLENCE IN THE MEDIA, DO YOU THINK THAT THERE HAS BEEN ENOUGH ATTENTION TO THE ISSUE?

	Respondents	
Media attention	Number	Percent
Not enough attention	271	56.7%
Just enough	122	25.5%
Too much attention	85	17.8%
Total	478	100.0%

*Cases not applicable = 24

Most Floridians (56.7%) believe the media do not direct enough attention to the issue of domestic violence. Only 17.8% believe that too much attention is being focused on the issue.

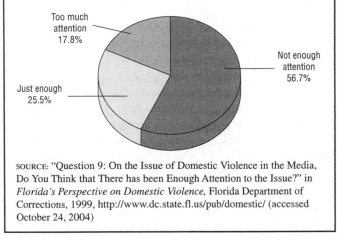

SOURCE: "Question 9: On the Issue of Domestic Violence in the Media, Do You Think that There has been Enough Attention to the Issue?" in *Florida's Perspective on Domestic Violence,* Florida Department of Corrections, 1999, http://www.dc.state.fl.us/pub/domestic/ (accessed October 24, 2004)

Michael Rodriguez et al., in "Mandatory Reporting of Domestic Violence Injuries to the Police: What Do Emergency Department Patients Think?" (*Journal of the American Medical Association,* vol. 286, no. 5, August 1, 2001), examine how female patients seen in emergency departments viewed mandatory reporting of domestic violence injuries to police. The investigators surveyed 1,218 female patients in twelve hospital emergency departments in California, where reporting is mandatory, and Pennsylvania, where there is no law requiring reporting of domestic violence cases. Twelve percent of the patients (140 women) reported physical or sexual abuse within the year preceding the study by a current or former intimate partner.

To determine patients' views about the mandatory reporting law, female nurses asked the patients, "Do you think the emergency department staff in hospitals should be required to call the police when they think that a husband, boyfriend, or partner (ex-husband, ex-boyfriend, ex-partner) has hurt or abused an adult patient?" Respondents could choose one of three answers: yes, every time; every time unless the patient objects; and never.

Rodriguez et al. found that more than half (55.7%) of the recently victimized female respondents supported mandatory reporting of intimate partner violence to police, while 36.4% thought physicians should report only with patient consent. About 44% of abused women opposed mandatory reporting. The women who opposed mandatory reporting tended to be younger and nonwhite.

Of the women with no prior history of abuse, 70.7% favored mandatory reporting and 29.3% opposed it. Women who were primarily non-English speaking were more likely to oppose mandatory reporting, perhaps because their experiences with police were different from the experiences of U.S.-born women or because they feared deportation.

There were no differences between the opinions expressed by women in California and those in Pennsylvania. Similarly, opposition to reporting did not vary by relationship status or income.

Rodriguez et al. conceded that one of the limitations of their study was that it very likely did not obtain the opinions of women who failed to seek care in California because they knew of the mandatory reporting requirement and did not wish to have their perpetrators identified. If abused women were choosing not to seek emergency department care because of reporting requirements, then this study may have underestimated the extent to which abused women would oppose laws that mandate reports to police.

THE AMERICAN PSYCHOLOGICAL ASSOCIATION CONSIDERS THE ISSUES

The *Report of the American Psychological Association Presidential Task Force on Violence and the Family* (Washington, DC: American Psychological Association, 1996) revealed some of the issues that challenge researchers and professionals seeking to prevent and stop domestic violence. The Task Force identified twelve dilemmas faced by family violence researchers and mental health practitioners, including these concerns:

• Privacy—There is an inescapable tension between the right of individuals to privacy and the need to penetrate the isolation and secrecy that often shield intimate partner violence from public scrutiny. One example of how this concern affects research is the preponderance of data suggesting that more violence occurs among low-income families. Researchers speculate that these data may simply indicate that low-income victims who must rely on hospital emergency departments and battered women's shelters are less able to conceal the consequences of abuse than persons with greater resources.

• Expectations of law enforcement—There are differing expectations of the police response to violence. Many victims want the police to intervene to stop abusive behavior, but they do not want the perpetrators punished. On the other hand, researchers, health professionals, and law enforcement personnel often contend that mandatory treatment and arrests are necessary to protect victims from further harm and to safeguard the community at large.

• Conflicting attitudes about abuse—Although most people feel sympathy for victims, there are those who believe that society inadvertently encourages victims by allowing them to use a history of abuse as an excuse for all subsequent bad behavior and problems. This viewpoint is different from blaming the victim for the abuse because it is intended to help victims assume individual responsibility for their behavior, and to heal and recover, rather than remain in the role of victim.

• Effectiveness of mandated treatment—There are ongoing debates about the effectiveness of different philosophies and models of treatment, as well as the use of court-ordered treatment. While some abusers who complete mandatory treatment programs do change their behavior, many studies confirm that these perpetrators are the most motivated and that many other offenders fail to complete court-ordered treatment. However, the American Psychological Association asserted that while the desire to change is linked to favorable outcomes of treatment, involuntary treatment can nevertheless be effective, especially when the perpetrator has been evaluated and enrolled in the most appropriate program.

PREVENTING RELATIONSHIP VIOLENCE

In 2000 the Working Group on Intimate Partner Abuse and Relationship Violence, a multidisciplinary group with members from five professional societies, published a curriculum for psychologists addressing issues related to researching, preventing, and treating intimate partner violence. The objectives of prevention were described as:

• stopping the violent behavior from ever occurring

• delaying the onset of violent behavior

• reducing the impact of existing violent behavior

• strengthening behaviors that promote emotional and physical well-being, thereby inoculating people from the negative effects of relationship violence

• supporting institutional, community, and government policies that promote the prevention of relational violence

The American Psychological Association recommends instituting violence prevention programs aimed at middle school, high school, and college students that are intended to heighten awareness and reduce rates of date rape. Furthermore, it is important that the prevention pro-

grams be repeated since there is considerable evidence that these education programs do produce measurable effects on knowledge and attitudes, though the effects are often not lasting.

Other special-needs populations that the curriculum targeted for prevention programs include immigrants, ethnic minorities, and persons who are gay, lesbian, or bisexual.

Levels of Violence Prevention

Many researchers believe that in order to effectively address the public health problem of intimate partner violence, health professionals, policy makers, educators, and women's advocates must intensify violence prevention efforts. There are three levels of prevention.

Primary prevention of intimate partner violence aims to reduce harmful circumstances before they can produce violence and includes global educational efforts to promote nonviolent interactions and relationships.

Secondary prevention of intimate partner violence is intended to break the pattern of violent behavior before it becomes deeply ingrained. Examples of such efforts are early identification and counseling of first-time offenders to challenge and change behavior as soon as possible after its occurrence. Unfortunately, few programs specifically targeting first-time offenders are available, and programs for chronic perpetrators often alienate first-time offenders who feel they do not belong with severe batterers.

Tertiary prevention of intimate partner violence involves services for victims, counseling, and mandatory treatment of offenders, and may also involve justice interventions including arrest and incarceration.

Primary Prevention Theories

The majority of efforts to date focus on tertiary prevention. However, changing attitudes about intimate partner violence and increasing recognition of violence as a societal problem that affects everyone, not simply the victims, emphasize the need for primary prevention. An example of this effort is the David and Lucile Packard Foundation's support of the "Next Generations: Strengthening Young Families and Communities through Prevention of Child Abuse, Youth Violence, and Domestic Violence" initiative. It aims to contribute "a research and evaluation perspective" to primary prevention efforts, according to Jeffrey L. Edleson, Deborah Daro, and Howard Pinderhughe in "Finding a Common Agenda for Preventing Child Maltreatment, Youth Violence, and Domestic Violence" (*Journal of Interpersonal Violence*, vol. 19, no. 3, March 2004). The Next Generation initiative is a collaboration with the Family Violence Prevention Fund and the National Funding Collaborative on Violence Prevention.

Neil B. Guterman, in "Advancing Prevention Research on Child Abuse, Youth Violence, and Domestic Violence: Emerging Strategies and Issues," argued that primary prevention programs are still in their infancy (*Journal of Interpersonal Violence,* vol. 19, no. 3, March 2004). He believes that in order for primary prevention programs to be truly effective, researchers need to do the following:

- formulate a universal definition of family violence to allow comparable measurements of family violence

- design research studies to advance knowledge of how to assess risk for future violence in order to target prevention efforts

- design research studies to advance knowledge on how to intervene in violent relationships to prevent future violence

While the author acknowledges there is often a gap between research into possibly effective prevention strategies and the implementation of those programs, he argued that "these tensions between prevention practice and research . . . can be viewed as instilling healthy and productive pressures in both directions. For researchers, such pressures mandate that research activities ultimately should be 'in the service of service' . . . and for practitioners . . . they mandate that their real world strategies are rigorously grounded, optimally evaluated in an objective fashion."

In *Primary Prevention of Intimate Partner Violence* (Washington, DC: National Institute of Mental Health, July 2002), researchers Martha Smithey and Murray Straus described the environmental changes and educational approaches they feel will serve to reduce the risk of intimate partner violence for the entire population. Smithey and Straus asserted that "the outcome envisioned as a result of primary prevention is that, although some individuals may continue to be violent, their number will be reduced."

Smithey and Straus feel primary prevention is consistent with the feminist approach to reducing intimate partner violence, since feminists view patriarchy and male dominance as the principle causes of violence. Feminists view societal change that promotes equality between men and women as primary prevention of partner violence. Underlying this view is the belief that the more humane a society becomes, the less likely that its individual members will resort to intimate partner violence.

Smithey and Straus found that while there are few programs specifically aimed at primary prevention of intimate partner violence, some programs offer both primary and secondary types of services. For example, in addition to aiding victims, battered women's shelters may offer community education and other programs to empower women. Furthermore, the presence of shelters in a community sends a clear message that victims have alternatives to remaining in abusive relationships and conveys the community's intolerance of partner violence.

Similarly, the justice concepts of "general deterrence" and "specific deterrence" have primary and secondary prevention objectives. Legal sanctions, such as arrest, prosecution, mandatory treatment, and incarceration, deliver the secondary prevention benefit of deterring an offender from further violence and may also perform a primary prevention function: deterring others from perpetrating violence by warning them of the consequences of their actions. Although there are no data linking legislative changes, such as the enactment of the 1994 Violence against Women Act and the criminalization of wife beating, to changing public attitudes about intimate partner violence, Smithey and Straus argued that the combination of legal reform and widespread access to and availability of services such as hotlines, shelters, and advocacy has resulted in social change.

Smithey and Straus presented eleven criminal justice theories and their implications for primary prevention of intimate partner violence. The following theories have practical applications for prevention programs:

- Deterrence Theory—Intensify formal and informal sanctions for abusive behavior by family, friends, and colleagues.

- Strain Theory—Create more opportunities for education and economic achievement, promote gender equality in the family, and foster realistic expectations of marriage and cohabitation.

- Social Learning Theory—Discourage corporal punishment of children and reduce celebration of violence in the media.

- Control Theory—Strengthen family ties by offering parenting education.

- Moral Justification Theory—Eliminate social approval of violence as a means of supporting moral standards, such as governments' use of capital punishment.

- Control-Balance Theory—Enhance gender equality in the family and reduce social isolation to enable social controls that condemn the use of violence to govern behavior.

- Conflict Theory—Promote economic, social, and political equality and increase access to and availability of marriage counseling.

- Feminist Theories of Criminal Justice—Treat all victims as reliable and truthful and strengthen criminal justice sanctions for intimate partner violence.

- Feminist Theories of Crime/Power-Control Theories—Eliminate male dominance in society and the home.

- Survival Strategy Theory—Increase the availability of escape options, such as shelters and safe houses, for victims of abuse.

- Convergence Theory—Eliminate differences between criminal justice treatment of victims by gender of victims and offenders and reduce cultural support and celebration of violence.

Smithey and Straus also commended the United Nations' leadership role in global primary prevention of partner violence, evidenced by its adoption of the Domestic Violence Resolution in 1985. In its *Progress of the World's Women 2000: UNIFEM Biennial Report,* UN officials stated that "violence against women and girls constitutes the single most prevalent and universal violation of human rights" (New York: UN Development Fund for Women, 2000).

Despite these promising observations about changing attitudes and reliable data indicating that intimate partner violence is decreasing, Smithey and Straus cautioned that there is no direct evidence demonstrating that declines in violence rates since the mid-1970s have resulted from prevention programs. They offered other factors that may contribute to declining rates of violence, such as an increase of three years in the average age at marriage between 1970 to 2000. Another possible explanation for the decline is that prevention programs have effectively stigmatized partner violence to the degree that there is even greater reluctance, on the part of both victims and perpetrators, to disclose it. Even so, there might be cause for cautious optimism—greater reluctance to admit to abusive behavior indicates that society is less tolerant of violent personal relationships.

Primary Prevention Programs

A number of primary prevention programs are emerging to address the problem of intimate partner violence. Some began during the 1990s and others have been instituted as recently as 2000. Research has not yet evaluated their effectiveness, but researchers and battered women's advocates are hopeful that these initiatives will further reduce public acceptance and tolerance of intimate partner violence. Some examples of primary prevention programs follow.

The National Center for Injury Prevention and Control, an agency of the Centers for Disease Control, developed and implemented the Family and Intimate Violence Prevention Program to focus on surveillance, research, evaluation, and training and to fund community-based prevention programs at all levels of prevention. In addition to supporting community-based projects, such as the Milwaukee Women's Center and Georgia's Men Stopping Violence, Inc., the agency also sponsors projects aimed at preventing intimate partner violence in specific populations, such as rural and Native American communities.

The National Crime Prevention Council offers school-based prevention programs that train teens to respond to hotline callers and perform peer counseling. The council focuses on violence in teen dating relationships, and its dating violence intervention projects teach boys and girls not to accept violence in their earliest relationships, even before they begin dating. The students are taught how to identify and resolve conflict, recognize abusive behavior, and communicate respectfully with their peers.

The National Advisory Council on Violence against Women was established in 1995 with the goal of eliminating social norms that support and condone violence against women. To achieve this ambitious goal, the council coordinates multidisciplinary efforts involving community leaders and representatives from health care agencies, the military, organized sports, the social welfare system, the justice system, the media, academia, businesses, and religious communities. The council also supports education of children about gender roles and stereotypes that condone violence against women.

The Family Violence Prevention Fund is a national, nonprofit organization that offers primary, secondary, and tertiary prevention programs. One of their aims is to educate the general public that when people fail to speak out against partner violence, they perpetuate the problem with their silence. To this end, the Fund produced the media campaign "There's No Excuse for Domestic Violence." The fund also provides services for abuse victims, offers community and professional education programs for the public at large, and actively seeks public policy reform. The fund is one of the organizations active in the initiative "Next Generations: Strengthening Young Families and Communities Through Prevention of Child Abuse, Youth Violence, and Domestic Violence."

IMPORTANT NAMES AND ADDRESSES

American Public Human Services Association (formerly American Public Welfare Association)
810 First St. NE, Ste. 500
Washington, DC 20002
(202) 682-0100
FAX: (202) 289-6555
URL: http://www.aphsa.org

Center for Women Policy Studies
1211 Connecticut Ave. NW, Ste. 312
Washington, DC 20036
(202) 872-1770
FAX: (202) 296-8962
E-mail: cwps@centerwomenpolicy.org
URL: http://www.centerwomenpolicy.org

FaithTrust Institute
2400 N. 45th St., #10
Seattle, WA 98103
(206) 634-1903
FAX: (206) 634-0115
E-mail: info@faithtrustinstitute.org
URL: http://www.faithtrustinstitute.org

Family Research Laboratory
University of New Hampshire
126 Horton
Social Science Center
Durham, NH 03824
(603) 862-1888
FAX: (603) 862-1122
URL: http://www.unh.edu/frl/index.html

Family Violence Prevention Fund
383 Rhode Island St., Ste. 304
San Francisco, CA 94103-5133
(415) 252-8900
FAX: (415) 252-8991
E-mail: info@endabuse.org
URL: http://endabuse.org

Minnesota Program Development, Inc.
202 E. Superior St.

Duluth, MN 55802
(218) 722-2781
URL: http://www.duluth-model.org

National Center for Victims of Crime
2000 M St. NW, Ste. 480
Washington, DC 20036
(202) 467-8700
FAX: (202) 467-8701
URL: http://www.ncvc.org

National Clearinghouse for the Defense of Battered Women
125 S. 9th St., Ste. 302
Philadelphia, PA 19107
(215) 351-0010
FAX: (215) 351-0779

National Coalition against Domestic Violence
P.O. Box 18749
Denver, CO 80218
(303) 839-1852
Toll-free: 1-800-799-7233
FAX: (303) 831-9251
URL: http://www.ncadv.org

National Council on Child Abuse and Family Violence
1025 Connecticut Ave. NW, Ste. 1012
Washington, DC 20036
(202) 429-6695
FAX: (831) 655-3930
E-mail: info@NCCAFV.org
URL: http://www.nccafv.org

National Criminal Justice Reference Service
P.O. Box 6000
Rockville, MD 20849-6000
(301) 519-5500
FAX: (301) 519-5212
Toll-free: 1-800-851-3420
URL: http://www.ncjrs.org

National Institute of Justice
810 7th St. NW
Washington, DC 20531
(202) 307-2942
URL: http://www.ojp.usdoj.gov/nij/

National Resource Center on Domestic Violence
Pennsylvania Coalition Against Domestic Violence
6400 Flank Dr., Ste. 1300
Harrisburg, PA 17112-2778
Toll-free: 1-800-537-2238
FAX: (717) 671-8149
URL: http://www.nrcdv.org

National Self-Help Clearinghouse
Graduate School and University Center of the City University of New York
365 5th Ave., Ste. 3300
New York, NY 10016
(212) 817-1822
E-mail: info@selfhelpweb.org
URL: http://www.selfhelpweb.org

National Sexual Violence Resource Center
123 North Enola Dr.
Enola, PA 17025
(717) 909-0710
Toll-free: 1-877-739-3895
FAX: (717) 909-0714
URL: http://www.nsvrc.org

Sexual Assault Recovery Anonymous Society (SARA)
P.O. Box 16
Surrey, BC V3T 4W4 Canada
(604) 874-2616
Toll-free: 1-866-466-7272
FAX: (604) 874-2620
E-mail: sarasociety@shaw.ca

RESOURCES

A number of studies were conducted on domestic violence when spouse abuse first became a public issue during the 1970s and 1980s. Since that time, however, there has been little government-funded statistical research on domestic abuse. The pioneering work done at the University of New Hampshire's Family Research Laboratory in Durham, New Hampshire, has become an authoritative source of information and insight about family violence.

Chief among the University of New Hampshire researchers who perform the landmark studies and in-depth work on intimate partner violence are Murray Straus, Richard Gelles, David Finkelhor, and Suzanne Steinmetz. Studies released by the Family Research Laboratory investigate all forms of domestic violence, many based on the National Family Violence Survey and the National Family Violence Resurvey. Murray A. Straus and Glenda Kaufman Kantor published data in 1994 in "Changes in Spouse Assault Rates from 1975 to 1992: A Comparison of Three National Surveys" (Durham, NH: The Family Research Laboratory at the University of New Hampshire, presented at the 13th World Congress of Sociology, July 19, 1994). Martha Smithey and Murray Straus published the report "Primary Prevention of Intimate Partner Violence" (Washington, DC: National Institute of Mental Health, July 2002). Murray A. Straus published "Prevalence of Violence against Dating Partners by Male and Female University Students Worldwide," in *Violence against Women*, vol. 10, July 2004.

International data about violence against women is collected by organizations such as the Statistical Commission and Economic Commission for Europe and the United Nations Interregional Crime and Justice Research Institute. Private sources on abuse include *The Commonwealth Fund's 1998 Survey of Women's Health* (Baltimore, MD: Commonwealth Fund, 1998) and Lori Heise's *Violence against Women: The Hidden Health Burden* (Washington, DC: The World Bank, 1994).

The following sources also provide information about medical and health care utilization by abused women: The National Academy of Sciences Institute of Medicine report *Confronting Chronic Neglect: The Education and Training of Health Professionals on Family Violence* (Washington, DC: National Academy Press, 2001); the American Medical Association (AMA) report *AMA Data on Violence Between Intimates* (Chicago: American Medical Association Council on Scientific Affairs, December 2000); the Centers for Disease Control and Prevention report *Intimate Partner Violence Surveillance: Uniform Definitions and Recommended Data Elements* by Linda E. Saltzman, Janet L. Fanslow, Pamela M. McMahon, and Gene A. Shelley (Atlanta: Centers for Disease Control and Prevention, revised edition, 2002); and the report *Violence against Women* (Washington, DC: Henry J. Kaiser Family Foundation, 2001).

National opinion poll research comes from Harris Interactive, Inc. (the Harris Poll) and from the 1999 Florida Department of Corrections' report *Florida's Perspective on Domestic Violence*. These provide insight into attitudes and beliefs about intimate partner violence.

Research cited in this publication was drawn from numerous books including *Against Our Will,* by Susan Brownmiller (New York: Simon and Schuster, 1975); *For Love of Country: Confronting Rape and Sexual Harassment in the Military*, by Teri Spahr Nelson (Binghamton, NY: Haworth Maltreatment and Trauma Press, September 2002); *Terrifying Love: Why Battered Women Kill and How Society Responds*, by Lenore Walker (New York: Harper and Row, 1989); *When Battered Women Kill*, by Angela Browne (New York: The Free Press, 1987); *Current Controversies on Family Violence*, edited by Richard Gelles and Donileen Loseke (Newbury Park, CA: Sage, 1994); *Legal Responses to Wife Assault*, edited by Zoe Hilton (Newbury Park, CA: Sage, 1993); *Wife Rape*, by Raquel Kennedy Bergen (Newbury Park, CA: Sage,

1996); *The Batterer: A Psychological Profile*, by Donald Dutton (New York: Basic Books, 1995); *Women At Risk*, by Evan Stark and Anne Flitcraft (Newbury Park, CA: Sage, 1996); *Do Arrests and Restraining Orders Work?*, edited by Eve Buzawa and Carl Buzawa (Newbury Park, CA: Sage, 1996); and *Abused Men: The Hidden Side of Domestic Violence*, by Philip W. Cook (Westport, CT: Praeger, 1997).

The federal government's Bureau of Justice Statistics in Washington, D.C., provides information on domestic violence from the National Crime Victimization Surveys in *Criminal Victimization, 2003* (2004); *Criminal Victimization in the United States, 2002 Statistical Tables* (2002); *Homicide Trends in the United States* (2002); *Criminal Victimization 2001: Changes 2000–01 with Trends 1993–2001* (2001); *Violence by Intimates, Findings from the National Violence against Women Survey* (1999); *Intimate Partner Violence and Age of Victim, 1993–99* (2001); *Batterer Intervention: Program Approaches and Criminal Justice Strategies* (1998); *The Sexual Victimization of College Women* (2000); *Stalking and Domestic Violence: The Third Annual Report to Congress under the Violence against Women Act* (1998); *Women Offenders: A Special Report* (2000); *Extent, Nature and Consequences of Intimate Violence* (2000); *Special Report on Intimate Partner Violence* (2000); *Background Checks for Firearm Transfers, 2003* (2004); *Enforcement of Protective Orders* (2002); *Drugs and Crime Facts* (2003); and *The Benefits and Limitations for Victims of Domestic Violence* (1997).

The National Institute of Justice, administered by the Office of Justice Programs in the U.S. Department of Justice, reports on a variety of studies on domestic violence.

Among them are *Batterer Intervention Programs: Where Do We Go From Here?* by Shelly Jackson, Lynette Feder, David R. Forde, Robert C. Davis, Christopher D. Maxwell, and Bruce G. Taylor (Washington, DC: National Institute of Justice, NCJ 195079, June 2003); a special issue of the *National Institute of Justice Journal* dedicated to battering and murder, no. 250, November 2003; and *Extent, Nature, and Consequences of Intimate Partner Violence: Findings from the National Violence against Women Survey* by Patricia Tjaden and Nancy Thoennes, (Washington, DC: National Institute of Justice, 2000).

The U.S. Merit Systems Protection Board, an agency of the federal government, provided data on trends and responses to sexual harassment in *Sexual Harassment in the Federal Workplace* (Washington, DC: U.S. Merit Systems Protection Board, 1995).

Medical, psychological, sociological, epidemiological, and other types of journals publish useful articles on abuse. The journal articles cited in this publication were published in *American Sociological Review*, *Archives of Internal Medicine*, *American Behavioral Scientist*, *British Journal of Criminology*, *Crime and Delinquency*, *Current Opinion in Obstetrics and Gynecology*, *Journal of General Internal Medicine*, *American Journal of Public Health*, *Journal of Marriage and the Family*, *Violence against Women*, *Violence and Victims*, *Journal of Comparative Family Studies*, *Journal of Research in Crime and Delinquency*, *Journal of the American Medical Association*, *Journal of Family Psychology*, *Journal of Family Practice*, *Journal of Emergency Nursing*, *Journal of Consulting and Clinical Psychology*, *Maternal and Child Health Journal*, *The Psychology of Women Quarterly*, and *Journal of Interpersonal Violence*.

INDEX

Page references in italics refer to photographs. References with the letter t following them indicate the presence of a table. The letter f indicates a figure. If more than one table or figure appears on a particular page, the exact item number for the table or figure being referenced is provided.

A

Abused Men: The Hidden Side of Domestic Violence (Cook), 17–18
Acquaintance rape
  as aggression, 60
  alcohol use, 60–61, 65
  college rape, 61–62, 61t, 62f, 62t, 64
  controversy over statistics, 66
  "date rape pill," 65–66, 102
  fraternities and athletics, 64–65
  sexual coercion, 61
"Acquaintance Rape and the College Social Scene" (Ward et al.), 64
Adams, David, 73
"Addressing Culture in Batterers Intervention: The Asian Indian Community as an Illustrative Example" (Ameida and Dolan-Delvecchio), 75
"Adolescent Dating Violence and Date Rape" (Rickert, Vaughan and Wiemann), 60
"Advancing Prevention Research on Child Abuse, Youth Violence, and Domestic Violence: Emerging Strategies and Issues" (Guterman), 127
"Affect, Verbal Content and Psychophysiology in the Arguments of Couples with a Violent Husband" (Jacobson), 48
Afghanistan, 5
Age and decrease in spouse/partner abuse, 39–40
Aggression
  acquaintance rape, 60
  marital rape, 58
"Aggression between Heterosexual Dating Partners" (Riggs and O'Leary), 60

Alabama, 2
Alcohol and drug use
  abuse and, 35–38, 35f, 106
  acquaintance rape, 60–61
  homicide, 36, 36t, 37t, 114–115
  spousal murder defendants, 111
"Alcohol and Other Drugs Are Key Causal Agents of Violence" (Flanzer), 35
"Alcohol and Other Drugs Are Not the Cause of Violence" (Gelles), 36
"Alcohol and Sexual Assault in a National Sample of College Women" (Ullman, Karabatsos and Koss), 60, 65
AMEND batterer intervention program, 74
American Psychological Association, 125–126
"An Analysis of Risk Markers in Husband to-Wife Violence: The Current State of Knowledge" (Hotaling and Sugarman), 38
Antistalking legislation, 94–95
"An Arresting Experiment: Domestic Violence Victim Experiences and Perceptions" (Miller), 92
Arrests
  deterrence, 89–91, 92
  mandatory, 91
  police attitudes, 88–89
  warrantless probable cause arrests, 91
Asian immigrants, 24, 25
"Assessing Risk Factors for Intimate Partner Homicide" (Campbell et al.), 41
Asylum, 7
Athletics, college, 64–65
"Attitudes Toward Wife Rape: Effects of Social Background and Victim Status" (Basile), 59–60
"The Attitudes Towards Violence Scale: A Measure for Adolescents" (Funk et al.), 32–33
Attitudinal research
  causes of domestic violence, 124(t10.2)
  domestic violence as a widespread problem, 122(f10.1)
  domestic violence in Florida, 122–124, 122(f10.2)

  gender and domestic violence views, 121–122
  marital rape, 59–60
  media attention to domestic violence, 125f
  percentage of physically abusive men, 123t
  police and domestic violence, 88–89, 124(t10.3)
  rape, 55
  violence, 32–33, 121
  wife beating, 5
  witnessing of spouse/partner abuse, 123f
Avoidance, 49

B

Baker v. The City of New York, 99
Balistreri v. Pacifica Police Department, 101
"Barriers to Screening for Domestic Violence" (Elliot et al.), 50
Battered woman syndrome, 45–46, 113, 115–118
"A Battered Woman's Problems Are Social, Not Psychological" (Bowker), 46–47
"Battered Women, Police and the Law" (Ferraro and Pope), 88
"Battered Women and Self-Defense: Myths and Misconceptions in Current Reform Proposals" (Maguigan), 117–118
Battered Women—Issues of Public Policy (Consultation on Battered Women), 9
The Batterer: A Psychological Profile (Dutton), 76
Batterer Intervention: Program Approaches and Criminal Justice Strategies (Healey and Smith), 71–74
Batterers. *See* Offenders
Behind Closed Doors: Violence in the American Family (Straus, Gelles and Steinmetz), 39
"Beyond the Conflict Tactics Scale: Assessing Gender Differences in Partner Violence" (Morse), 20–21
Bosnia, 6
Boyer, Amy, 96
Brady Handgun Prevention Act, 103–104

Brain dysfunction and injuries, 72
Bride burning, 4–5
Brown, James, 9
Brzonkala, Christy, 3, 102
Burlington Industries v. Ellerth, 68
The Burning Bed, 9

C

California, 3, 118–119
California laws, 96
Calvin Bradley v. The State, 2
Carswell, Dwayne, 10
Causes of domestic violence
  gender roles, 32
  intergenerational abuse, 38–39
  patriarchal theory, 33
  poverty, 30
  power struggles, 31–32
  pregnant women, 38
  psychological explanations, 33–34
  public opinion on, 124(*t*10.2)
  sociological explanations, 34–35
  stress, 39
  substance abuse, 35–38
  violence, attitudes towards, 32–33
Celebrities, 9–10
Changes in Spouse Assault Rates from 1975 to 1992: A Comparison of Three National Surveys in the United States (Straus and Kantor), 15–16
Chastisement, 2
Child abuse
  DeShaney v. Winnebago County Department of Social Services, 100–101
  gays and lesbians, 67
  and later abuse, 39
China, 7–8
City of Boca Raton, Faragher v., 68
City of Indianapolis, Gillespie v., 103–104
The City of New York, Baker v., 99
City of Torrington, Thurman v., 99–100
Civil Protection Orders: The Benefits and Limitations for Victims of Domestic Violence (National Center for State Court), 108
"Civil Protection Orders and Risk of Subsequent Police-Reported Violence" (Holt et al.), 108–109
Civil Rights Act of 1964, Title VII, 67, 68
Civil Rights Act of 1991, 67–68
Cognitive-behavioral group therapy, 72, 74
College sexual behavior
  alcohol use, 65
  controversy over rape statistics, 66
  fraternities and athletics, 64–65
  nonreporting incidents by reason, 63*t*
  rape, 61–62, 61*t*, 64
  victimization among women college students, 62*f*, 62*t*
"College Women's Experiences of Sexual Coercion" (Adams-Curtis and Forbes), 61
Colombia, 5–6
Colonial America, 2
Commonwealth v. McAfee, 3

"Conceptualization and Measurement of Battering: Implications for Public Policy" (Straus), 20
Conflict Tactics Scale, 19–20
Confronting Chronic Neglect: The Education and Training of Health Professionals on Family Violence (National Academy of Sciences Institute of Medicine), 51
Confronting Domestic Violence: A Guide for Criminal Justice Agencies (National Institute of Justice), 104–106
"Constructing the Symbolic Complainant: Police Subculture and Nonenforcement of Protective Orders from Battered Women" (Rigakos), 88–89
"Consultation on Battered Women," 9
Controversies
  college rape statistics, 66
  Conflict Tactics Scale, 19–20
  family violence model of spouse abuse, 18–20
  gender and domestic violence rates, 15–18
Coping strategies of victims, 48–50
"Coping with an Abusive Relationship: How and Why Do Women Stay?" (Herbert et al.), 48–49
"Coping with Partner Abuse among Mexican American and Anglo Women: Ethnic and Socioeconomic Influences" (Fernandez-Esquer and McCloskey), 49–50
"Cops and Docs" initiative, 52–53
Court cases
  Baker v. The City of New York, 99
  Balistreri v. Pacifica Police Department, 101
  Burlington Industries v. Ellerth, 68
  Calvin Bradley v. The State, 2
  Commonwealth v. McAfee, 3
  DeShaney v. Winnebago County Department of Social Services, 100–101
  Faragher v. City of Boca Raton, 68
  Fulgham v. State, 2
  Gebser v. Lago Vista Independent School District, 68
  Gillespie v. City of Indianapolis, 103–104
  Macias v. Ihde, 101
  Meritor Savings Bank v. Vinson, 67
  Self v. Self, 3, 99
  State v. Jesse Black, 2
  State v. Norman, 116–117
  State v. Rhodes, 3
  State v. Richard Oliver, 2
  Thompson v. Thompson, 3
  Thurman v. City of Torrington, 99–100
  U.S. v. Morrison, 3
Criminal justice system
  battered women murder defendants, 116–119
  batterer intervention programs, 75–76
  family preservation, 105–106
  filing charges, responsibility for, 104–105
  stalking, 94
  victim cooperation, 106–107

  victim/offender relationship, 107
Criminal justice theories, 127–128
Cultural Context Model, 75
Cultural issues
  batterer intervention programs, 75
  bride burning, 4–5
  female genital mutilation, 6–7
  immigrants and domestic violence, 25–26
  missing women, 7–8
  police response to domestic violence, 88
  rape, 5–6
  wife beating, 5
Cyberstalking, 96–97
Cyberstalking: A New Challenge for Law Enforcement and Industry (U.S. Attorney General), 96–97

D

Darfur, Sudan, 6
Data collection and sources
  marital rape, 57
  reliability, 11–12
  See also Reporting
Date rape. *See* Acquaintance rape
"Date rape" pills, 65–66, 102
Dating violence, 31
Declaration of Sentiments, 2
Declaration on the Elimination of Violence against Women, United Nations, 1
Definitions
  domestic abuse, 10–11, 11*t*
  intimate partner violence, 121
  intimate partners, 29*t*
  sexual harassment, 67
DeShaney v. Winnebago County Department of Social Services, 100–101
"Determining Police Response to Domestic Violence Victims" (Buzawa and Austin), 84, 86
Deterrence and arrest, 89–91, 92
Developing countries, 56
Domestic violence gun ban, 103–104, 103*t*
Dowry and bride burning, 4–5
Dropout rates for batterer treatment programs, 77–78
Drug abuse. *See* Alcohol and drug use
"The 'Drunken Bum' Theory of Wife Beating" (Kantor and Straus), 36–37
Due Process Clause, 100–101
Duluth batterer intervention program model, 73

E

Egypt, 5, 7
Elder abuse, 40
Ellerth, Burlington Industries v., 68
Ellis, Dale, 10
Emerge batterer intervention program, 3, 73–74
Emotional and psychological abuse, 23–24, 24*t*, 26*f*
Empowerment of victims, 51–52
"Ending the Continuous Reign of Terror" (Bennett), 117
Enforcement of Protective Orders (U.S. Department of Justice), 108

Equal force and self-defense, 115–116
Equal Protection Clause, 99–100
"Estrangement, Interventions and Male Violence Toward Female Partners" (Ellis and Wight), 51–52
Ethnicity. See Race/ethnicity
Europe, 1–2
Exchange/social control theory, 34
Expert testimony, 116–117
"Explaining Women's Double Jeopardy: Factors that Mediate the Association between Harsh Treatment as a Child and Violence by a Husband" (Simons et al.), 39
Extent, Nature and Consequences of Intimate Violence: Findings from the National Violence against Women Survey (Tjaden and Thoennes), 12–13

F
Family and Intimate Violence Prevention Program, 128
Family preservation, 105–106
Family systems model, 72
Family Violence Prevention and Services Act, 102
Family Violence Prevention Fund, 9, 128
Faragher v. City of Boca Raton, 68
"Fear and Expectations: Differences among Female Victims of Domestic Violence Who Come to the Attention of Police" (Apsler, Cummins and Carl), 89
Federal Prohibition of Female Genital Mutilation Act, 7
Federal workplace harassment, 69–70
Female genital mutilation, 6–7
Female infanticide, 7–8
Feminism
    battered women's shelters, 9
    batterer treatment programs, 71–72
    criticism of the family violence model of spouse abuse, 18–20
    gender roles and wife abuse, 32
    psychological explanations of wife abuse, 34
    violence, theories of, 34–35
Firearms ban, domestic violence, 103–104, 103t
Florida, 122–124
Fort Bragg, NC, 10
Fourteenth Amendment
    Due Process Clause, 100–101
    Equal Protection Clause, 99–100
France, 1–2
Fraternities, 64–65
Frazier, Joe, 10
Fulgham v. State, 2

G
Gays and lesbians
    rape, 66–67
    sexual harassment, 68
    See also Same-sex couples
Gebser v. Lago Vista Independent School District, 68
Gelles, Richard, 34
Gender
    abuse by women, 18–21

collegiate sexual behavior, 64
Conflict Tactics Scale, 19–20
controversy over 1985 National Family Violence Survey, 15–18
domestic violence attitudes, 121–122
intimate homicides, 21–22, 21(t2.8), 114f
National Youth Survey on intimate partner violence, 20–21
reporting by type of crime, gender and race/ethnicity of victim, 84(t7.4)
reporting of crime, 84(t7.3)
roles, 32
same-sex couple violence, 13, 23, 67
sexual coercion, 61
sexual harassment perceptions, 69
spouse/partner abuse, 30t
spouse/partner victimization by perpetrator gender, victim gender and history of same-sex/opposite-sex cohabitation, 15f
victim/offender relationships, 18(t2.6)
victimization by intimate partners, 12–13, 12t, 13t
violence, attitudes towards, 32–33
violent victimization rates, 16(f2.3), 19t
Gender preference, 7–8
'Gender Symmetry' in Domestic Violence: A Substantive and Methodological Research Review" (Kimmel), 19
General systems theory, 34
Genital mutilation, 6–7
Geoffrey de la Tour de Landry, 1
Gillespie v. City of Indianapolis, 103–104
Goldman, Ronald, 9
Guilt, 39
Guns, domestic violence ban on, 103–104, 103t

H
Harassment, sexual, 67–70
Health issues, 50–51
Health professionals, 50–53, 81–82, 124–125
Helplessness, 45–46
Helplessness: On Depression, Development and Death (Seligman), 45
Hillory J. Farias and Samantha Reid Date Rape Drug Prohibition Act, 102
History, 1–2
Homicide
    age, 21t
    alcohol and drug use of victims, 114–115
    changing state laws, 117–118
    defenses of abused women, 113
    gender, 114f
    Homicide Trends in the United States (Fox and Zawitz), 20–21
    imminent *vs.* immediate danger, 116
    marital rape, 114
    race/ethnicity, gender and relationship to murderer, 22(f2.4)
    rates among black females, 113f
    rates among white females, 112f
    relationship characteristics, 113–114
    risk factors, 41
    self-defense, 115–119
    sentencing and jail time served, 112–113

spouse/partner abuse, 44–45
substance abuse, 36, 36t, 37t
weapons used, 22(f2.5), 111
Homosexuals. *See* Gays and lesbians; Same-sex couples
Hospitalization, 50–51
"How Can Practitioners Help an Abused Woman Lower Her Risk of Death?" (Block), 52
Hudood ordinances, 5, 55–56
Hughes, Francine, 9

I
Ihde, Macias v., 101
Immediate *vs.* imminent danger, 116
Immigrant women, 24–27, 26f
Immigration and Naturalization Service, U.S., 7
Immigration law, 25, 102–103
Imminent *vs.* immediate danger, 116
"Implications of Personality Profiles for Batterer Treatment" (White and Gondolf), 77
Income and violent crime, 31t
India, 4–5, 8
Infanticide, female, 7–8
Infibulation, 7
Injuries, 50, 58
Intergenerational abuse, 38–39
International Criminal Court (ICC), 6
International issues
    data sources, 3–4
    marital rape, 56–60
    missing women, 7–8
    primary prevention programs, 128
    rape, 5–6, 55
    wife beating, 5
Internet, 96–97
Intervention
    stalking, 95
    for victims, 52–53
    See also Treatment for male batterers
"Interventions That Help Victims of Domestic Violence: A Quantitative Analysis of Physicians' Experiences" (Gerbert et al.), 52
Intimate partner abuse. *See* Spouse/partner abuse
Intimate Partner Violence and Age of Victim, 1993–99 (Rennison), 83–84
"Intimate Partner Violence and Physical Health Consequences," 50
Intimate Violence: The Definitive Study of the Causes and Consequences of Abuse in the American Family (Gelles and Straus), 49
Intimate Violence (Gelles and Straus), 38
Iran, 5
Islam
    infibulation, 7
    rape, 55
    wife beating, 5

J
Janjawid, 6
Jesse Black, State v., 2
Juries, 116–117